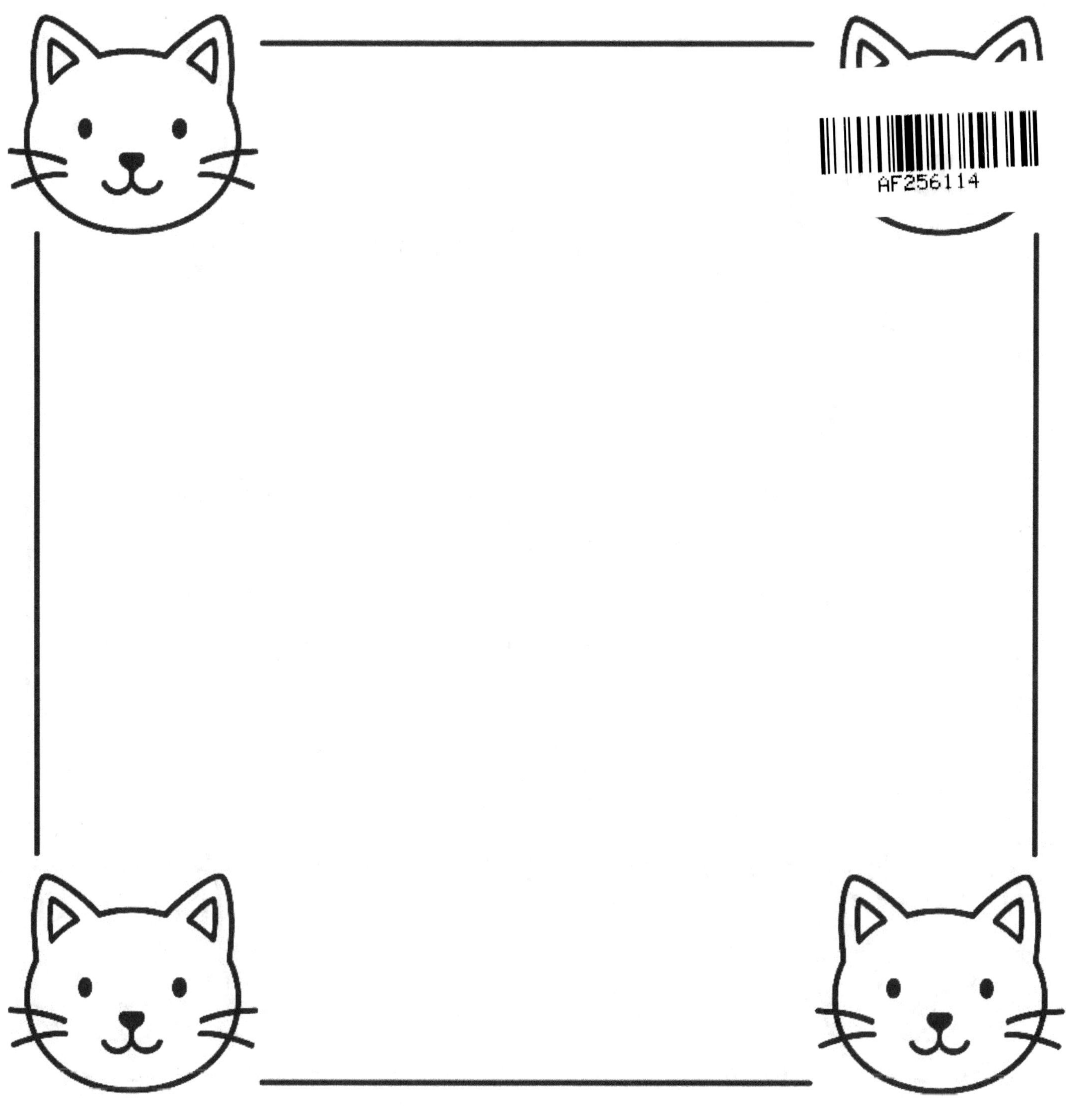
AF256114

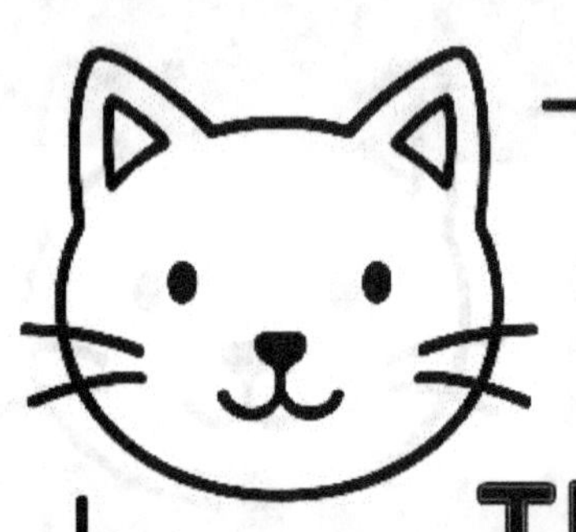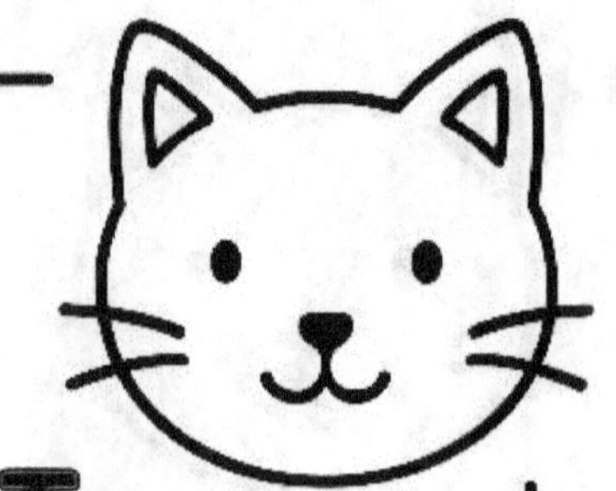

This Book belongs To:

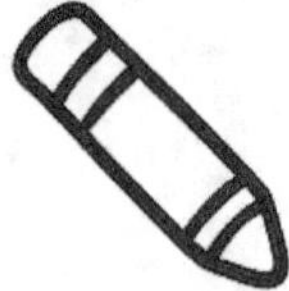

____

Welcome to your Color Me Cats – Kids Edition
coloring adventure!

Filled with fun facts and furry friends, this book
is all yours to color, learn, and enjoy.

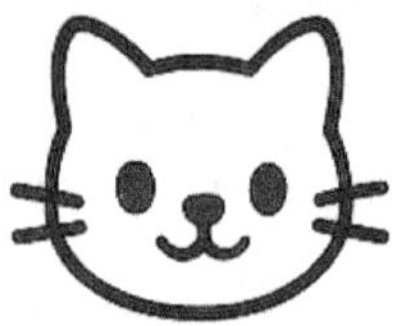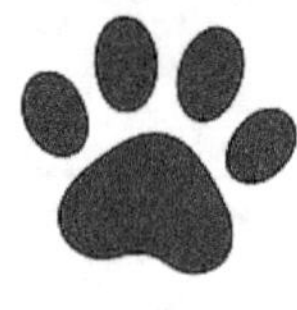

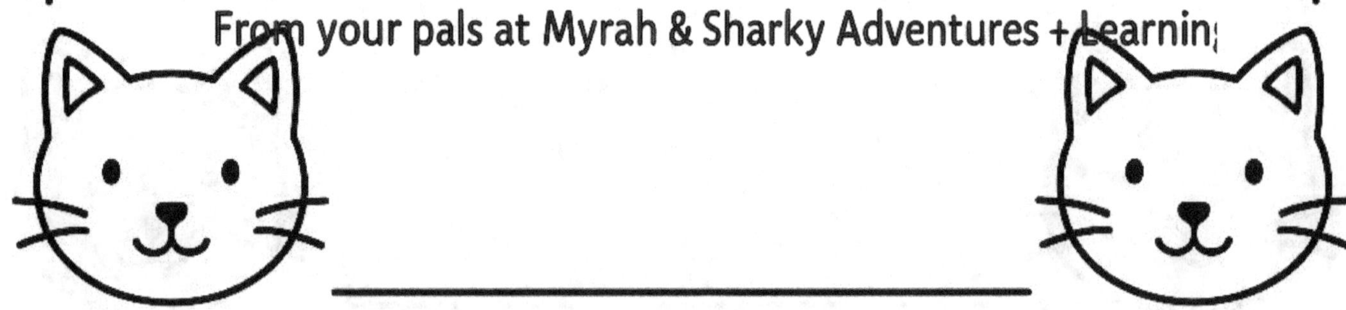

From your pals at Myrah & Sharky Adventures + Learning

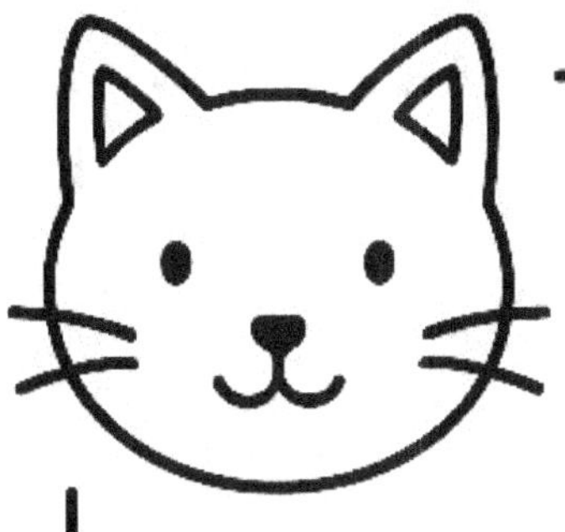
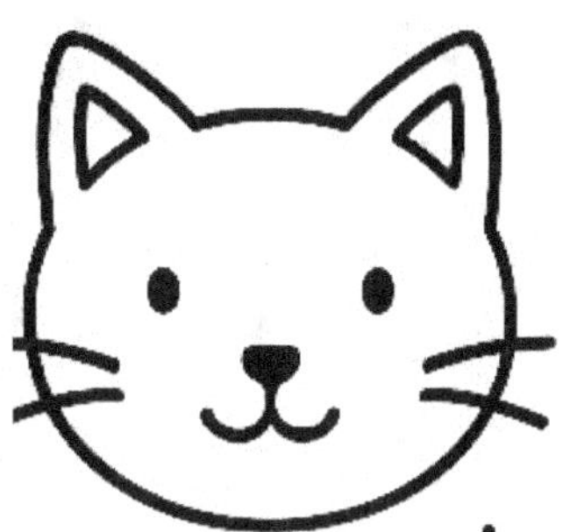

Este libro pertenece a:

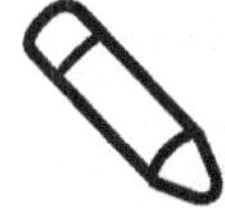

____

(¡Escribe tu nombre aquí!)

Bienvenido/a a tu aventura de colorear con Color Me Cats – Edición para Niños".

Este libro está lleno de datos curiosos y amigos peludos.
¡Es todo tuyo para colorear, aprender y disfutar!

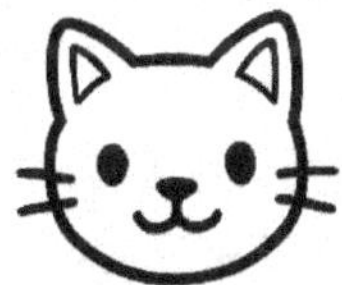 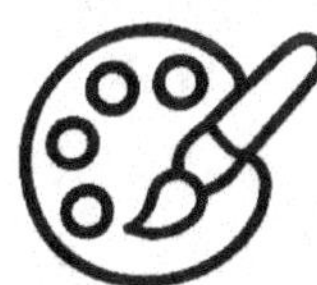 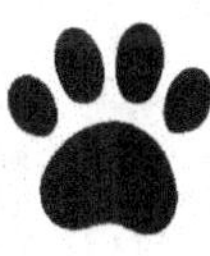

De parte de tus amigos en Myrah & Sharky Aventuras + Aprendizaje

Graccias por tus amigos

en Myrah & Sharky Aventuras + Aprendizaje

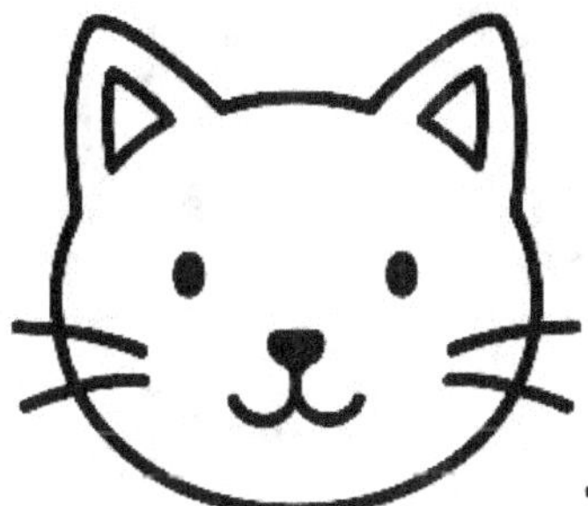
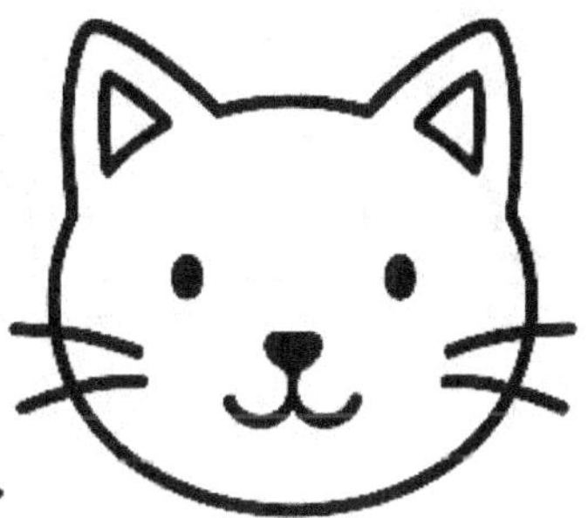

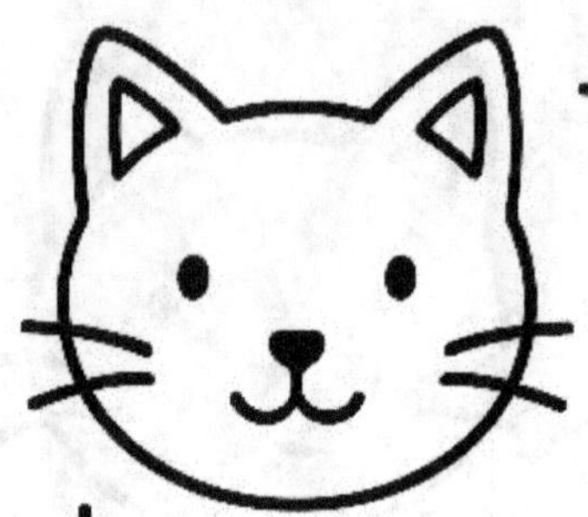
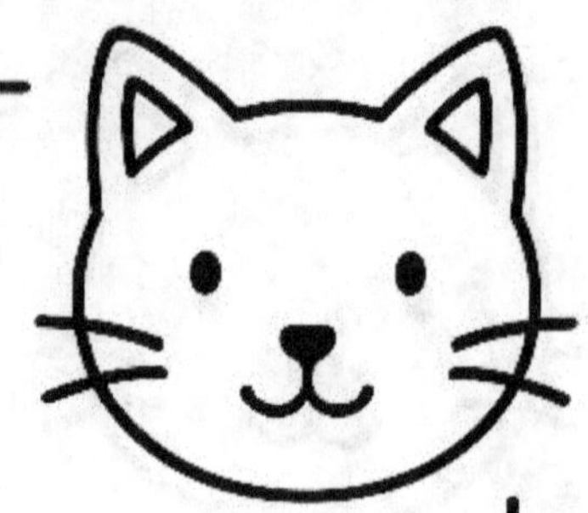

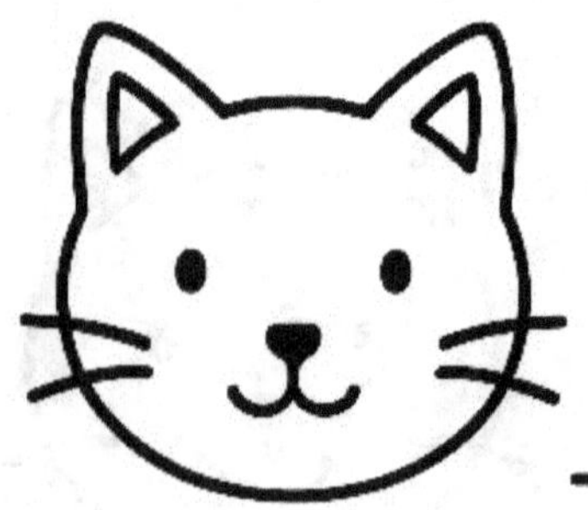
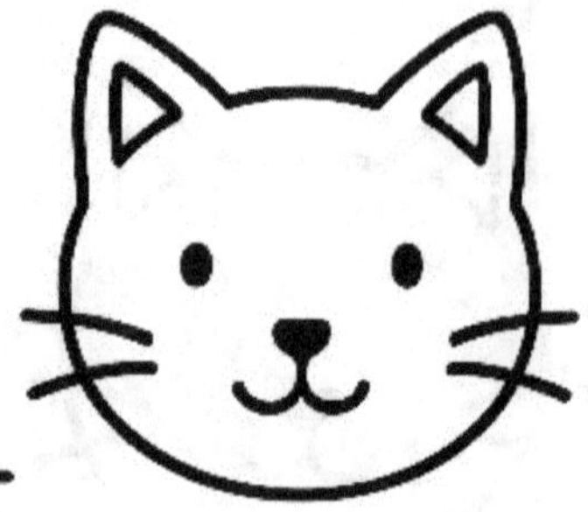

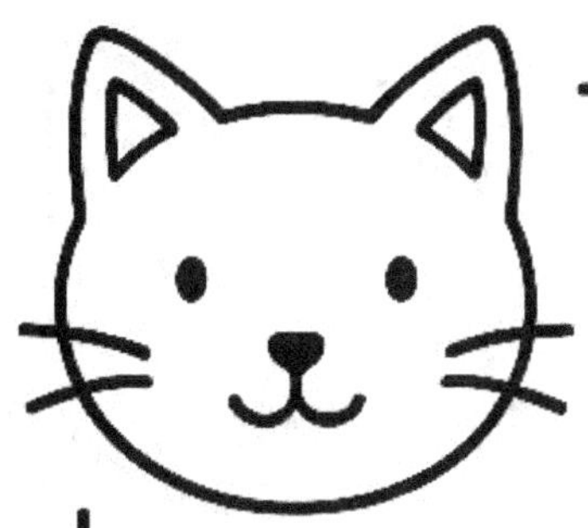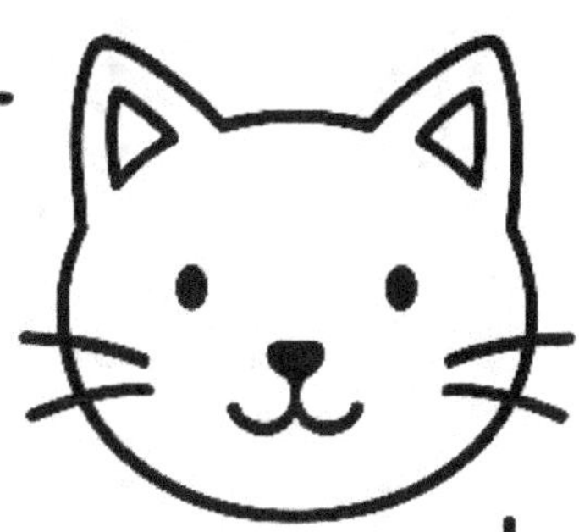

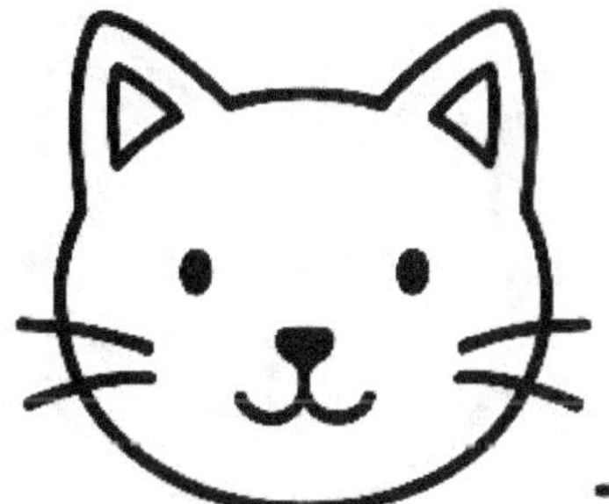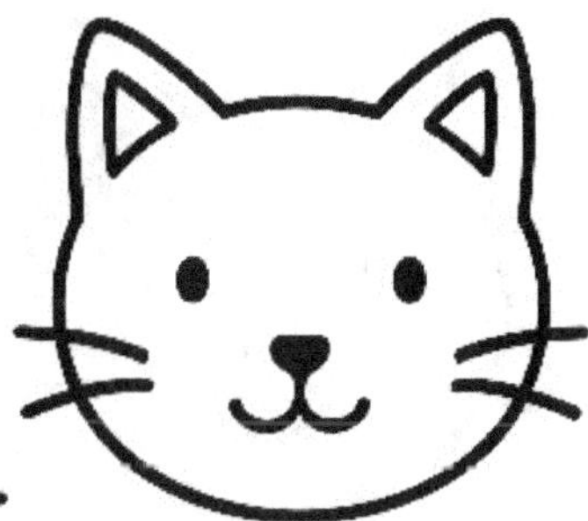

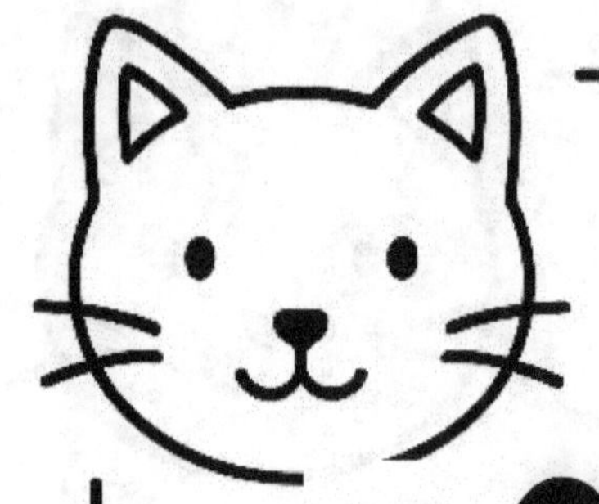 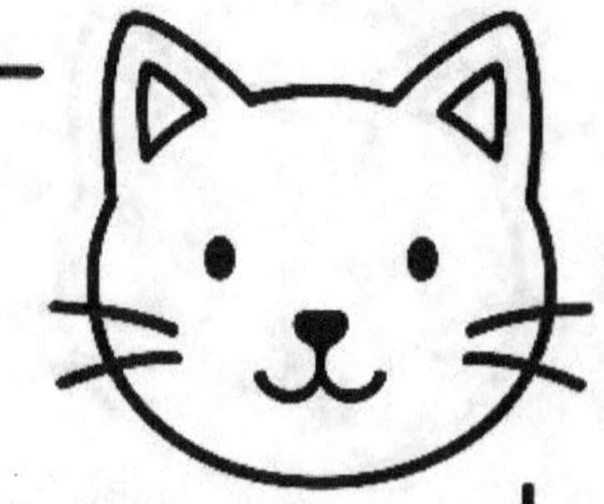

 Dedication

This book is lovingly dedicated to
all the curious little cat lovers out ther—

May your days be full of whiskers,
your hearts be full of wonder,
and your crayons never run out of color!

With love and purrs,
Myrah, Sharky & Friends

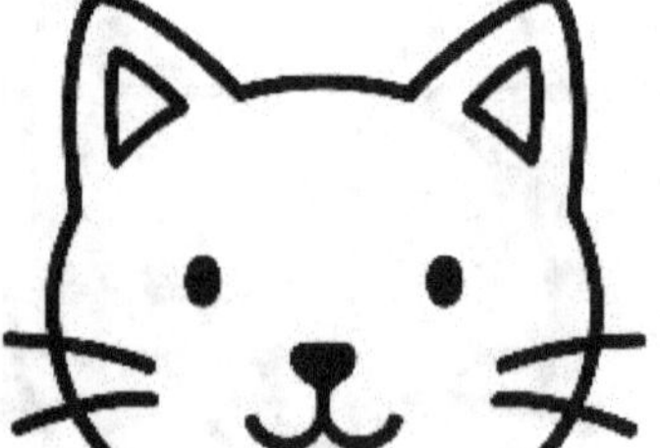 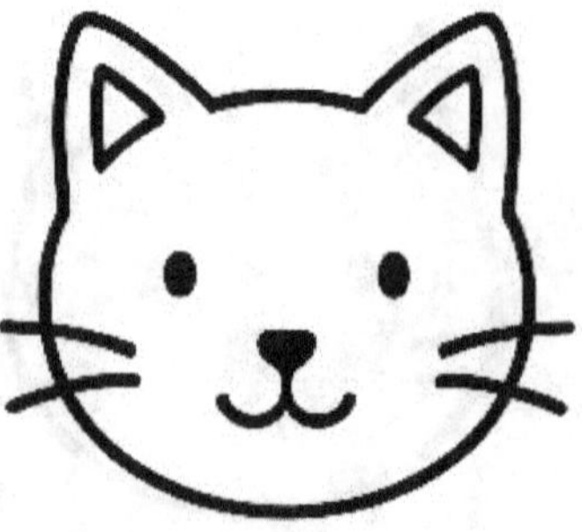

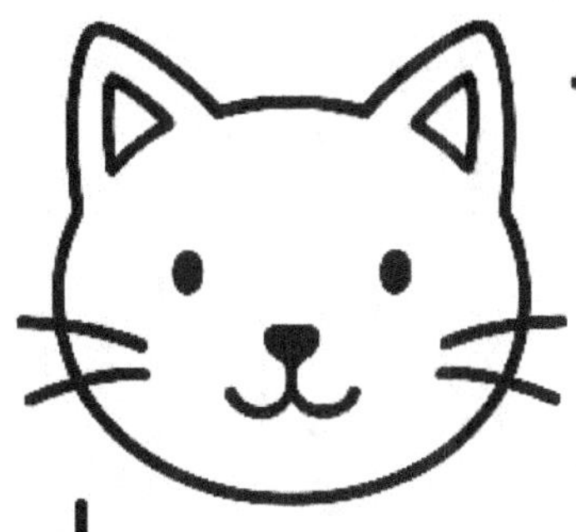
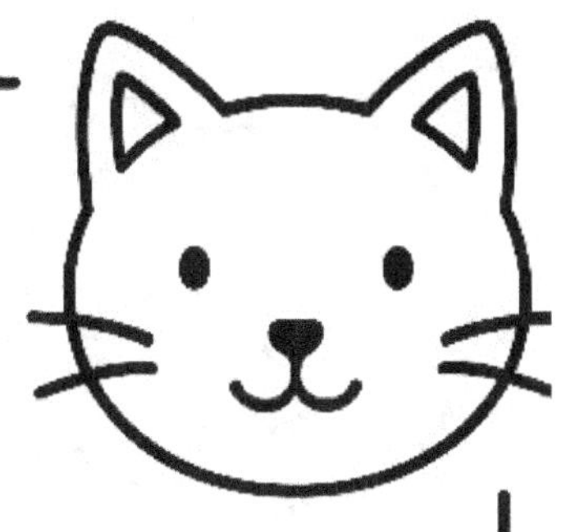

 # Dedicación

Este libro está dedicado con mucho
cariño a todos los pequeños amantes
curiosos de los gatos —

Que tus días estén llenos de bigotes,
tu corazón rebose de asombro,
¡y nunca se te acaben los crayones
de colores!

Con amor y ronroneos,
Myrah, Sharky y sus Amigos

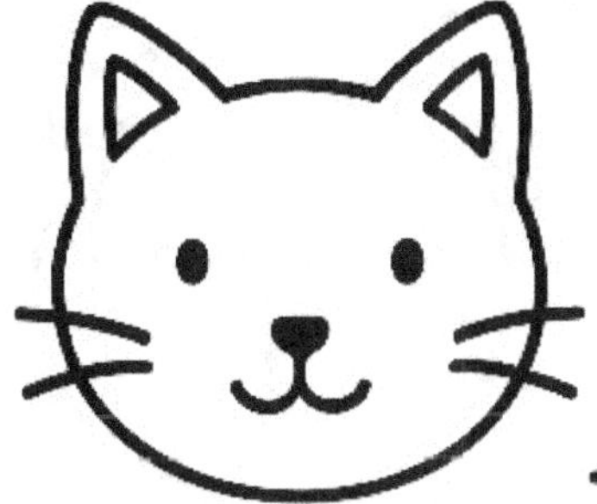
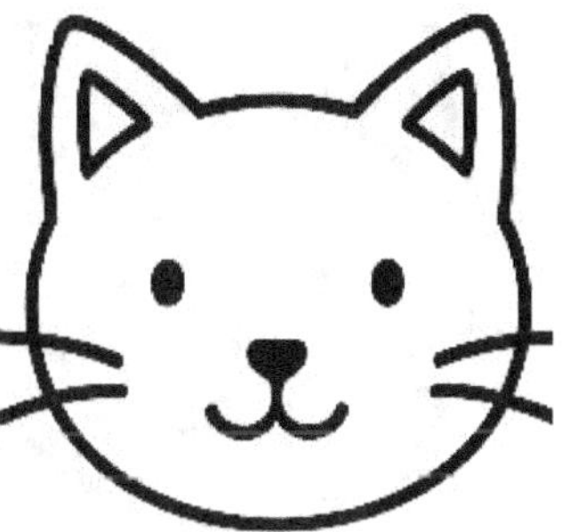

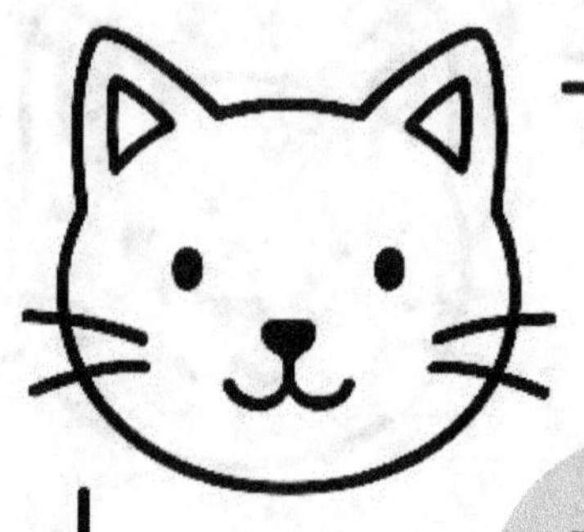
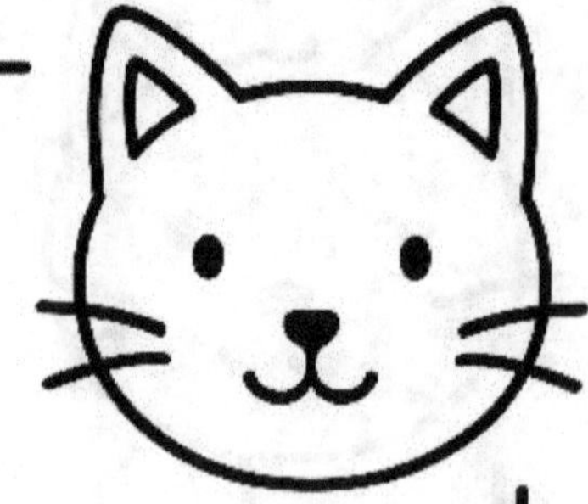

CATS HAVE WHISKERS TO HELP THEM FEEL.

Los gatos tienen bigotes para ayudarles a sentir.

Category 1: 10 Fun Bilingual Cat Facts

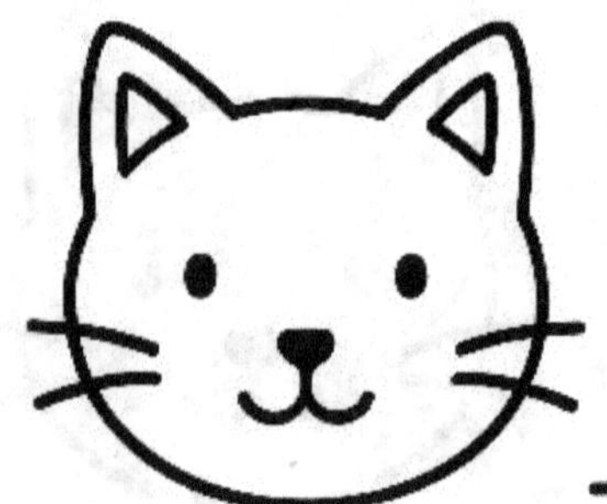
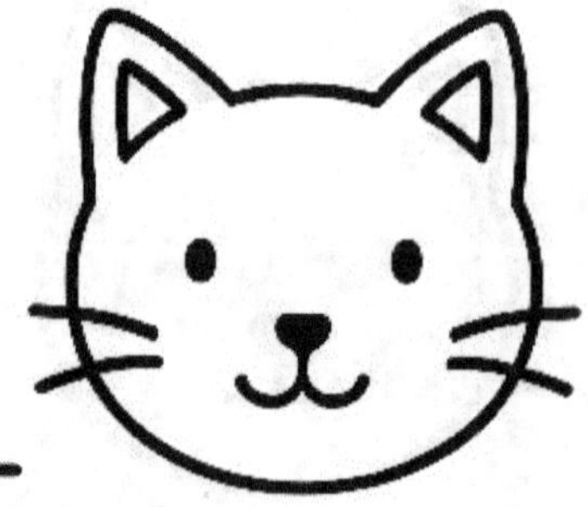

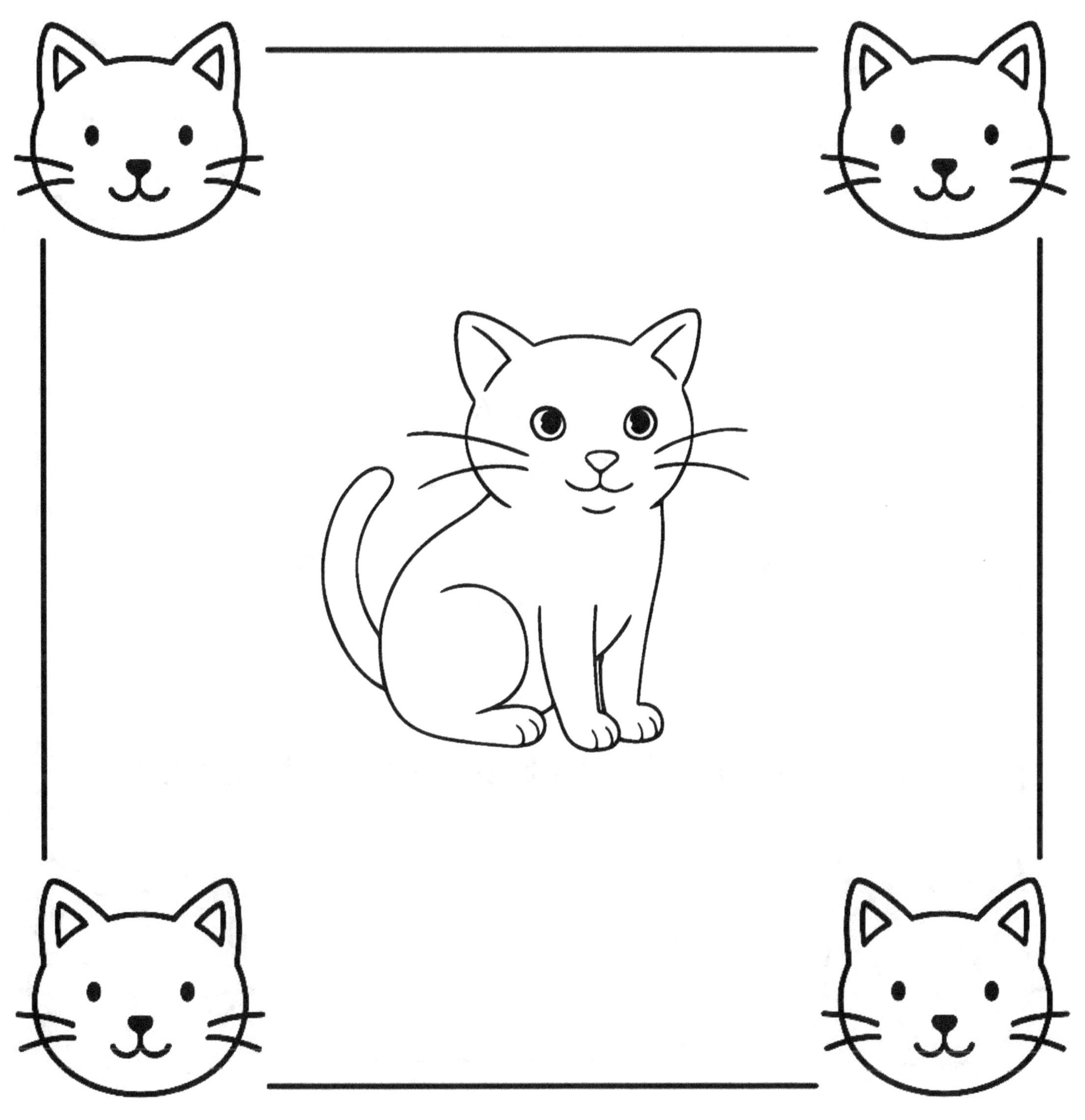

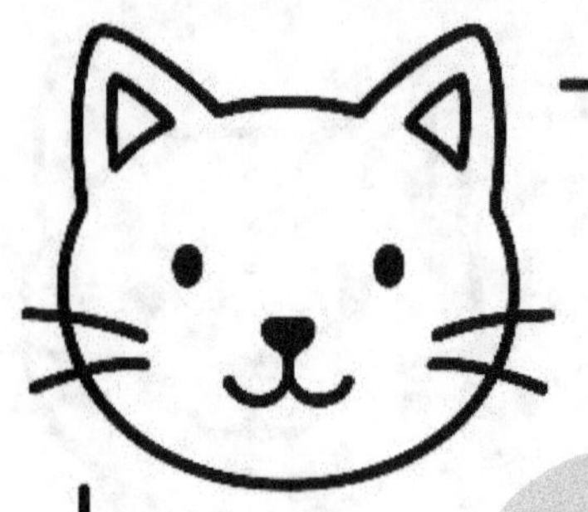
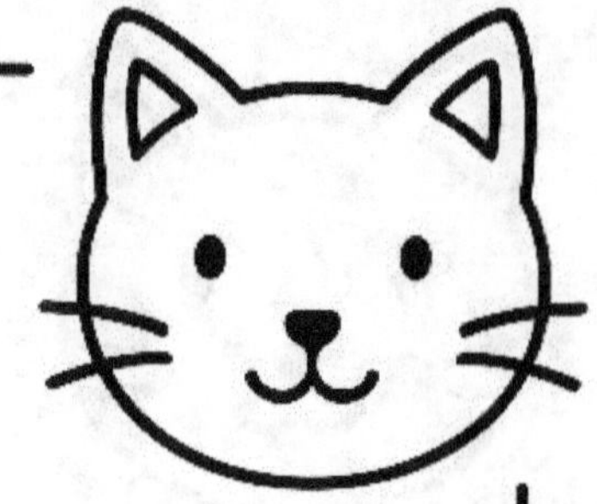

KITTENS ARE BORN WITH THEIR EYES CLOSED.

Los gatitos nacen con los ojos cerrados.

Category 1: 10 Fun Bilingual Cat Facts

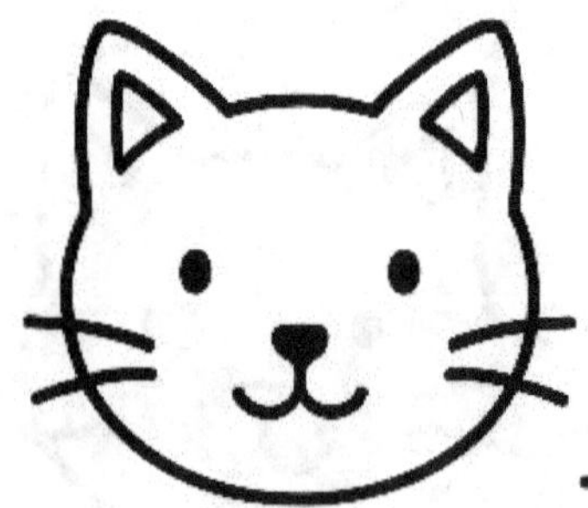
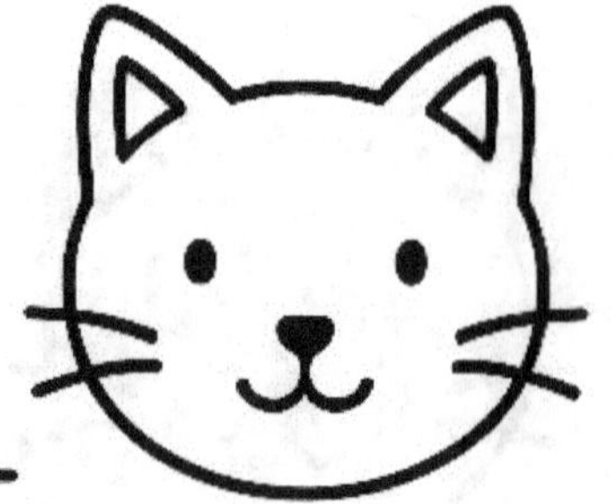

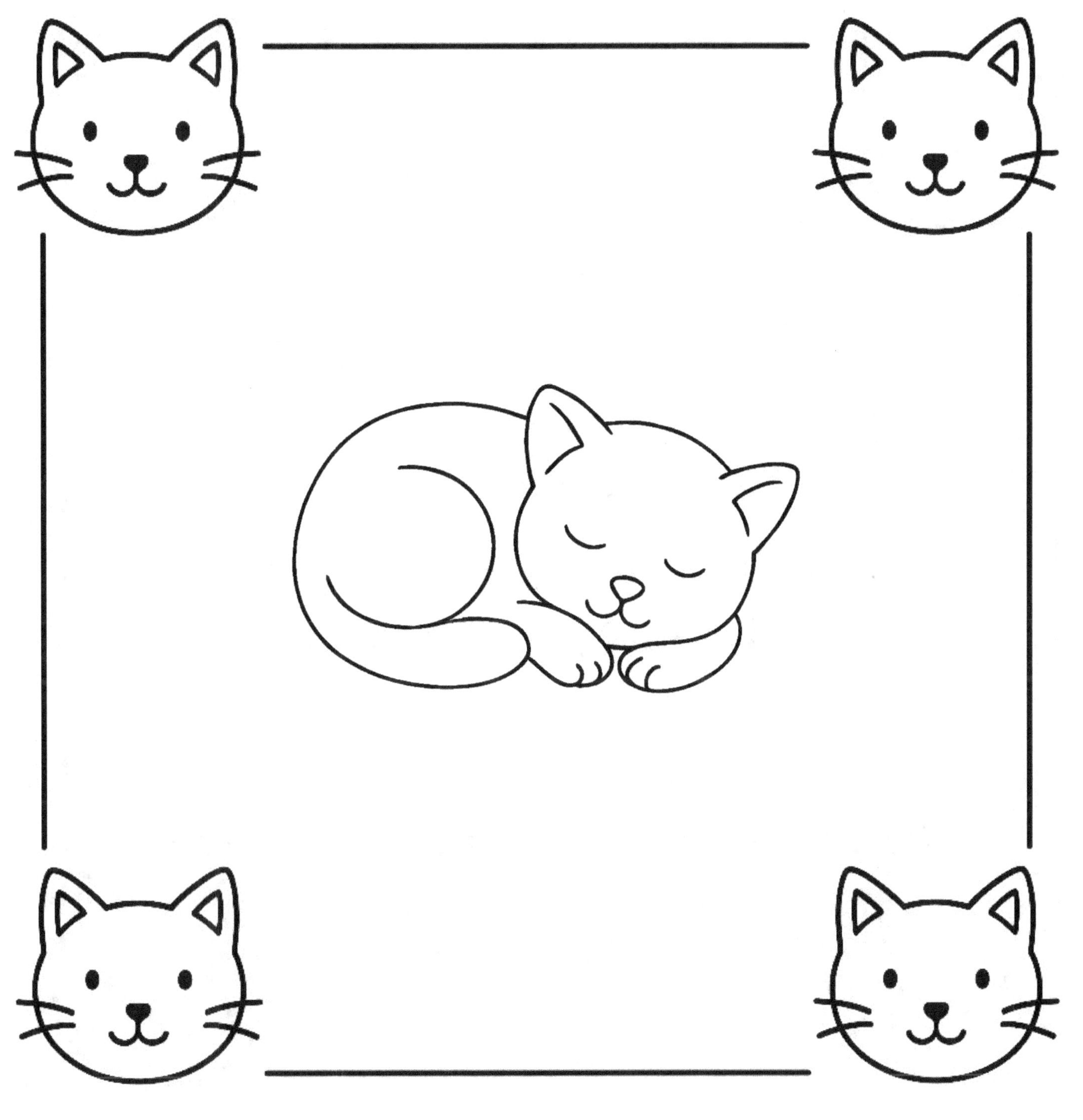

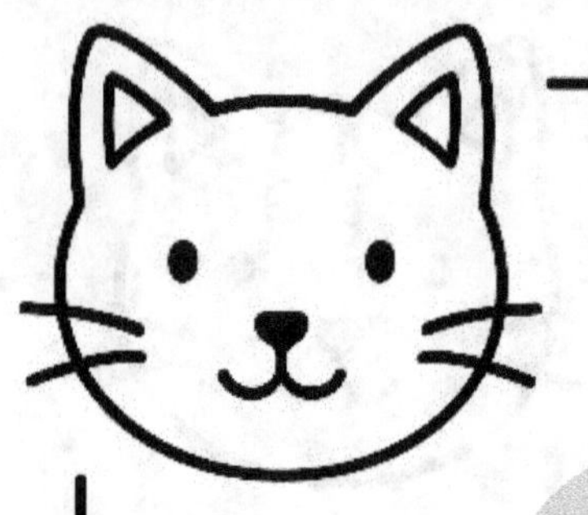
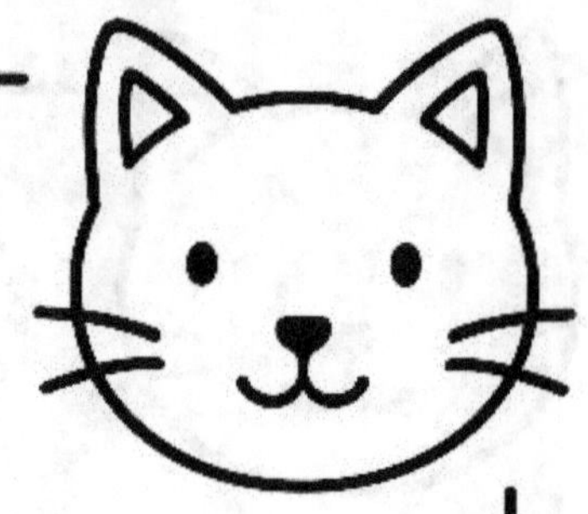

CATS LOVE TO CLIMB AND JUMP HIGH!

¡A los gatos les encanta trepar y saltar alto!

Category 1: 10 Fun Bilingual Cat Facts

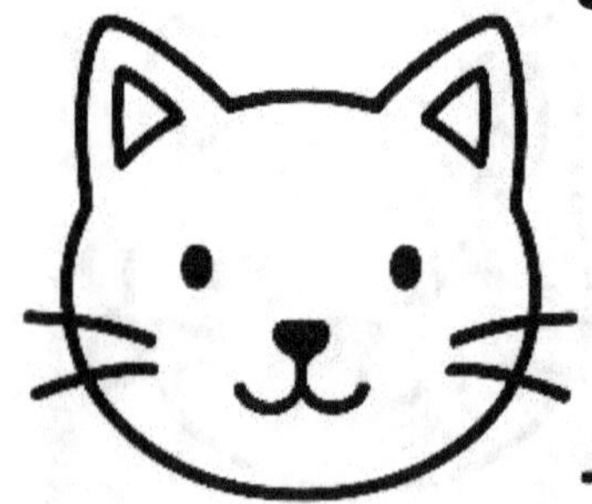
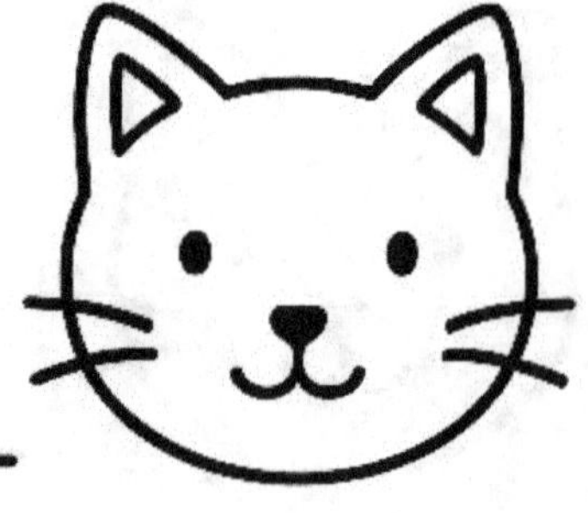

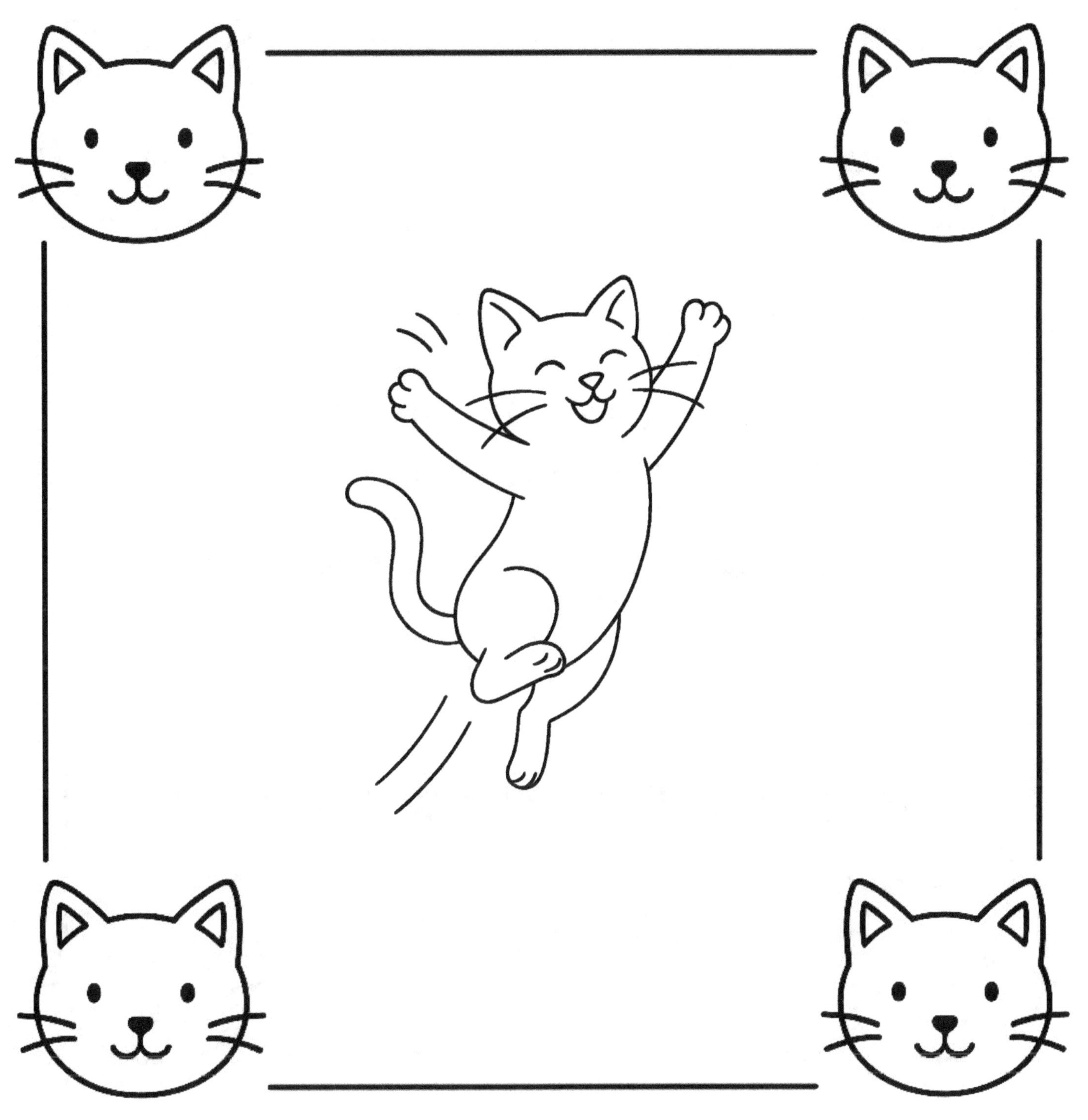

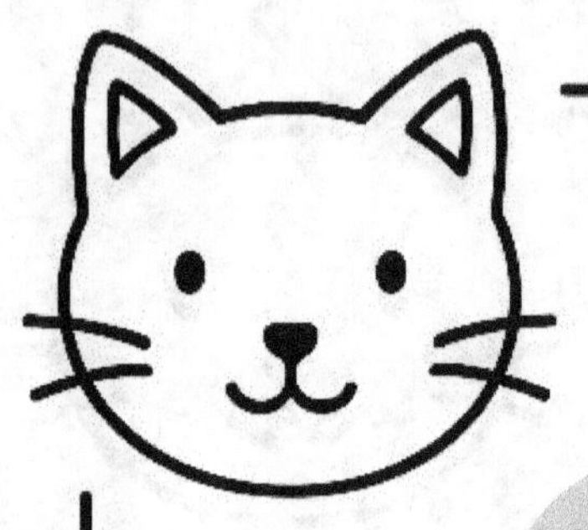
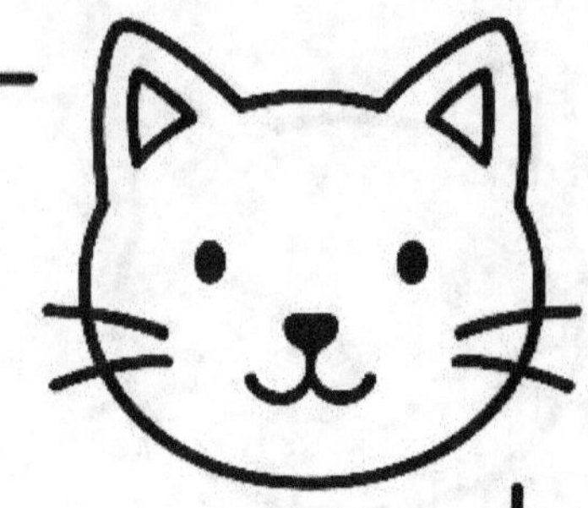

CATS CAN SLEEP UP TO 16 HOURS A DAY.

Los gatos pueden dormir hasta 16 horas al día.

Category 1: 10 Fun Bilingual Cat Facts

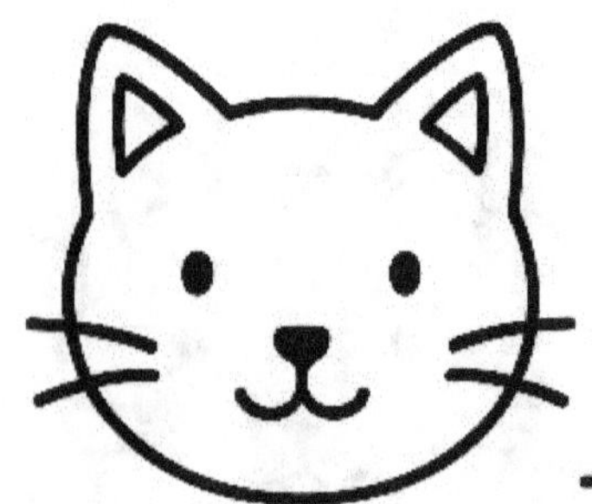
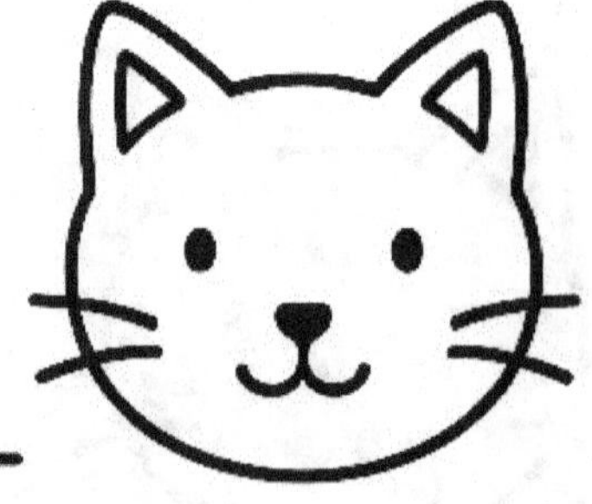

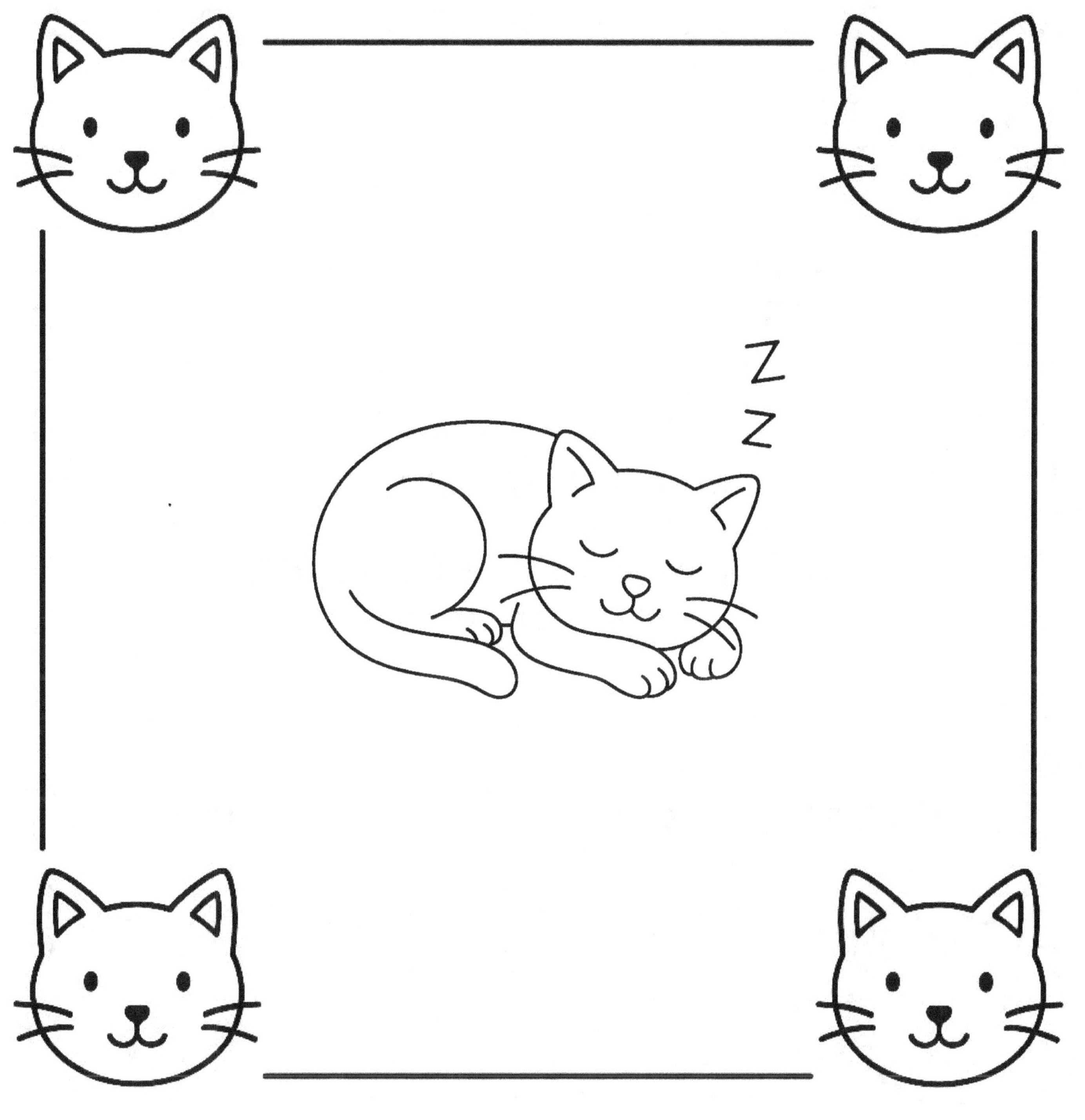

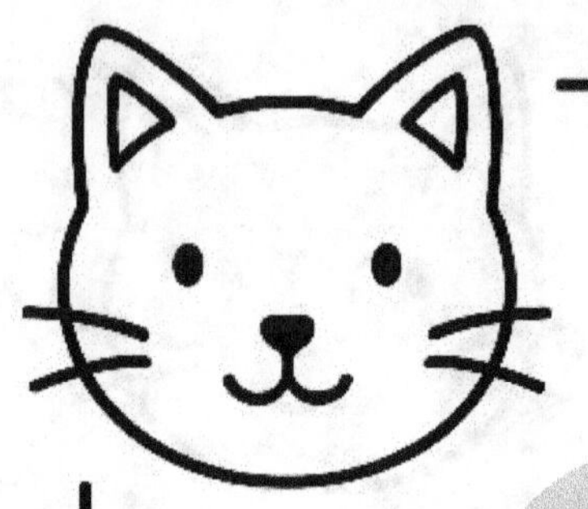
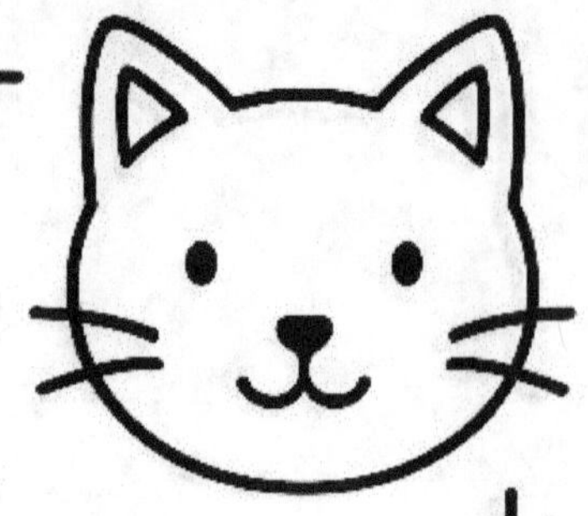

A CAT'S PURR MEANS IT FEELS SAFE AND HAPPY.

El ronroneo de un gato significa que se siente seguro y feliz.

Category 1: 10 Fun Bilingual Cat Facts

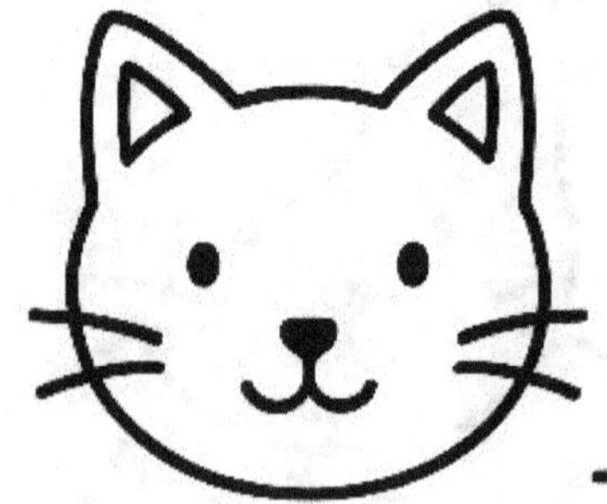
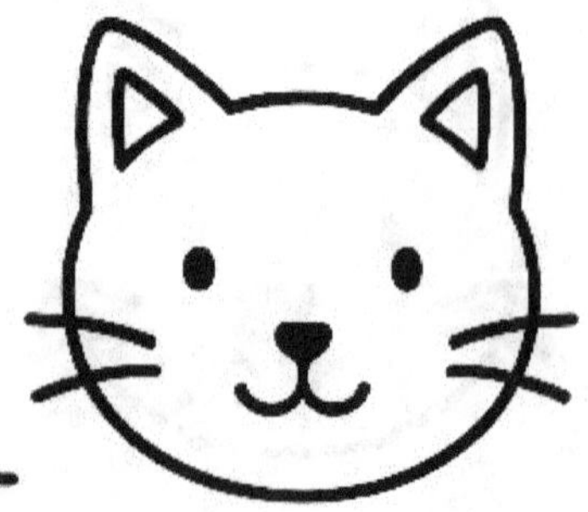

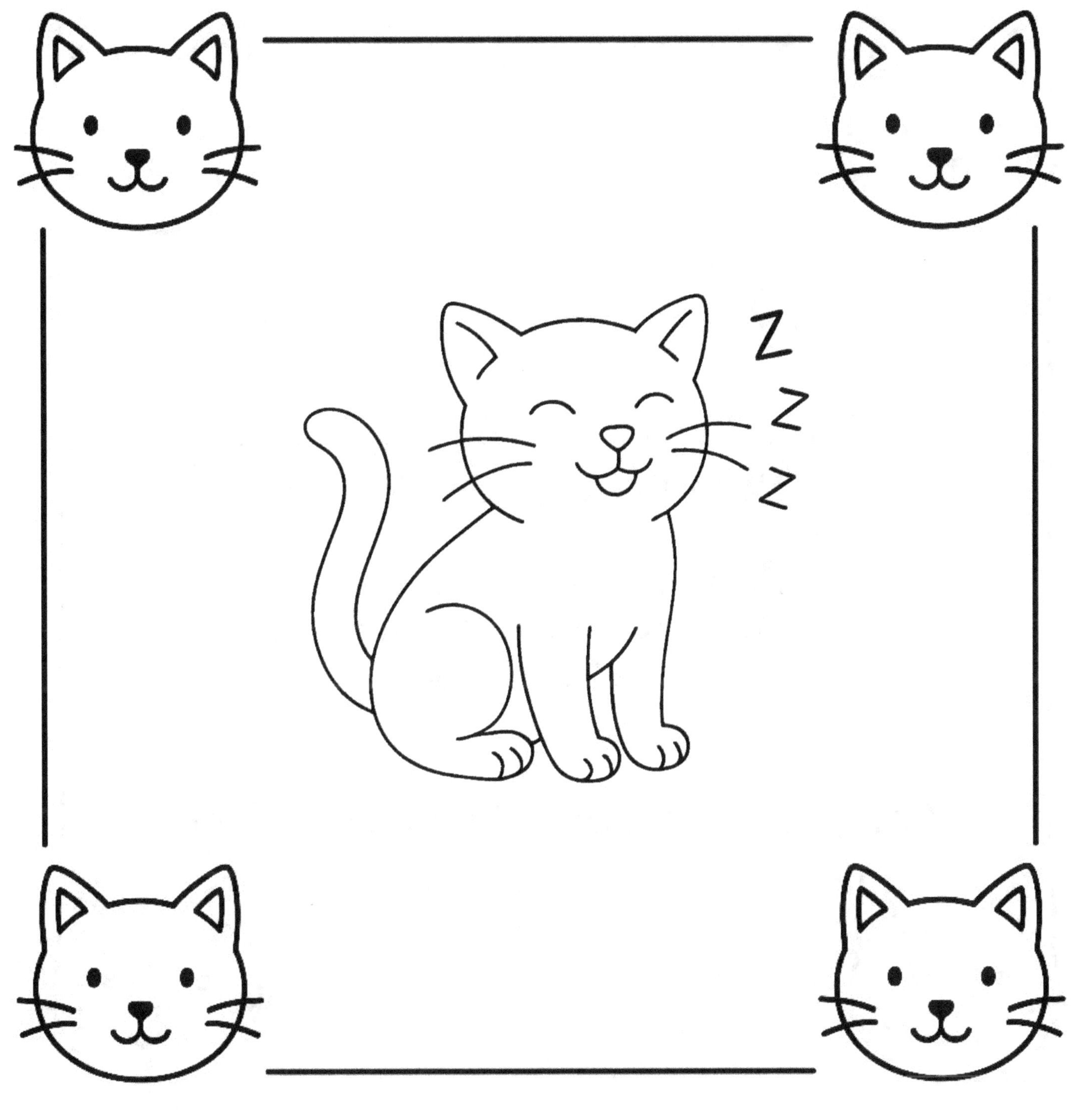

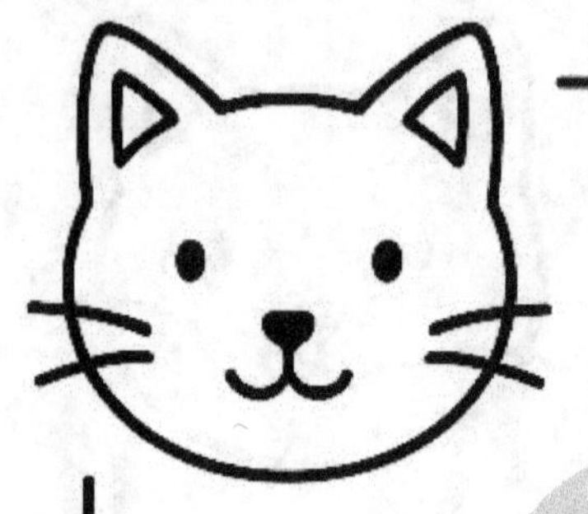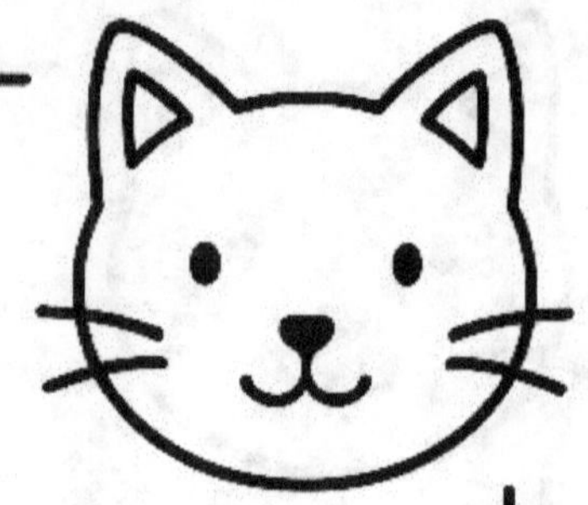

Fact #6

SOME CATS HAVE BLUE, GREEN, OR EVEN YELLOW EYES.

Algunos gatos tienen ojos azules, verdes o incluso amarillos.

Category 1: 10 Fun Bilingual Cat Facts

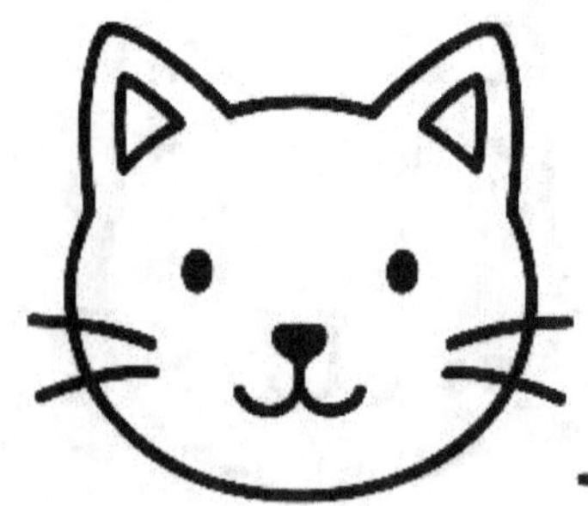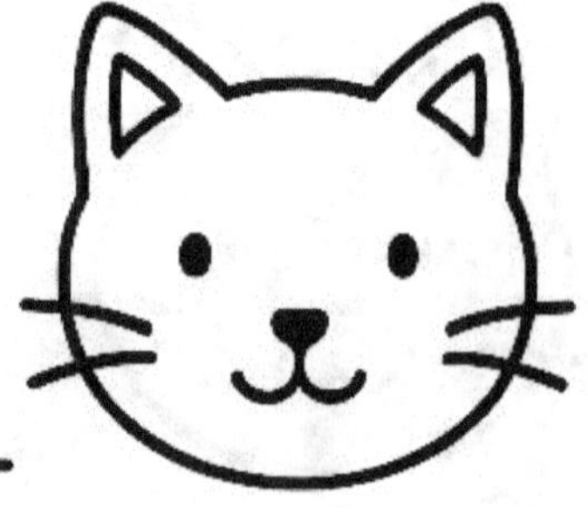

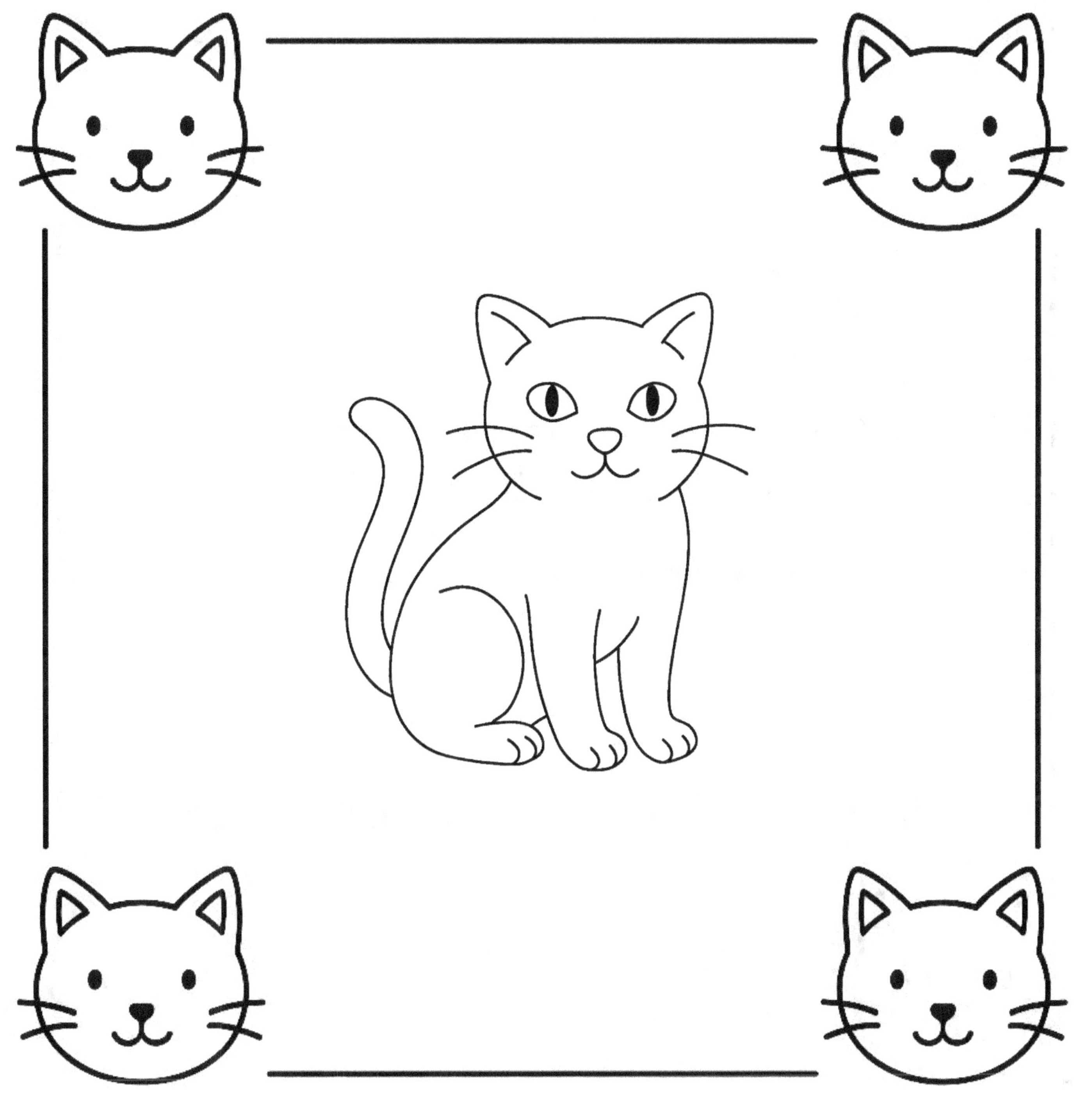

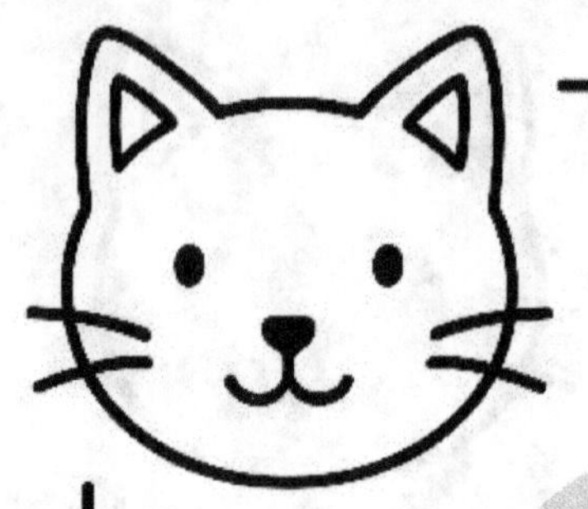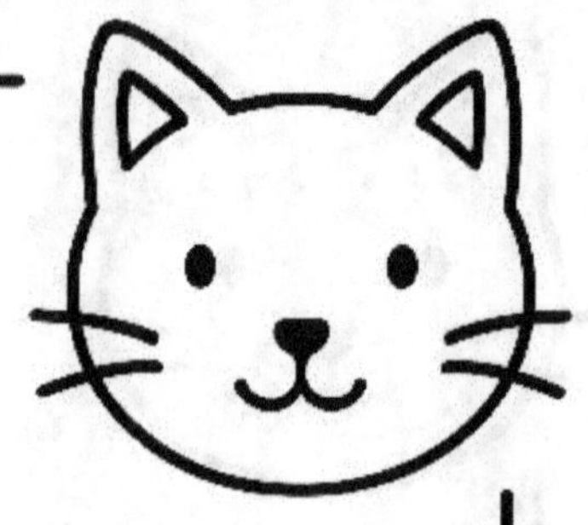

CATS CLEAN THEMSELVES BY LICKING THEIR FUR.

Los gatos se limpian lamiendo su pelaje.

Category 1: 10 Fun Bilingual Cat Facts

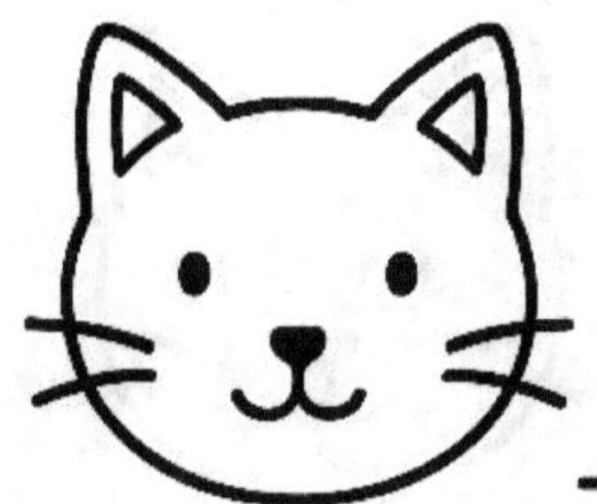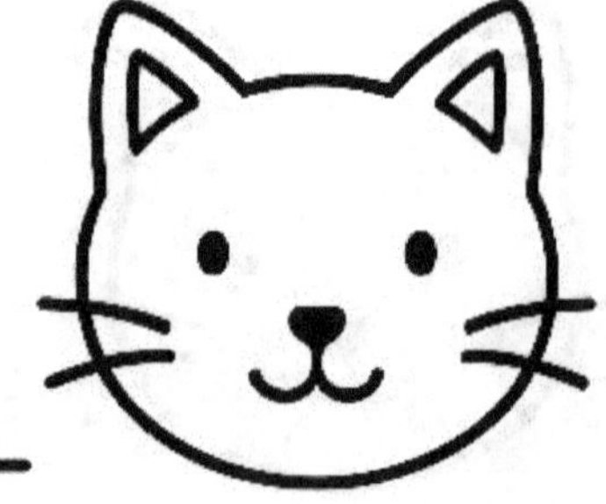

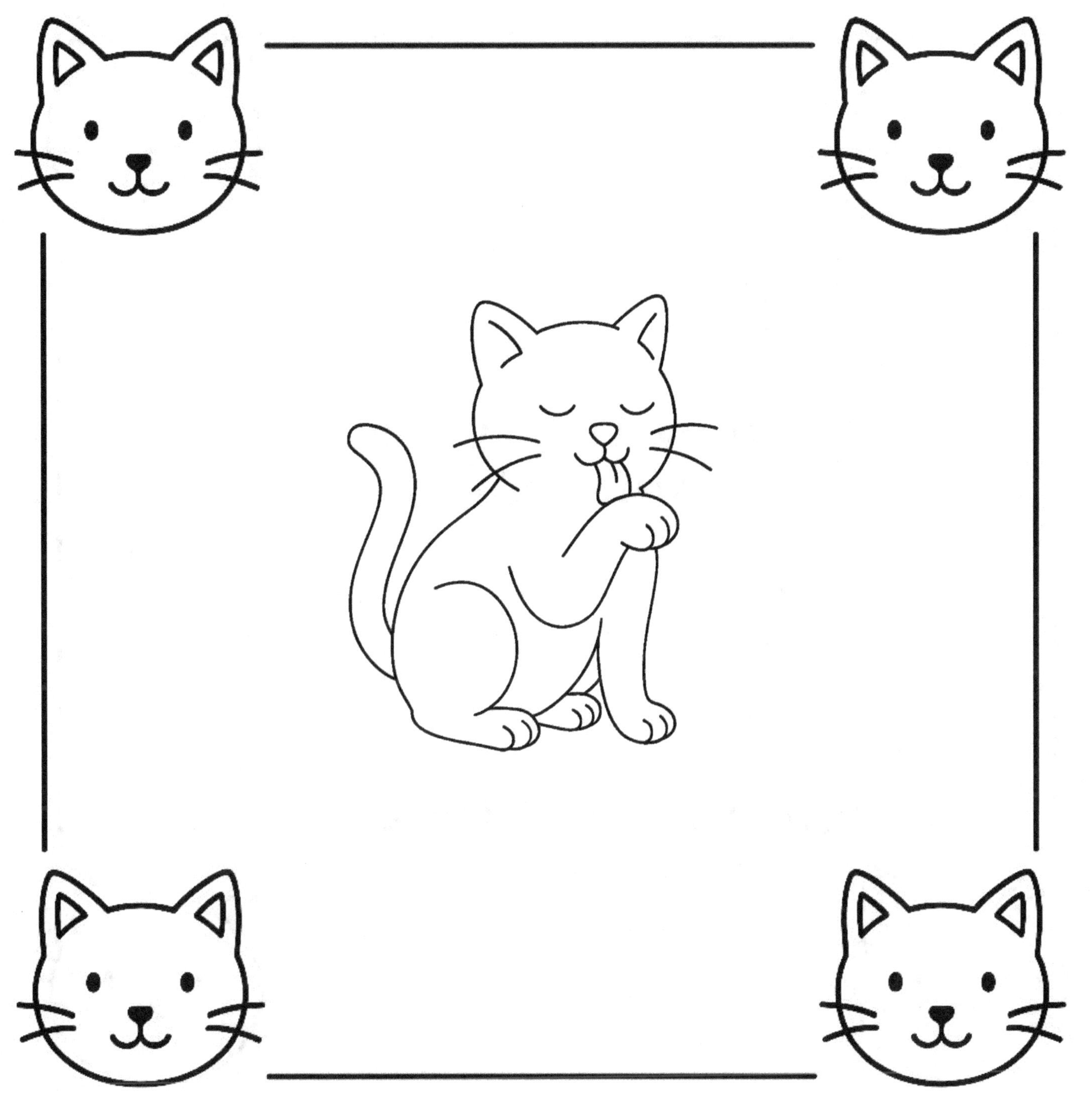

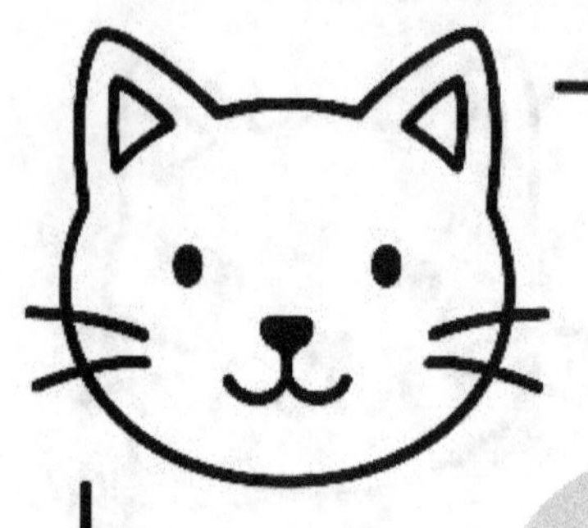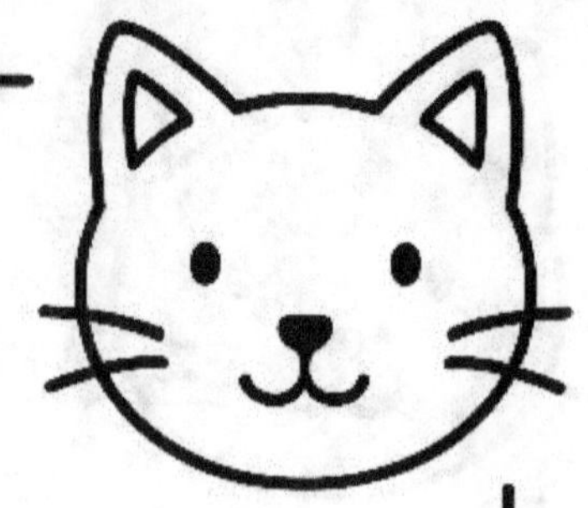

KITTENS LOVE TO CHASE TOYS AND STRING.

A los gatitos les encanta perseguir juguetes y cuerdas.

Category 1: 10 Fun Bilingual Cat Facts

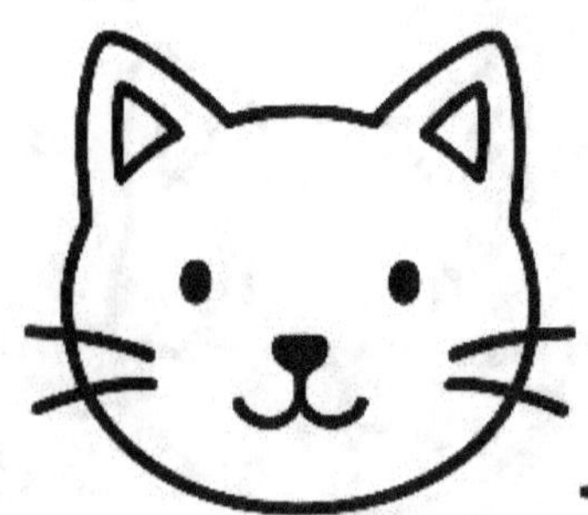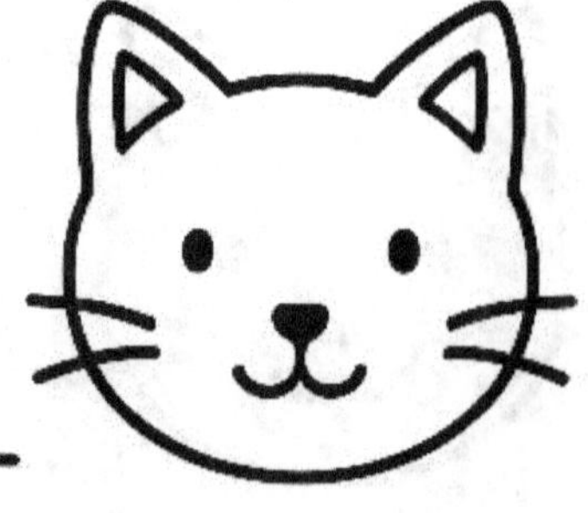

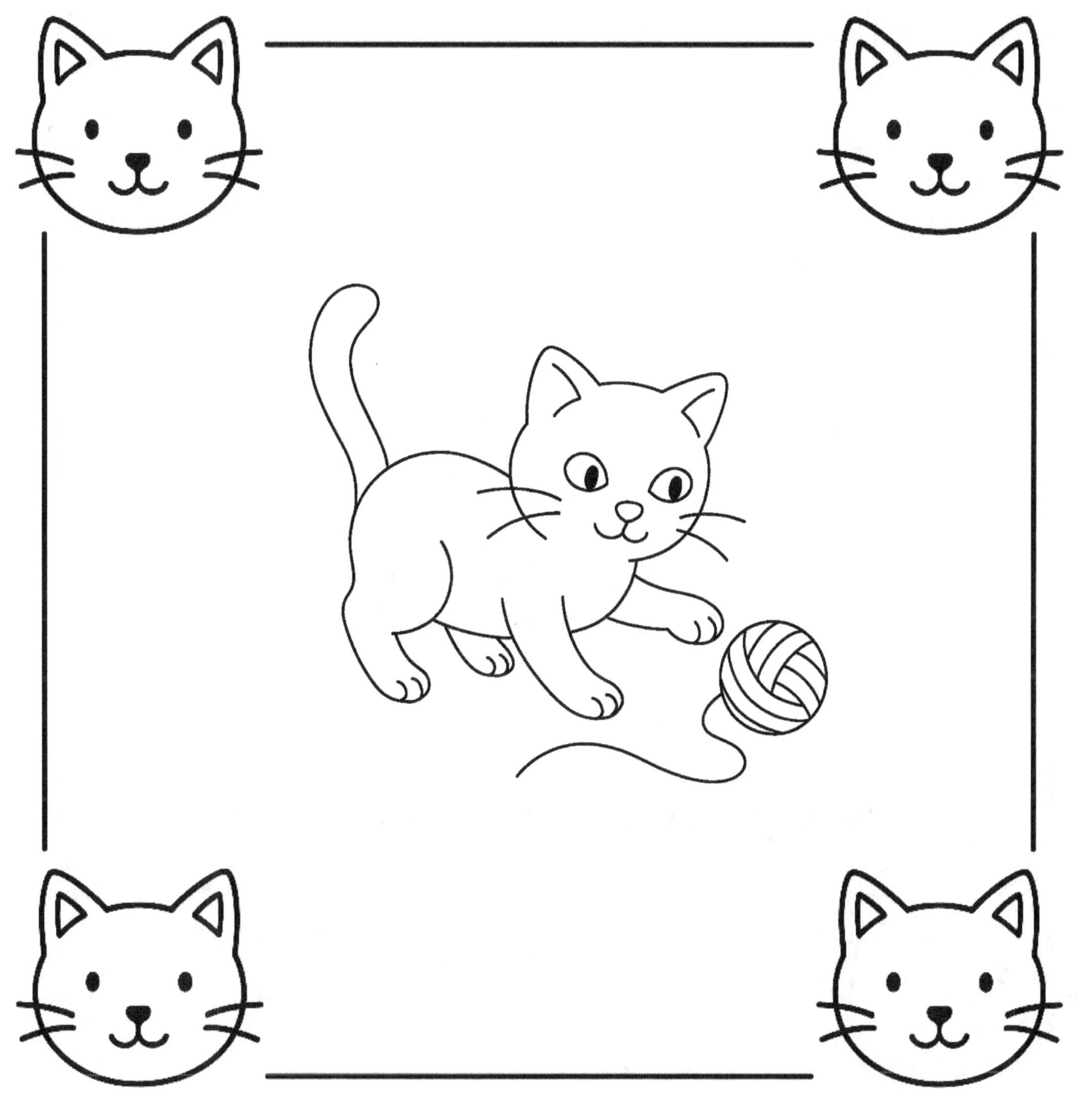

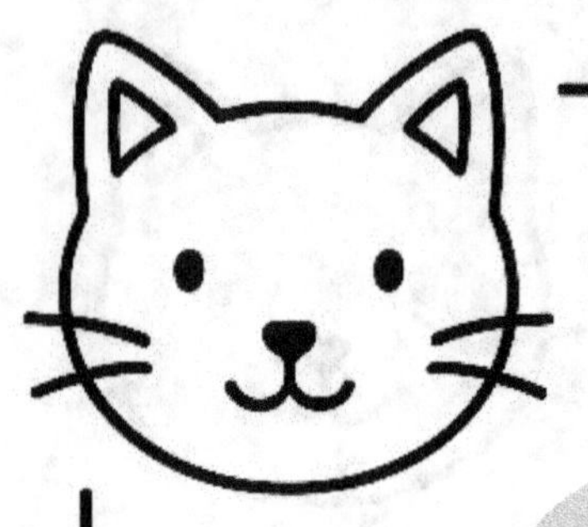 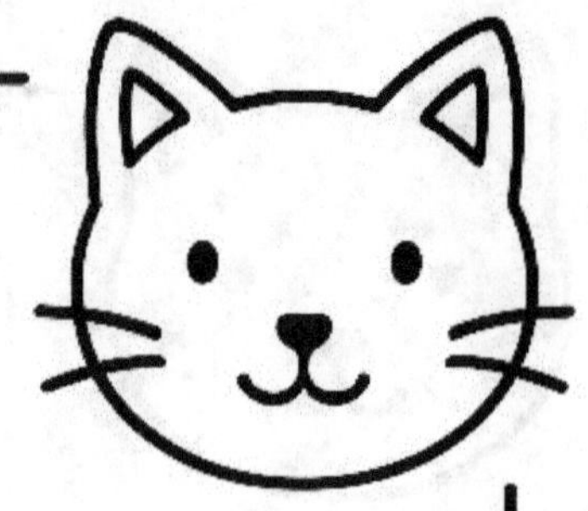

CATS USE THEIR TAILS TO HELP WITH BALANCE.

Los gatos usan la cola para mantener el equilibrio.

Category 1: 10 Fun Bilingual Cat Facts

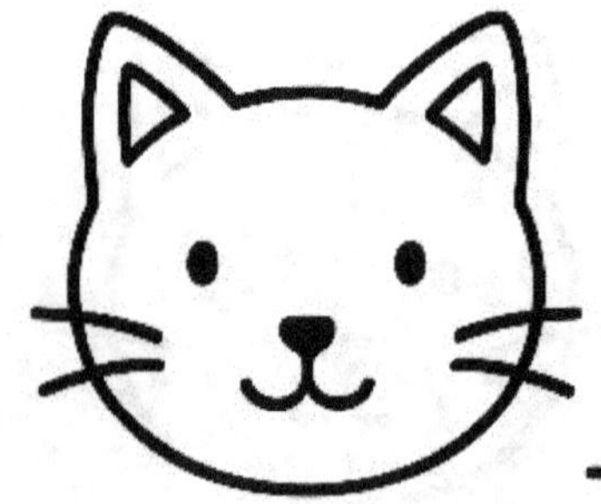 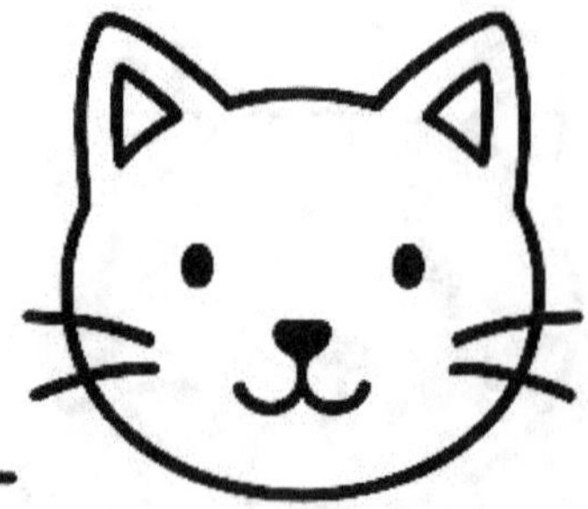

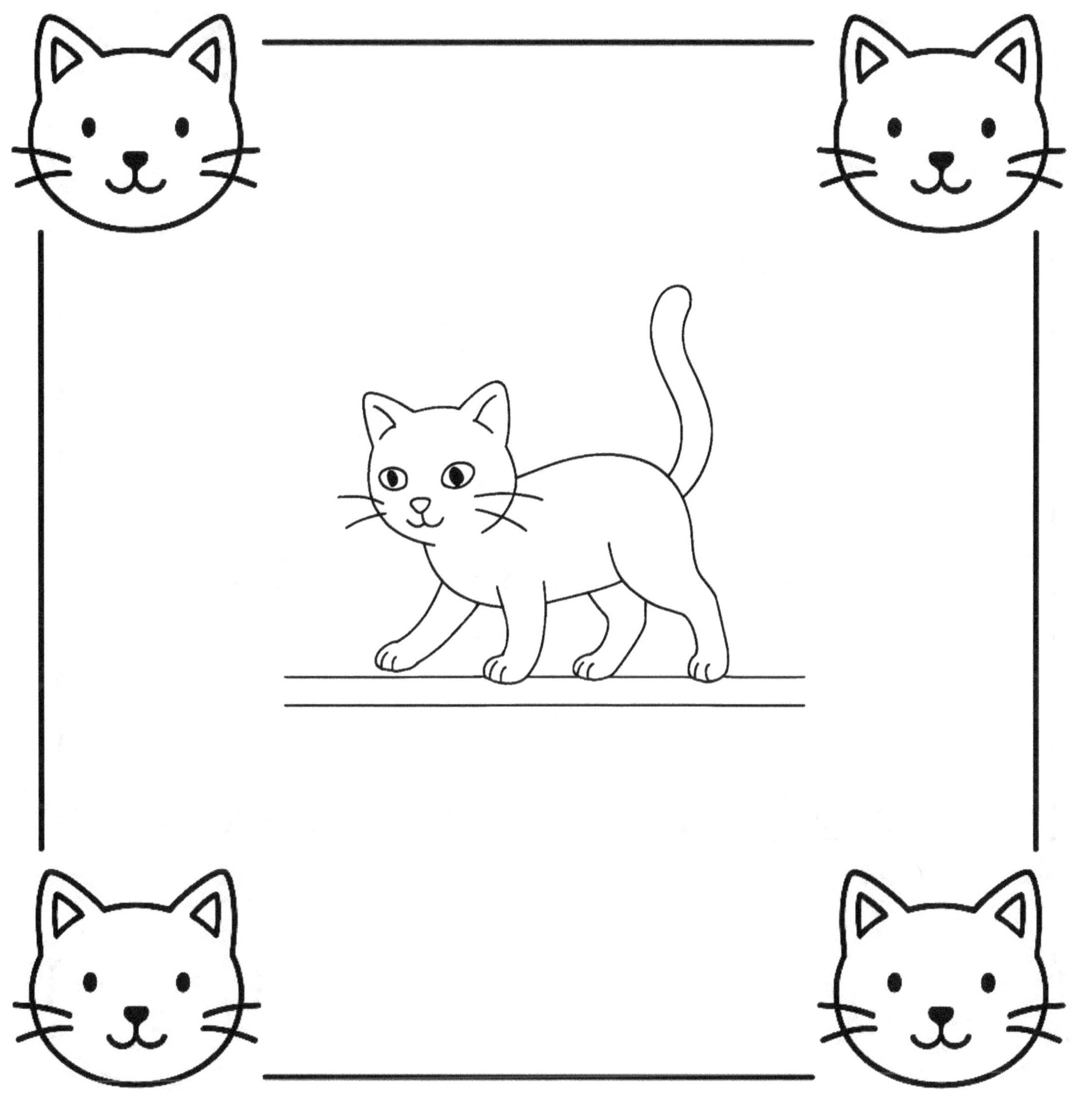

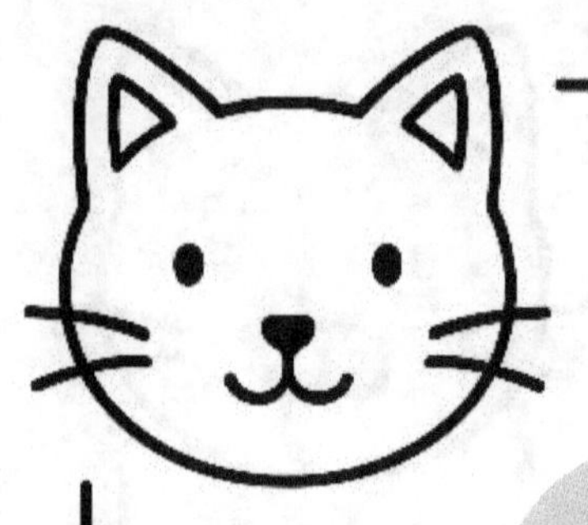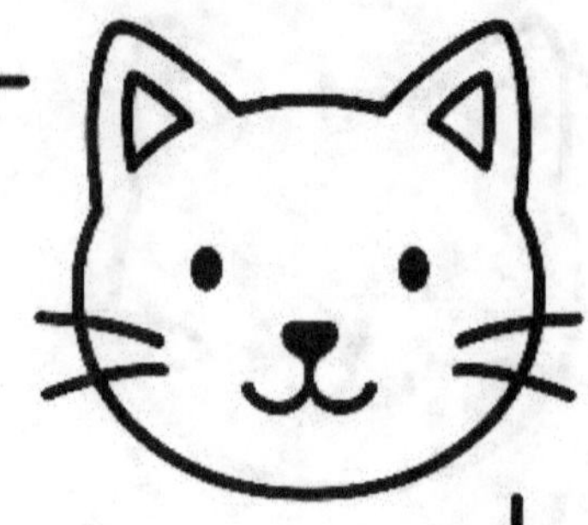

EACH CAT HAS A UNIQUE MEOW!

¡Cada gato tiene un maullido único!

Category 1: 10 Fun Bilingual Cat Facts

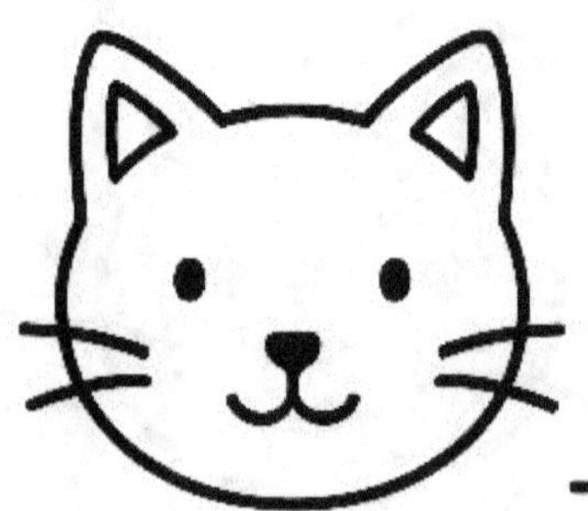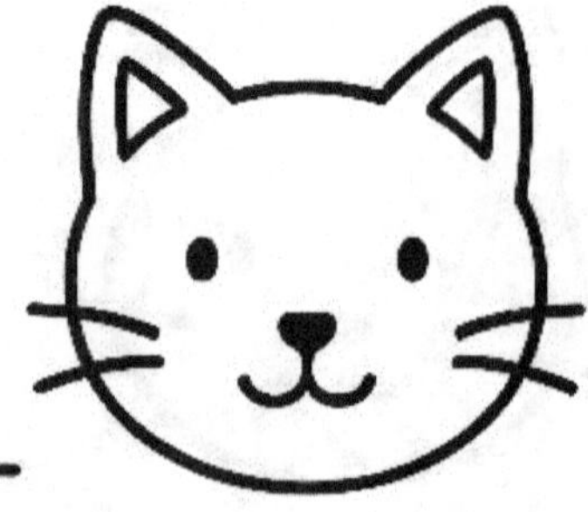

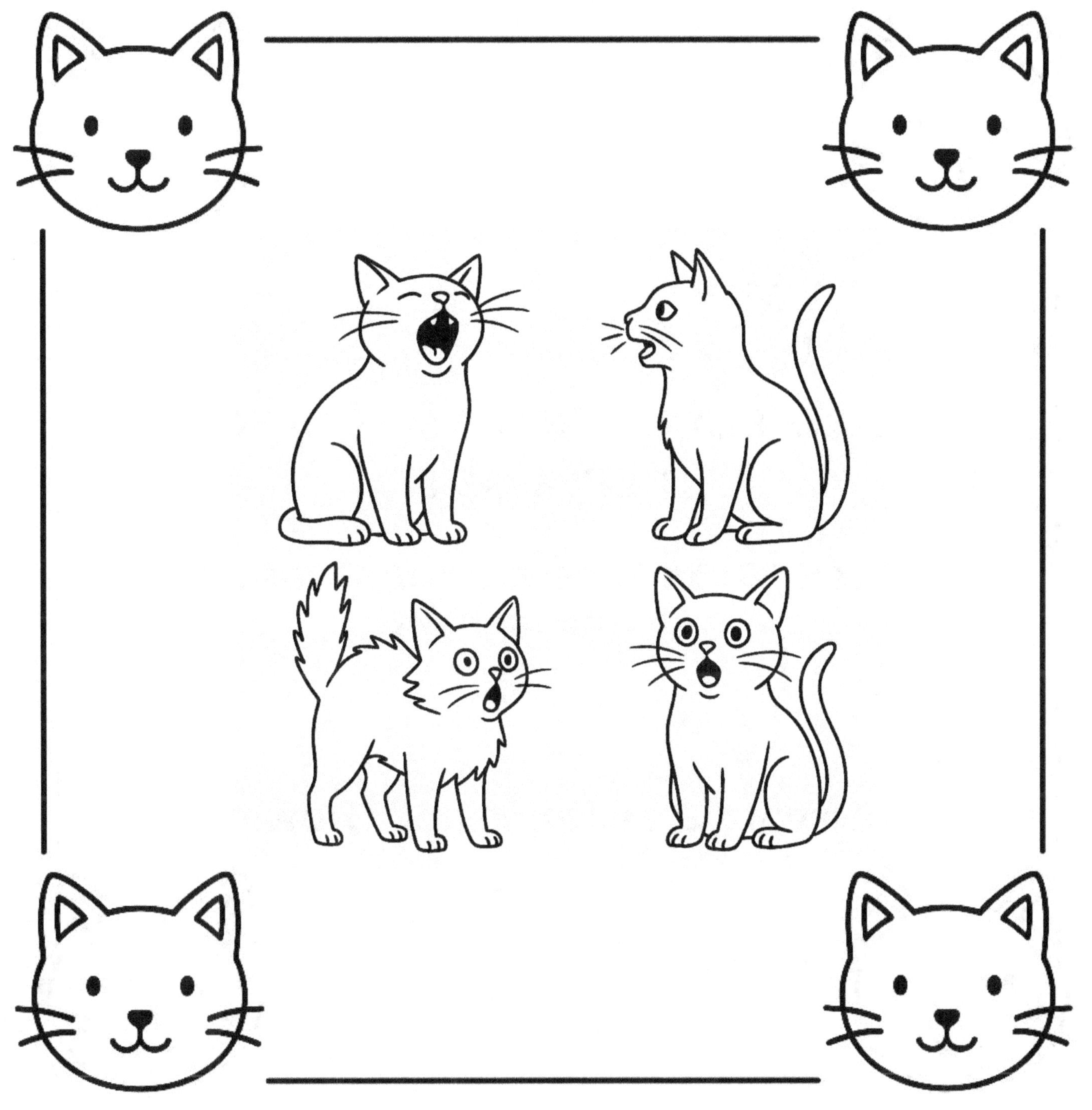

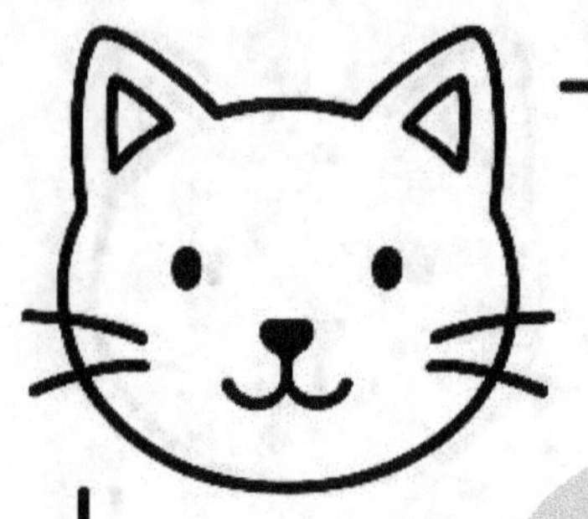
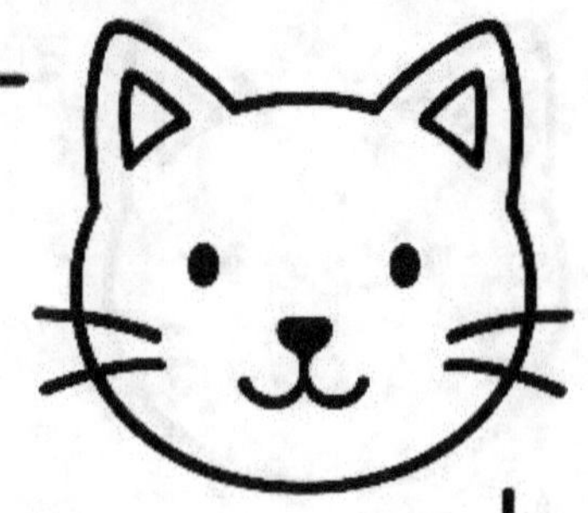

CATS LEARN FROM WATCHING THEIR MOMS.

Los gatos aprenden observando a sus mamás.

Category 2: Learning and Growing

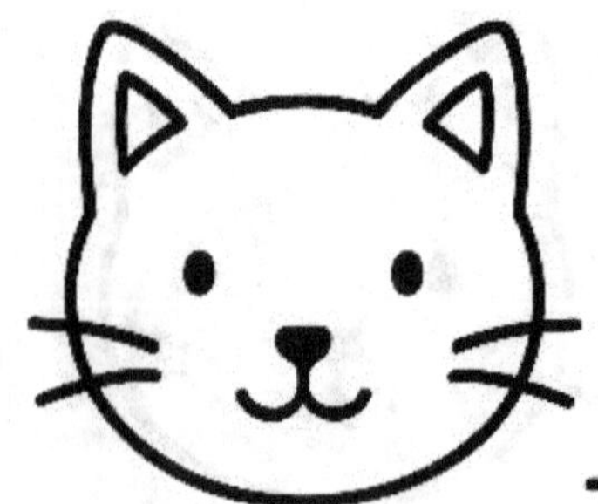
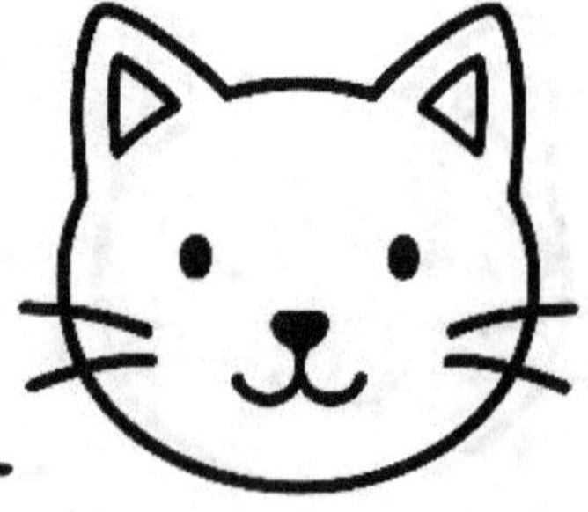

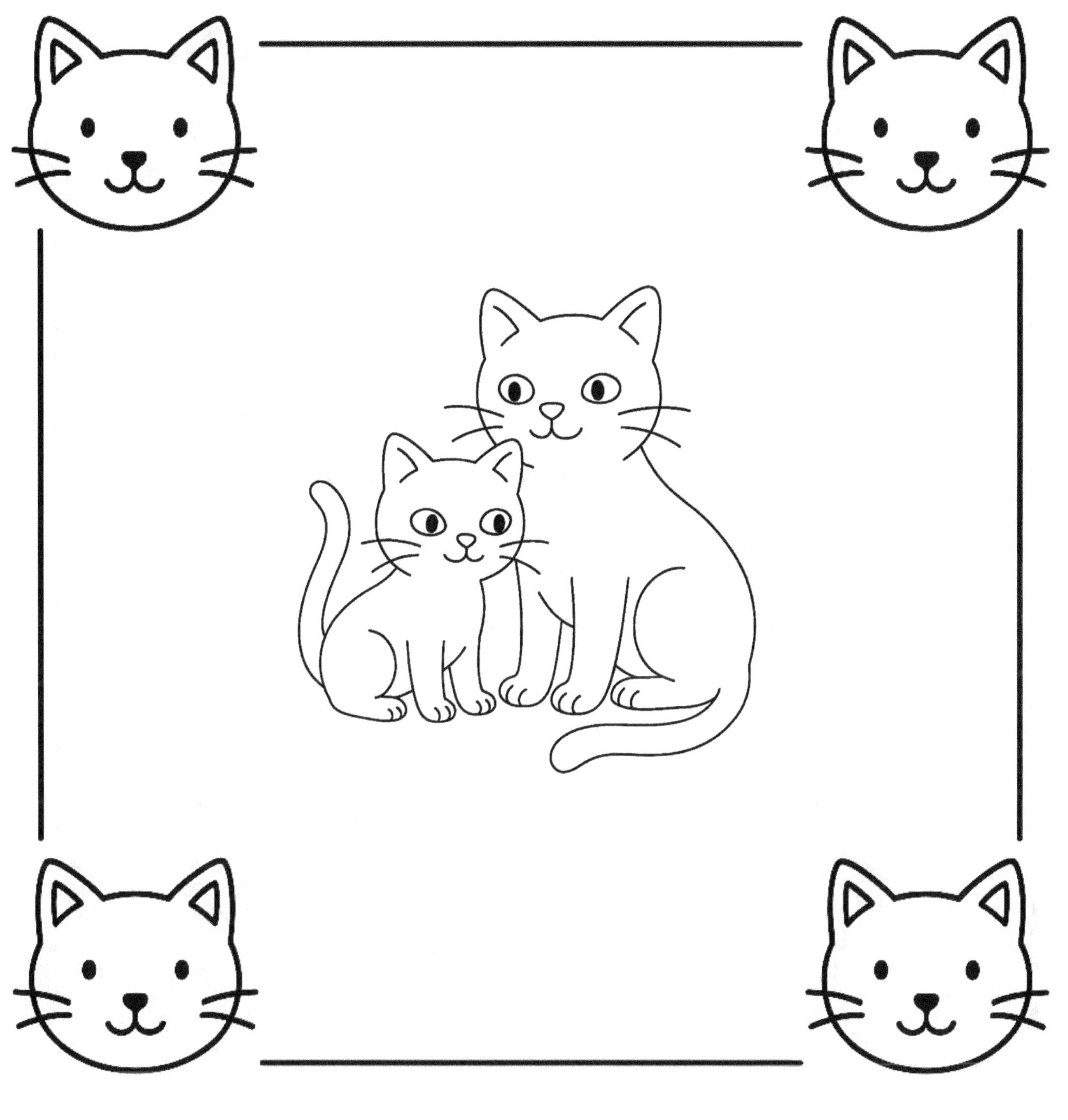

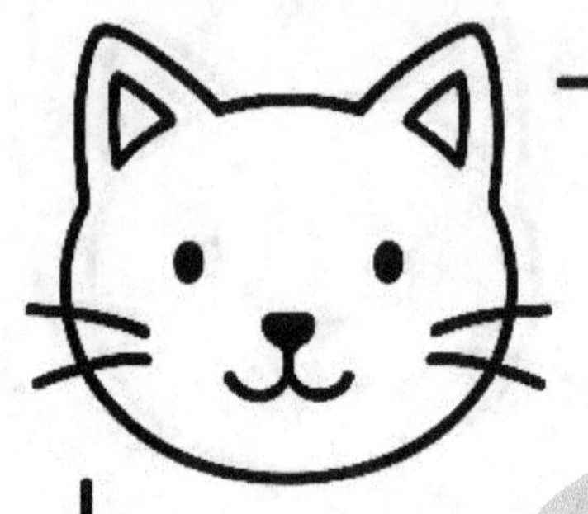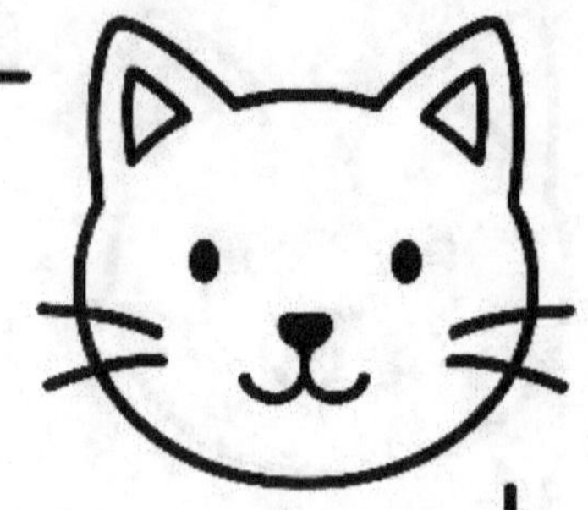

Fact #12

KITTENS START WALKING AT ABOUT 3 WEEKS OLD.

Los gatitos empiezan a caminar alrededor de las 3 semanas.

Category 2: Learning and Growing

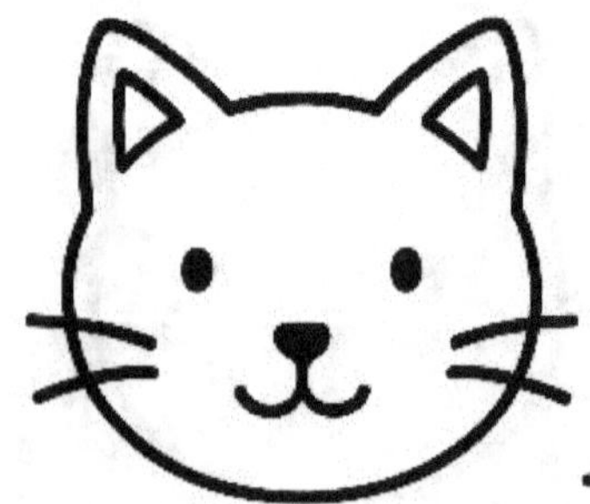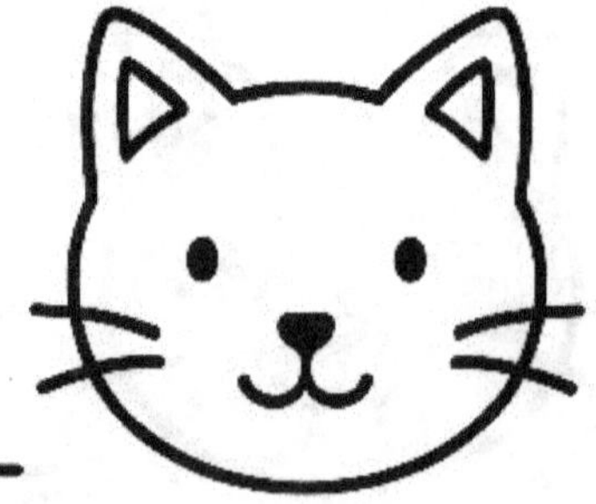

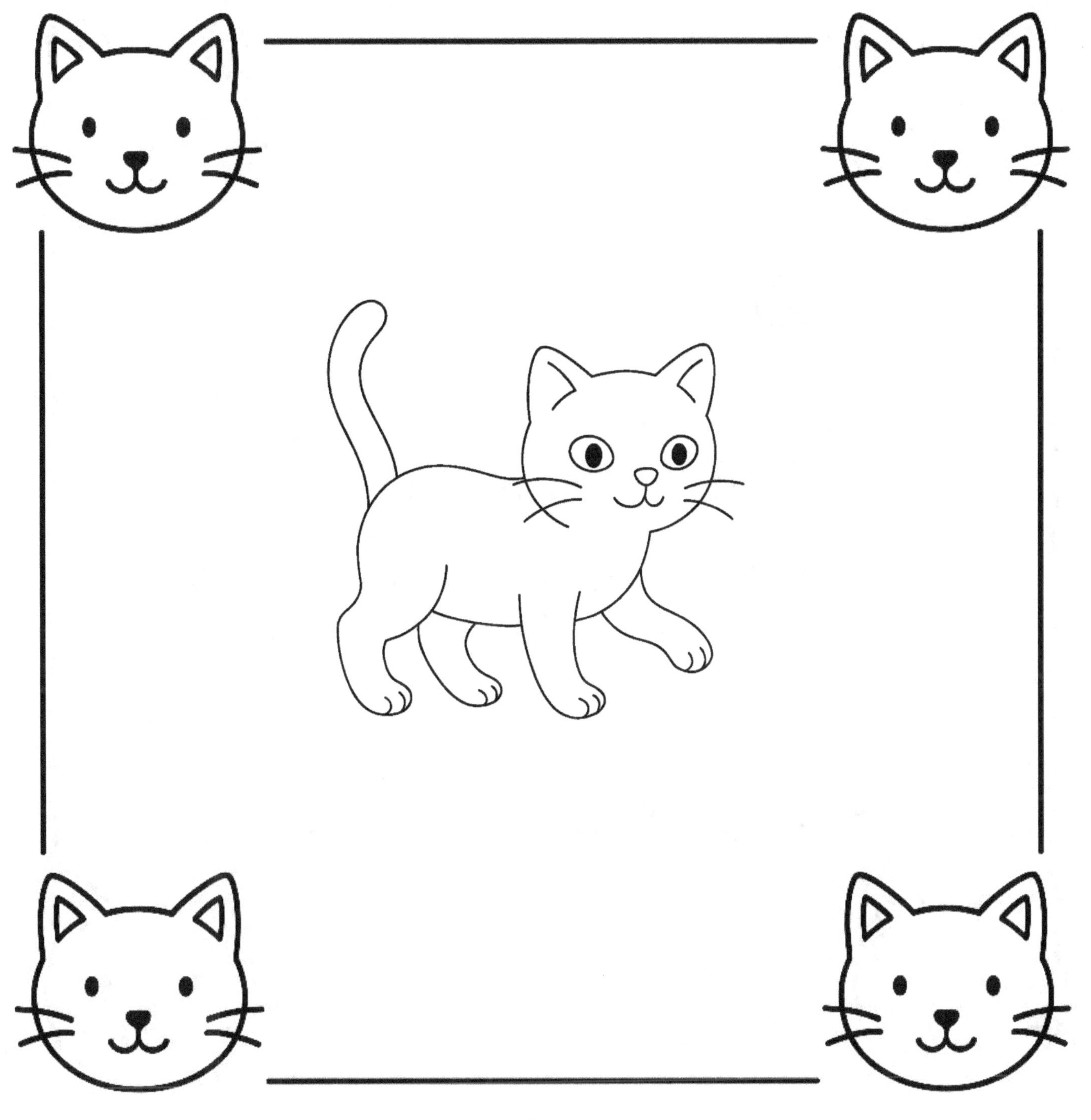

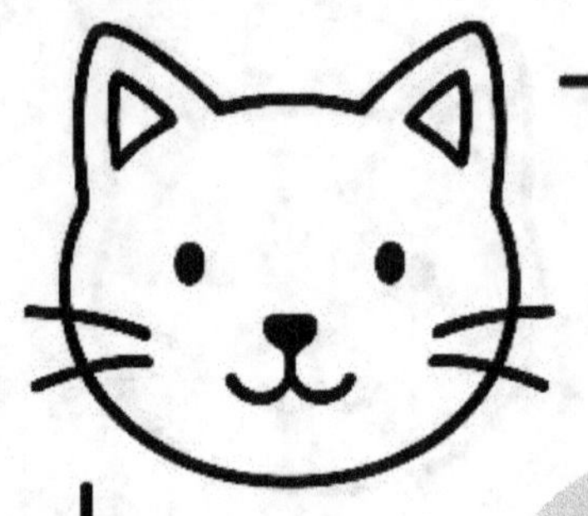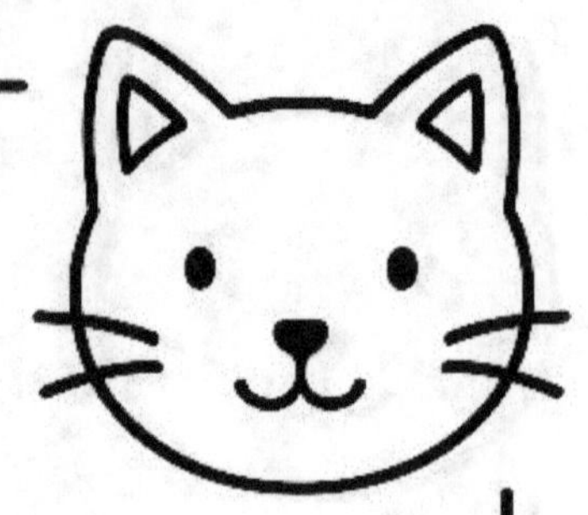

CATS USE THEIR PAWS TO EXPLORE NEW THINGS.

Los gatos usan sus patas para explorar cosas nuevas.

Category 2: Learning and Growing

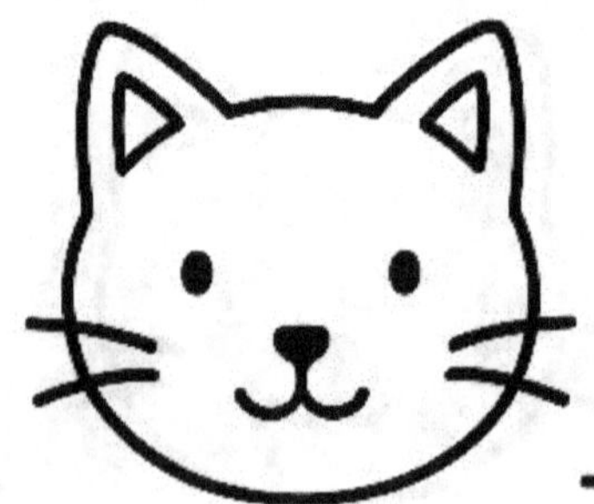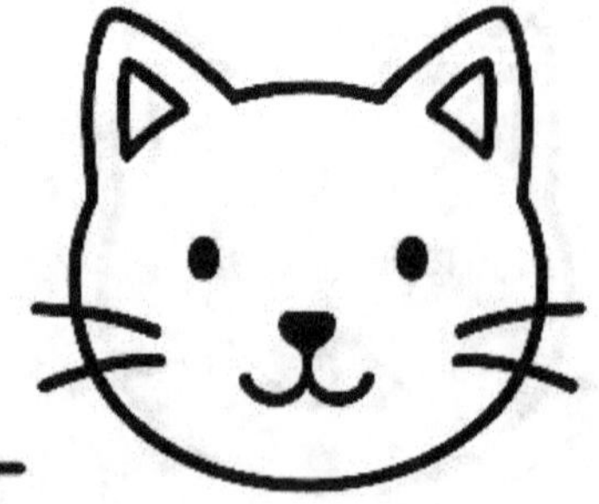

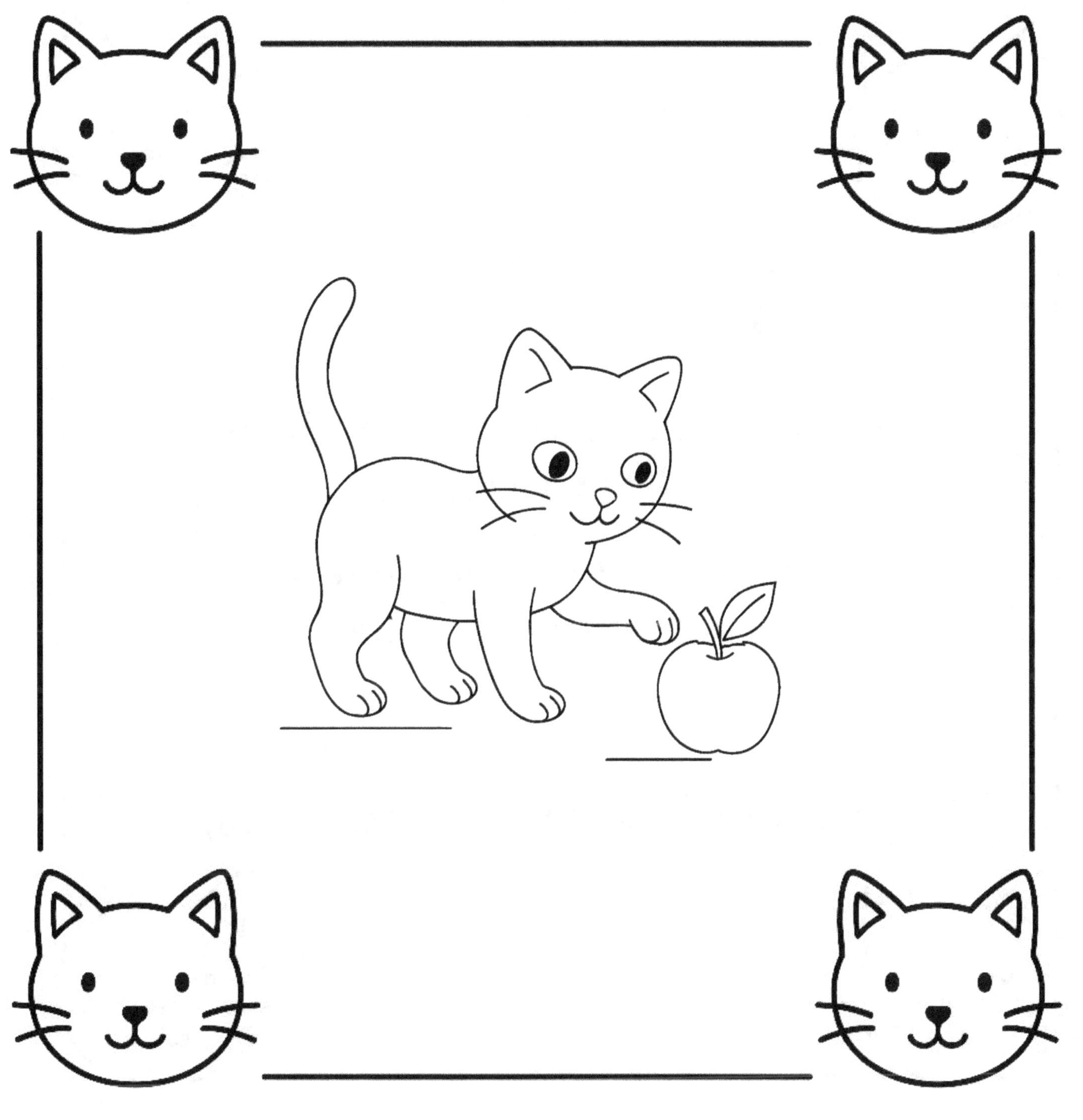

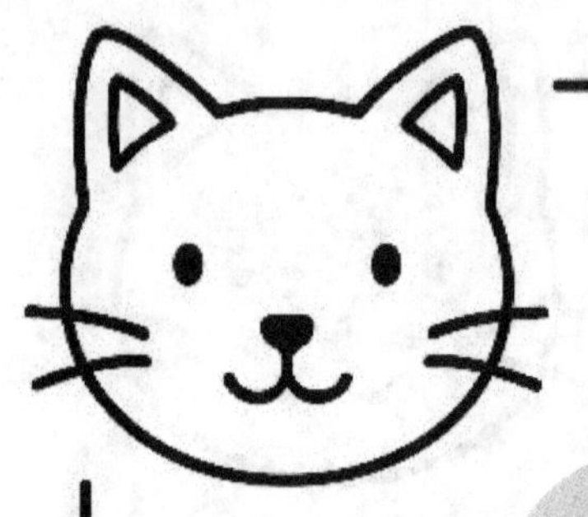
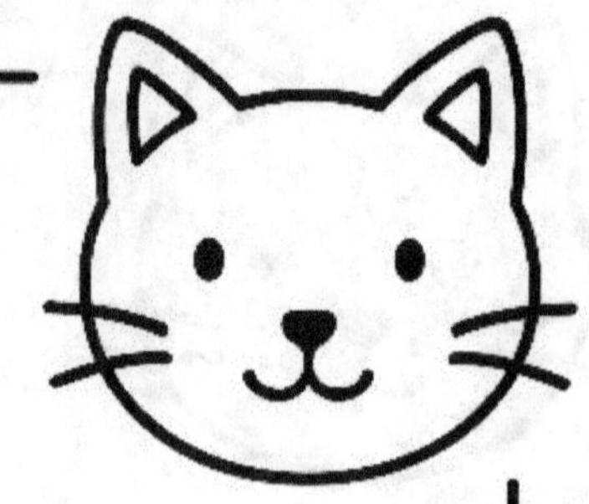

KITTENS PLAY TO LEARN HOW TO HUNT.

Los gatitos juegan para aprender a cazar.

Category 2: Learning and Growing

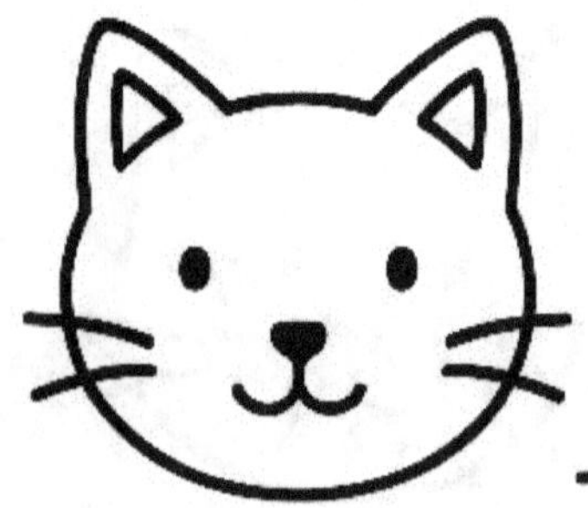
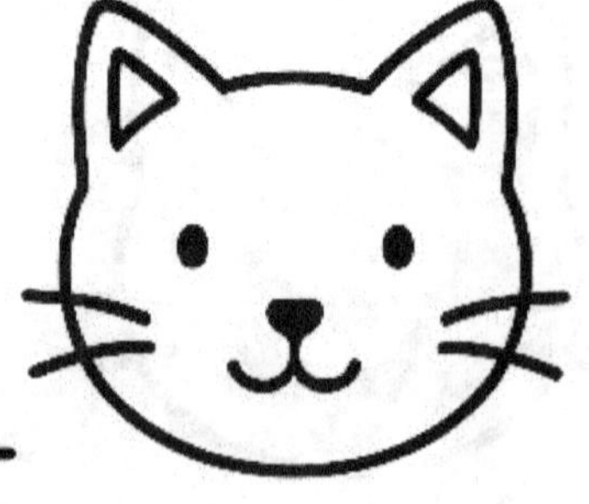

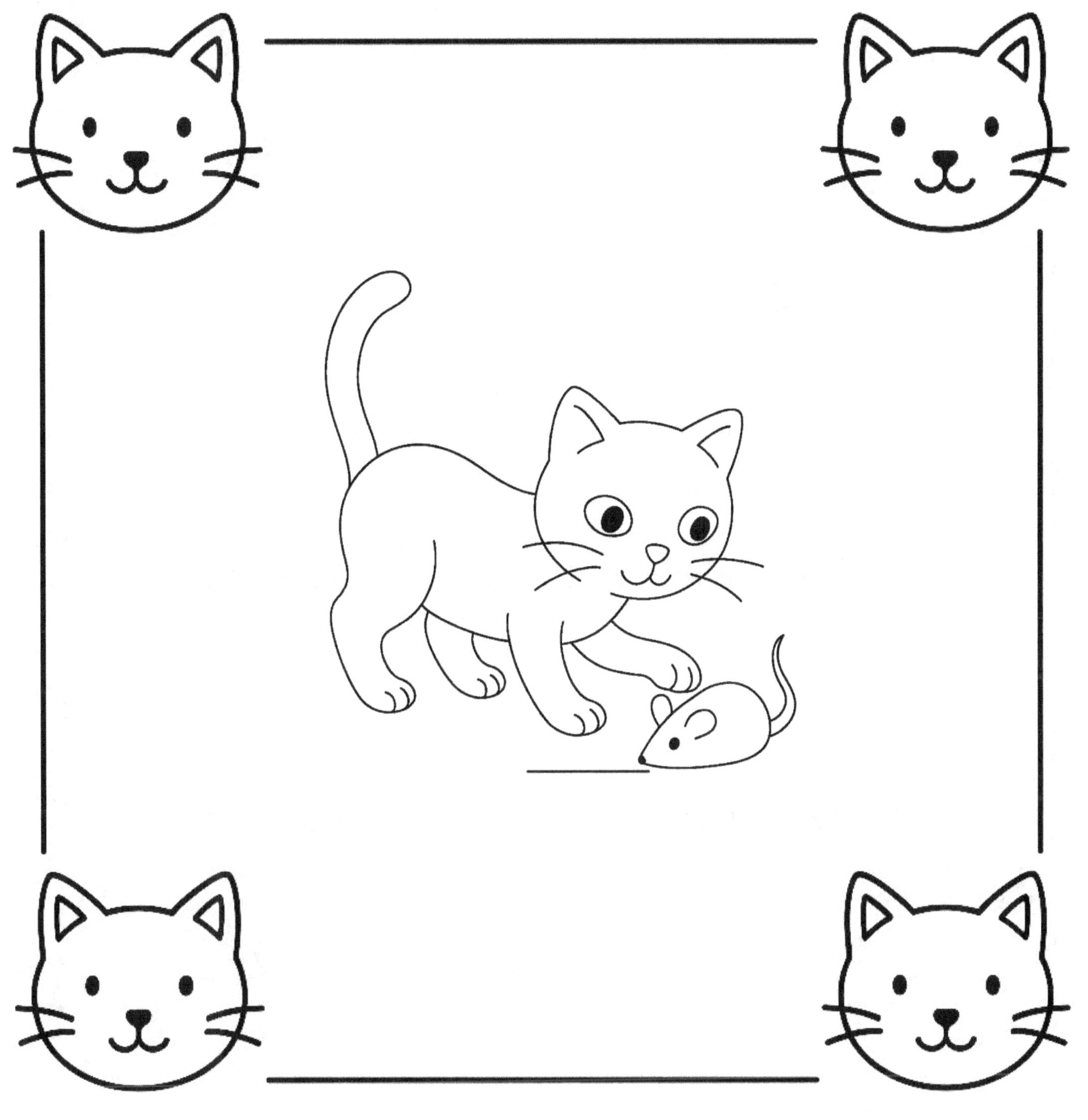

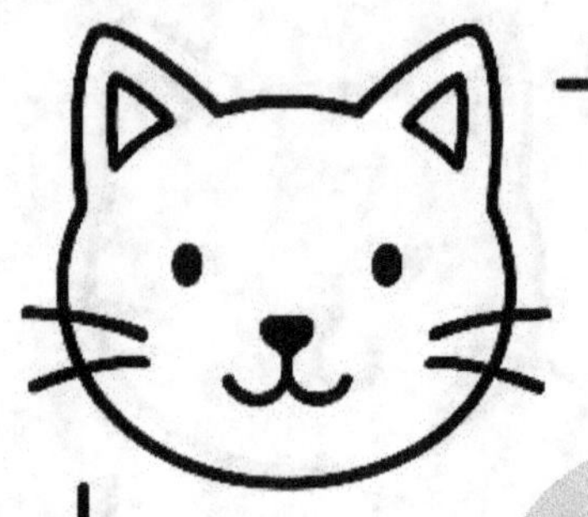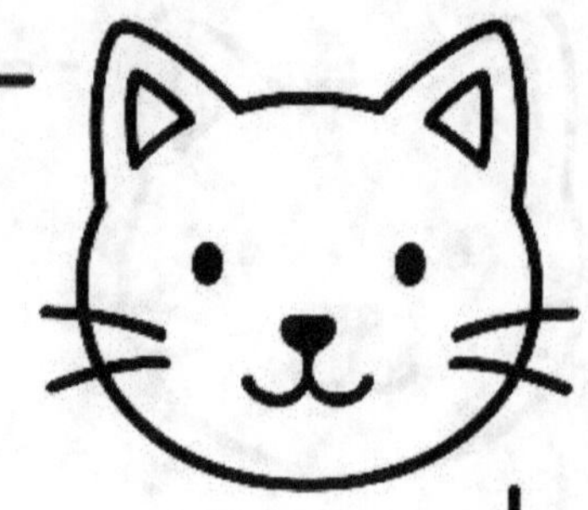

A CAT'S BRAIN IS SIMILAR TO A HUMAN BRAIN!

¡El cerebro de un gato es parecido al de un humano!

Category 2: Learning and Growing

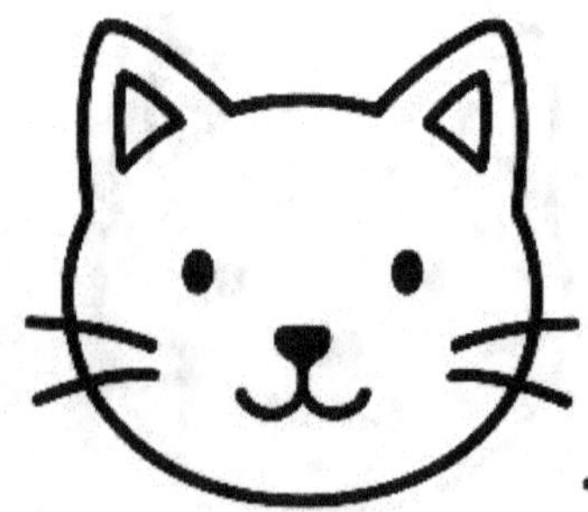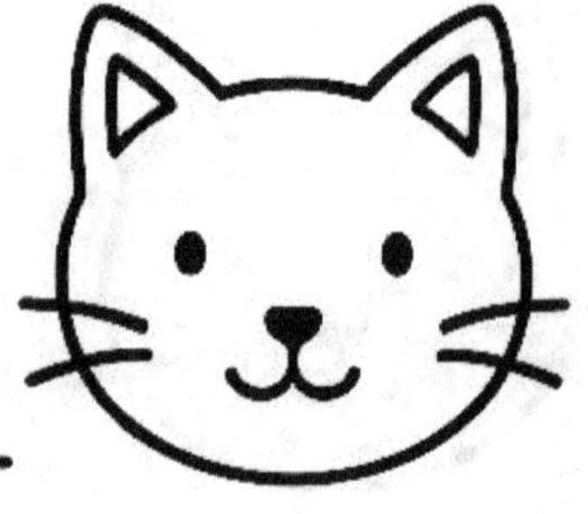

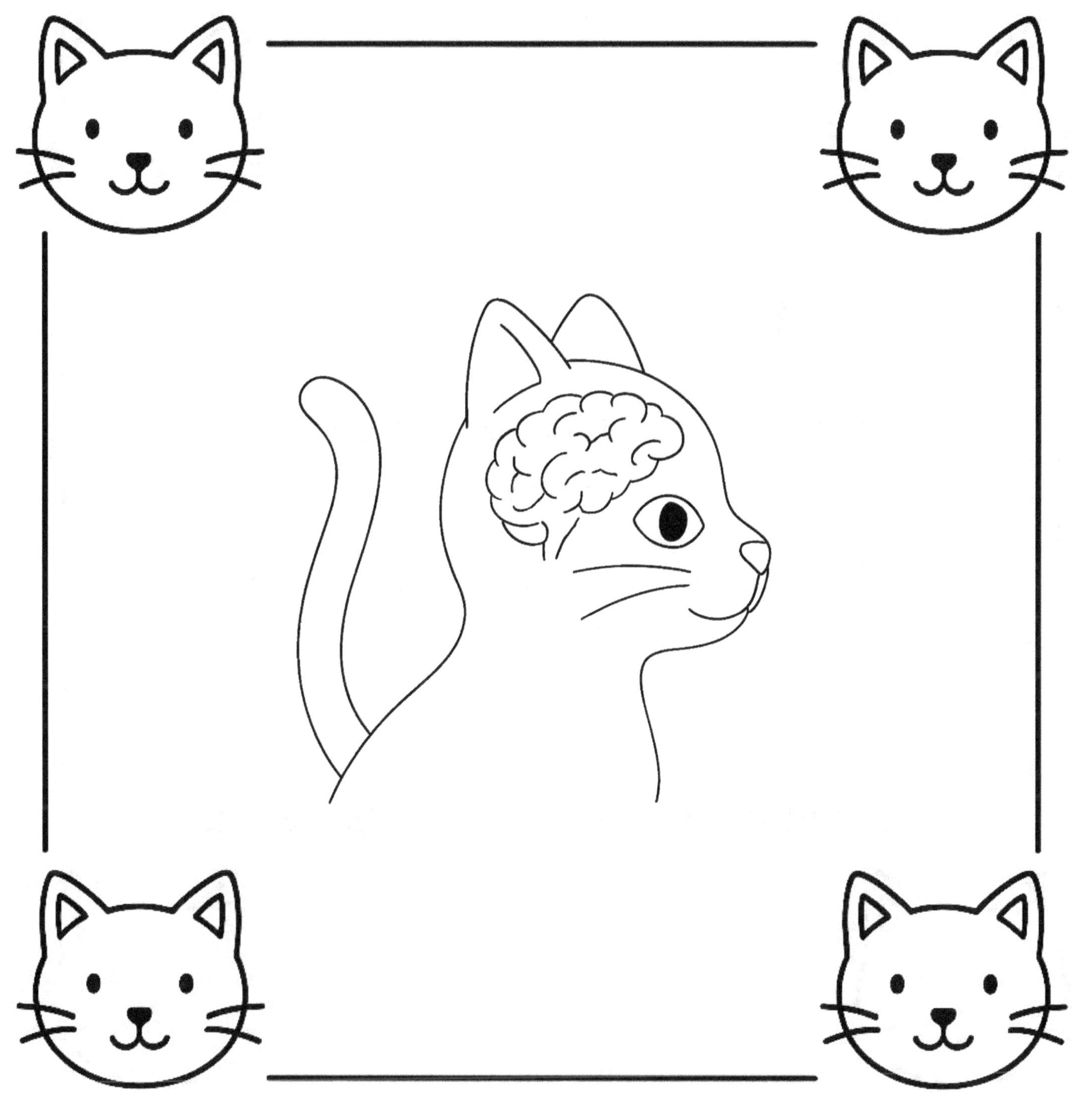

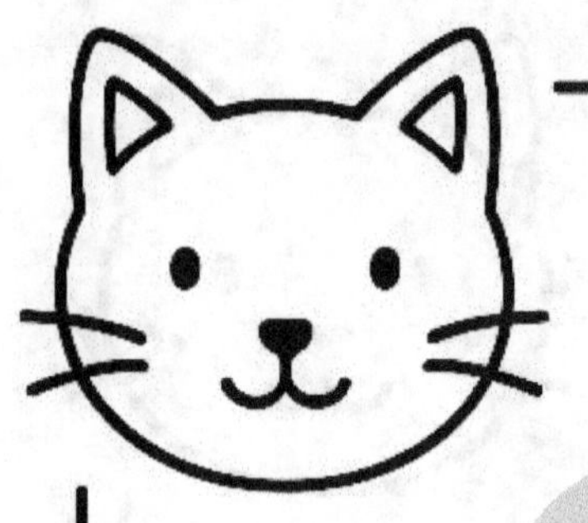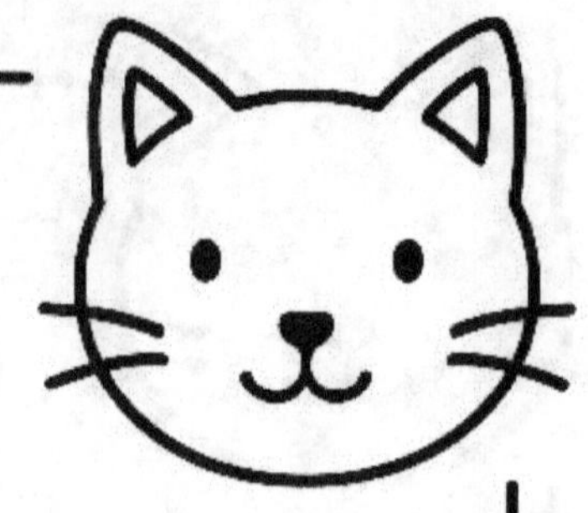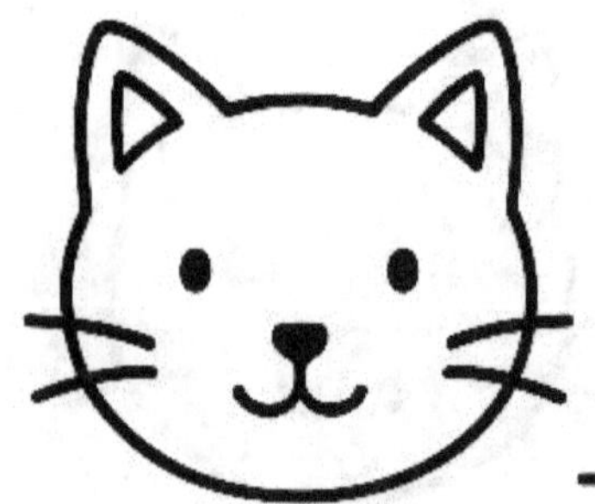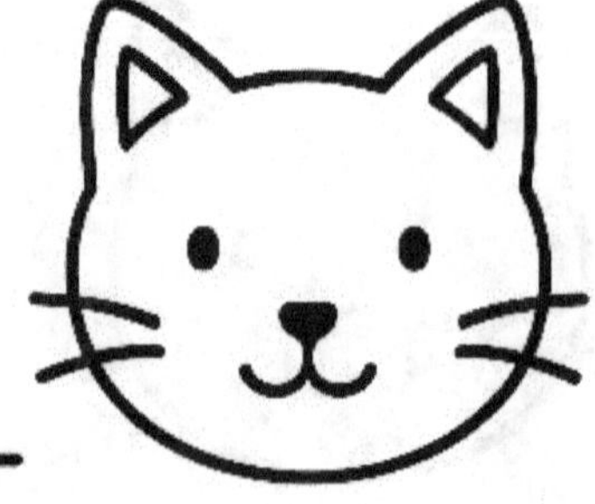

CATS STRETCH AFTER EVERY NAP.

Los gatos se estiran después de cada siesta.

Category 2: Learning and Growing

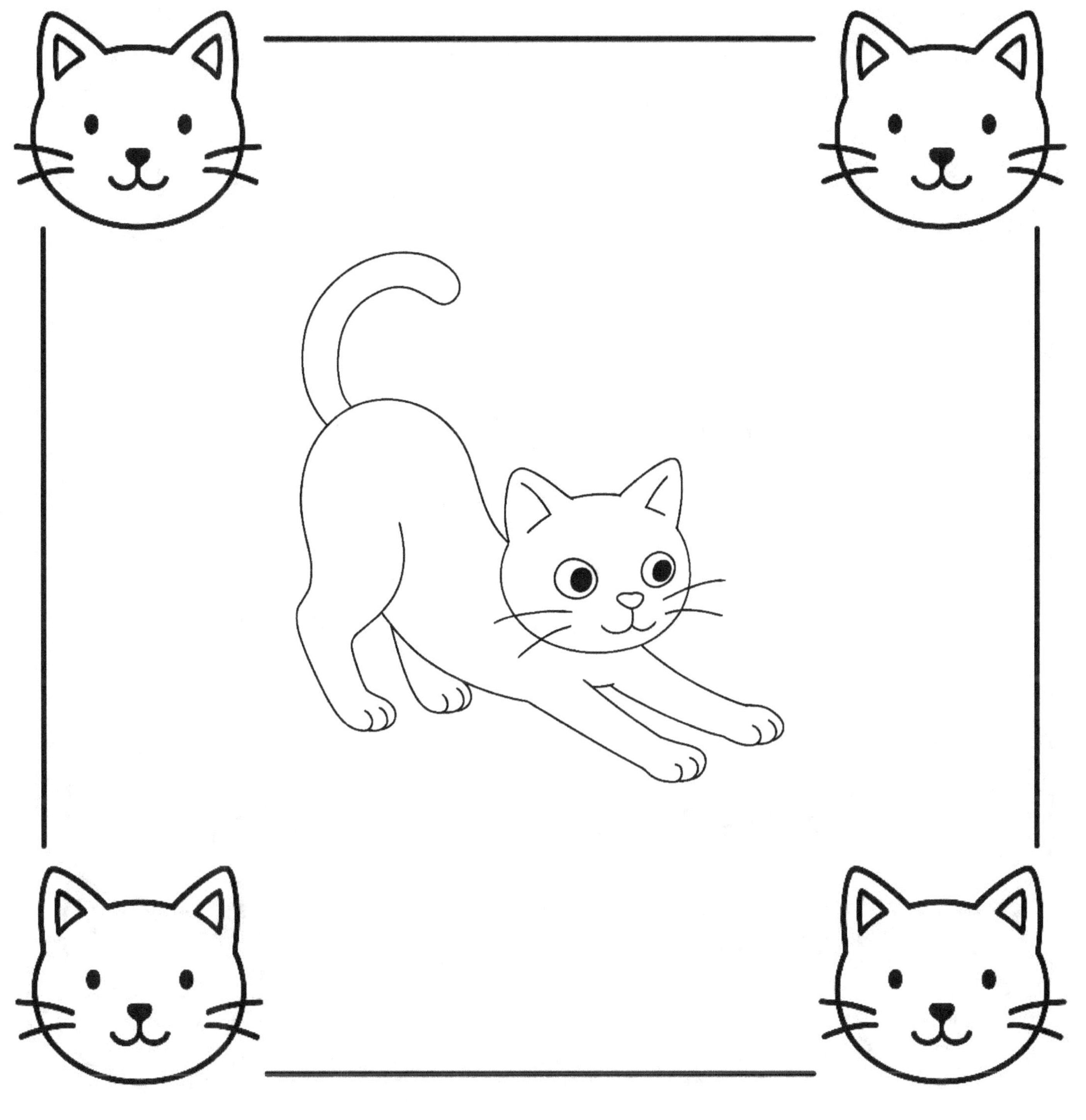

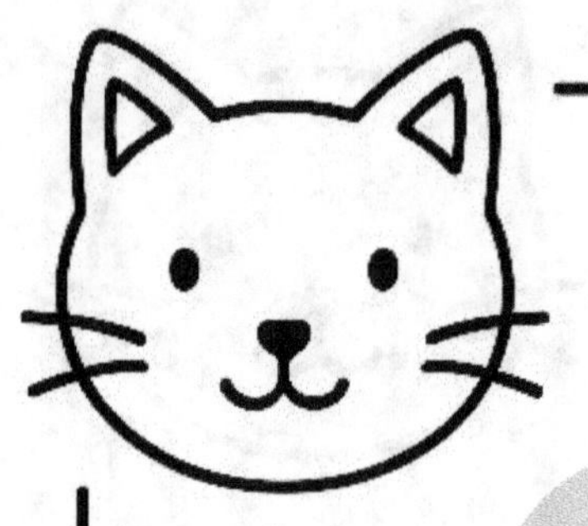
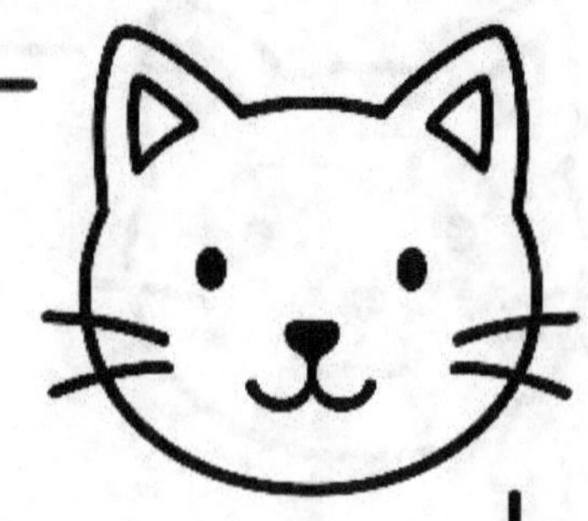

Fact #17

CATS LOVE TO HIDE IN BOXES AND BAGS.

A los gatos les encanta esconderse en cajas y bolsas.

Category 2: Learning and Growing

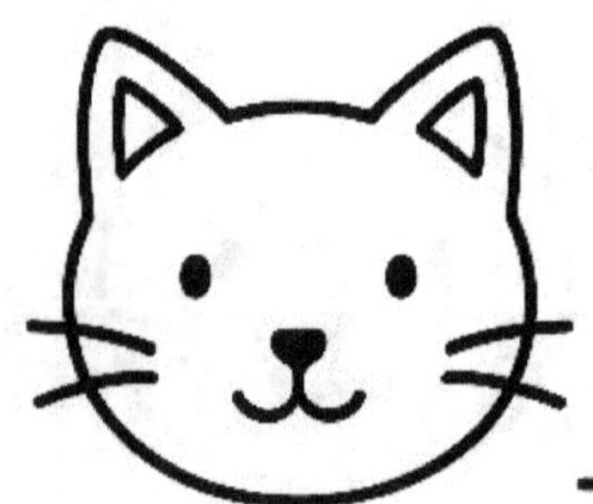
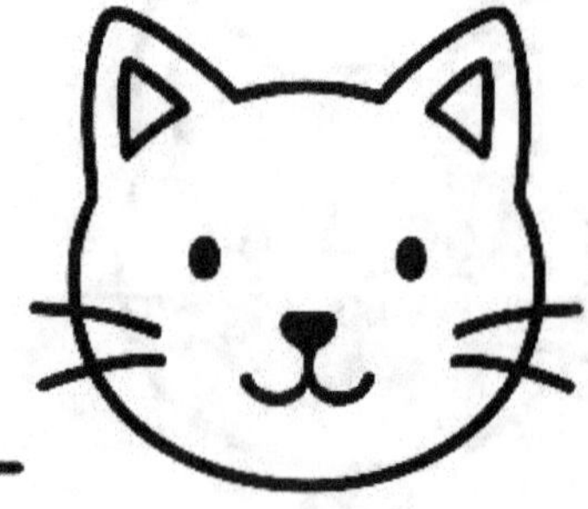

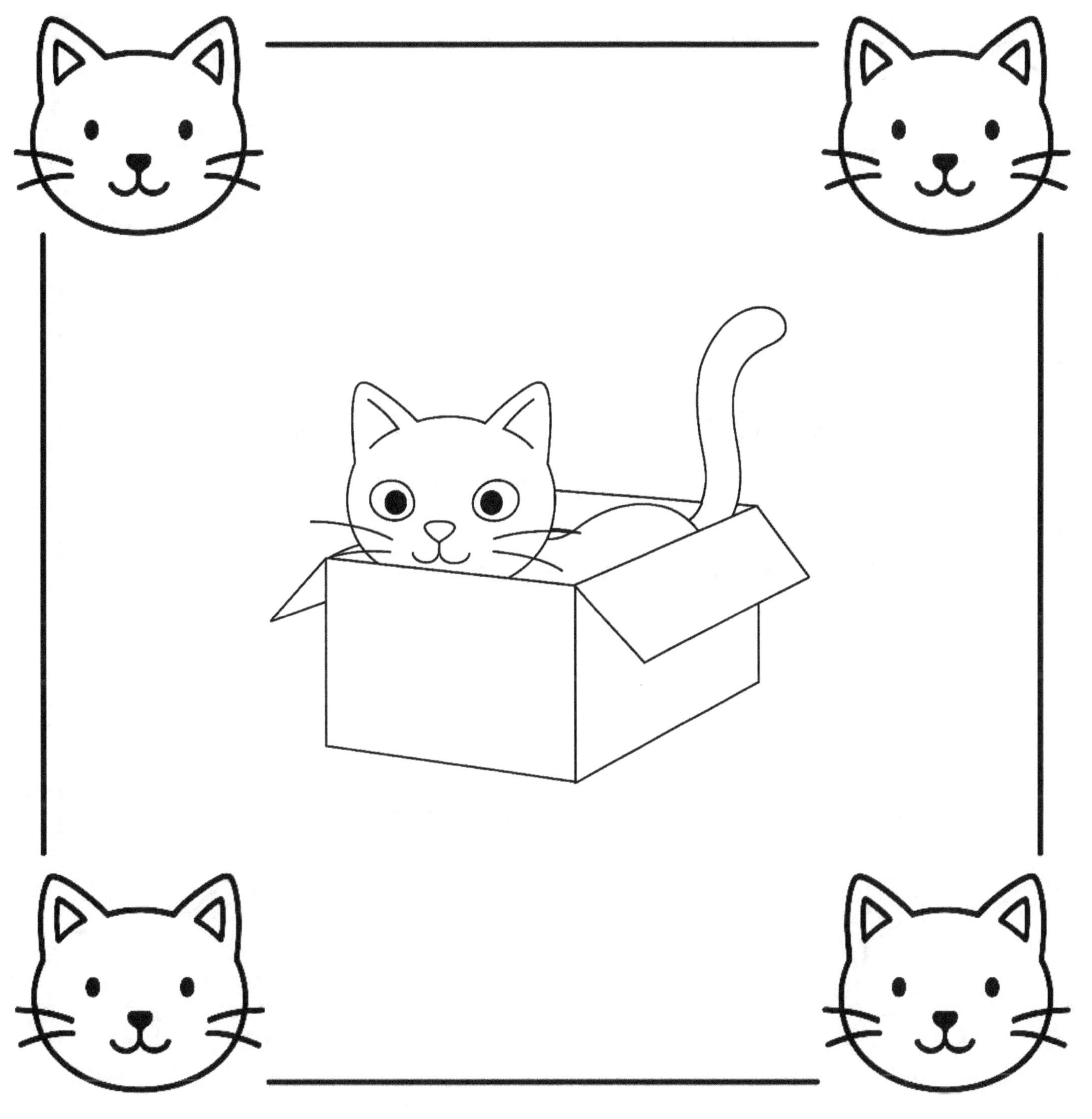

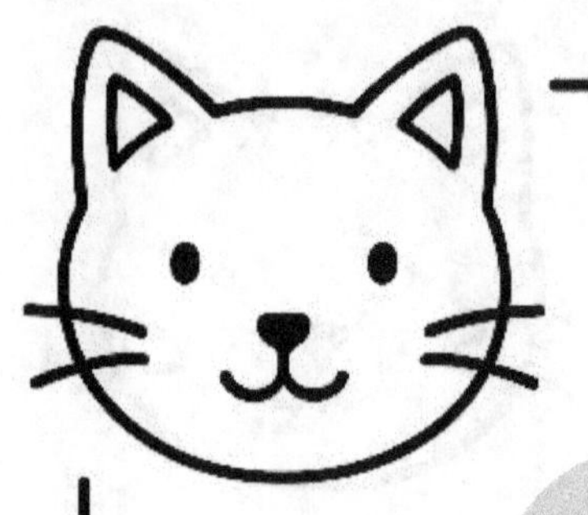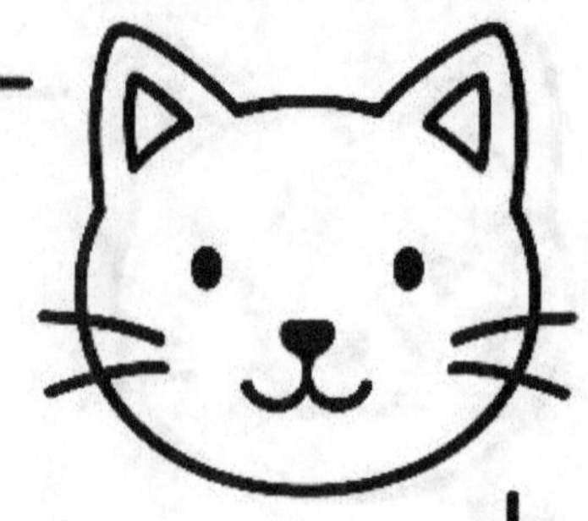

SOME CATS LIKE TO DRINK FROM THE SINK!

¡A algunos gatos les gusta beber del grifo!

Category 2: Learning and Growing

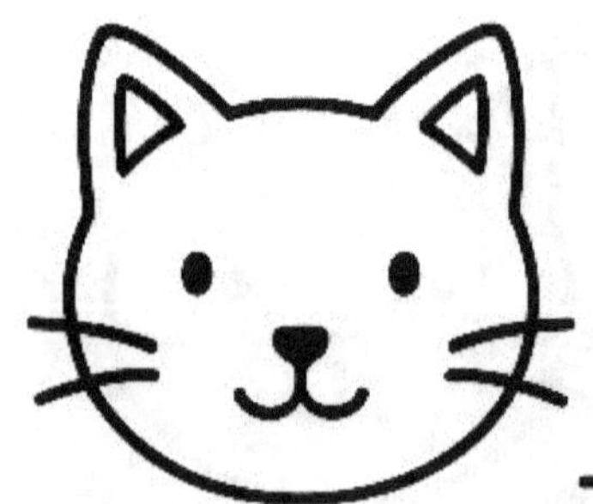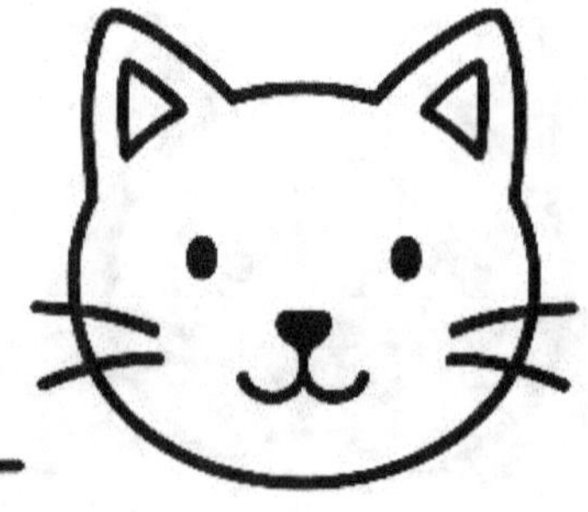

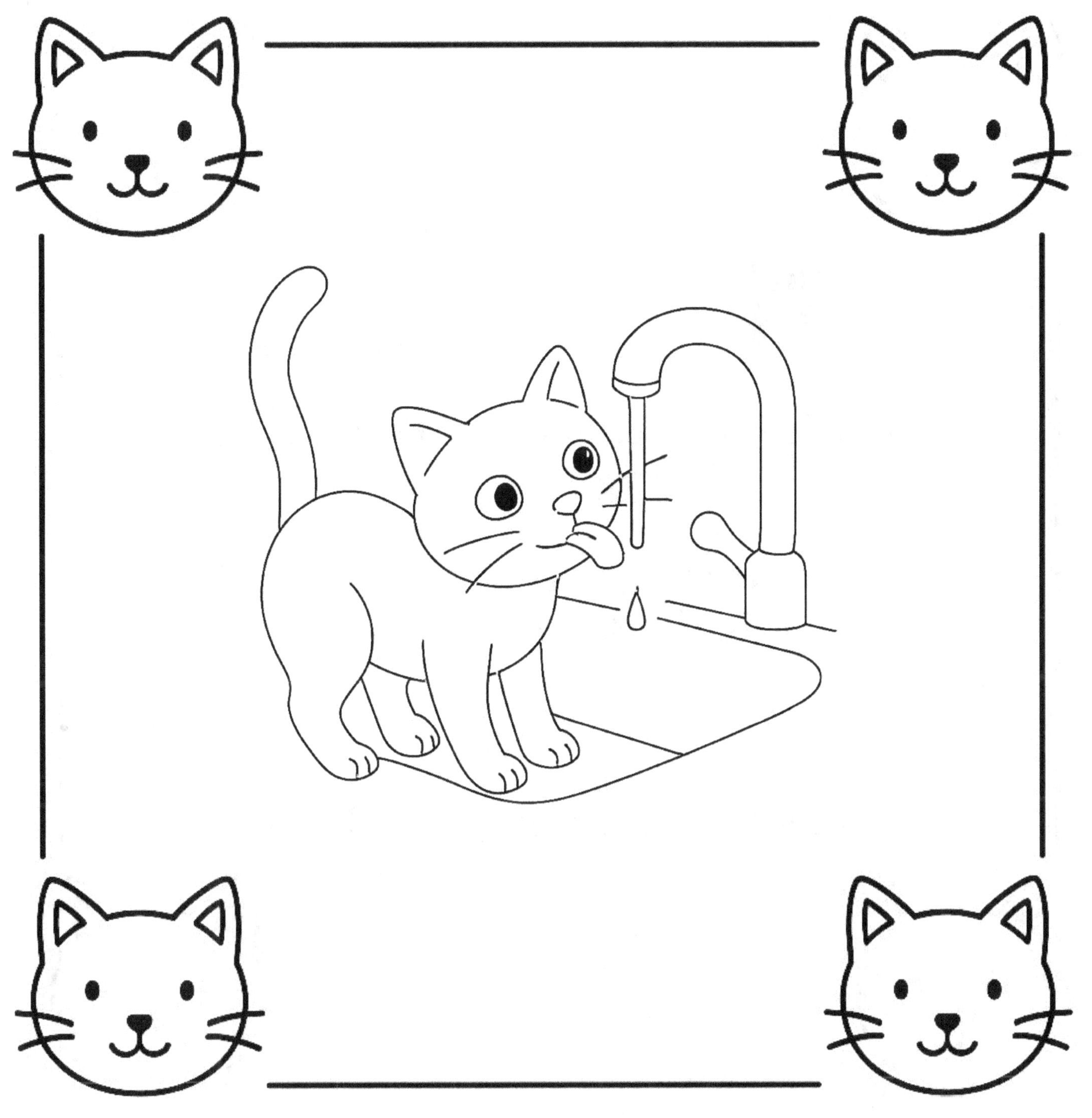

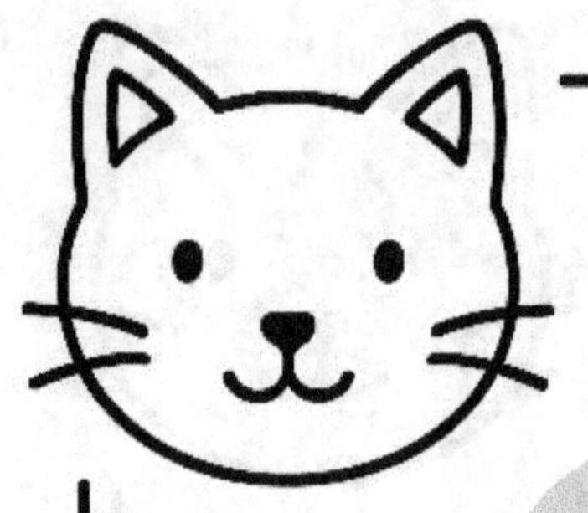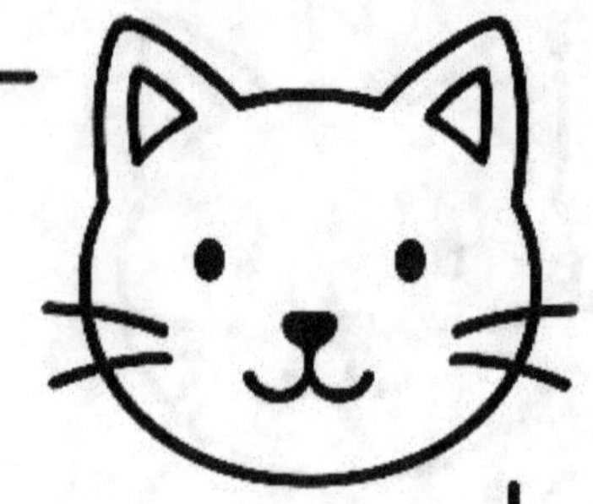

CATS CAN RUN UP TO 30 MILES PER HOUR.

Los gatos pueden correr hasta 48 kilómetros por hora.

Category 2: Learning and Growing

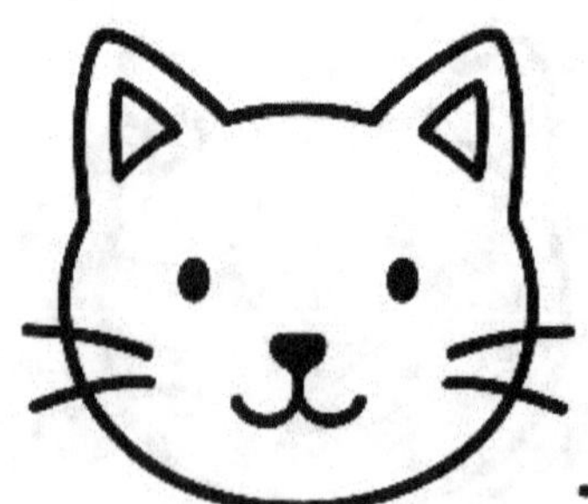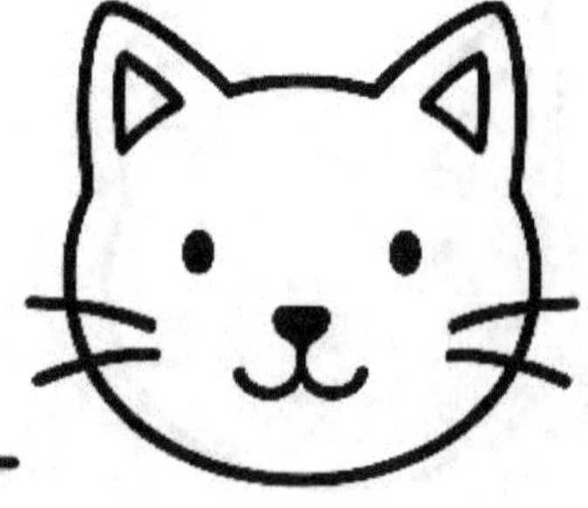

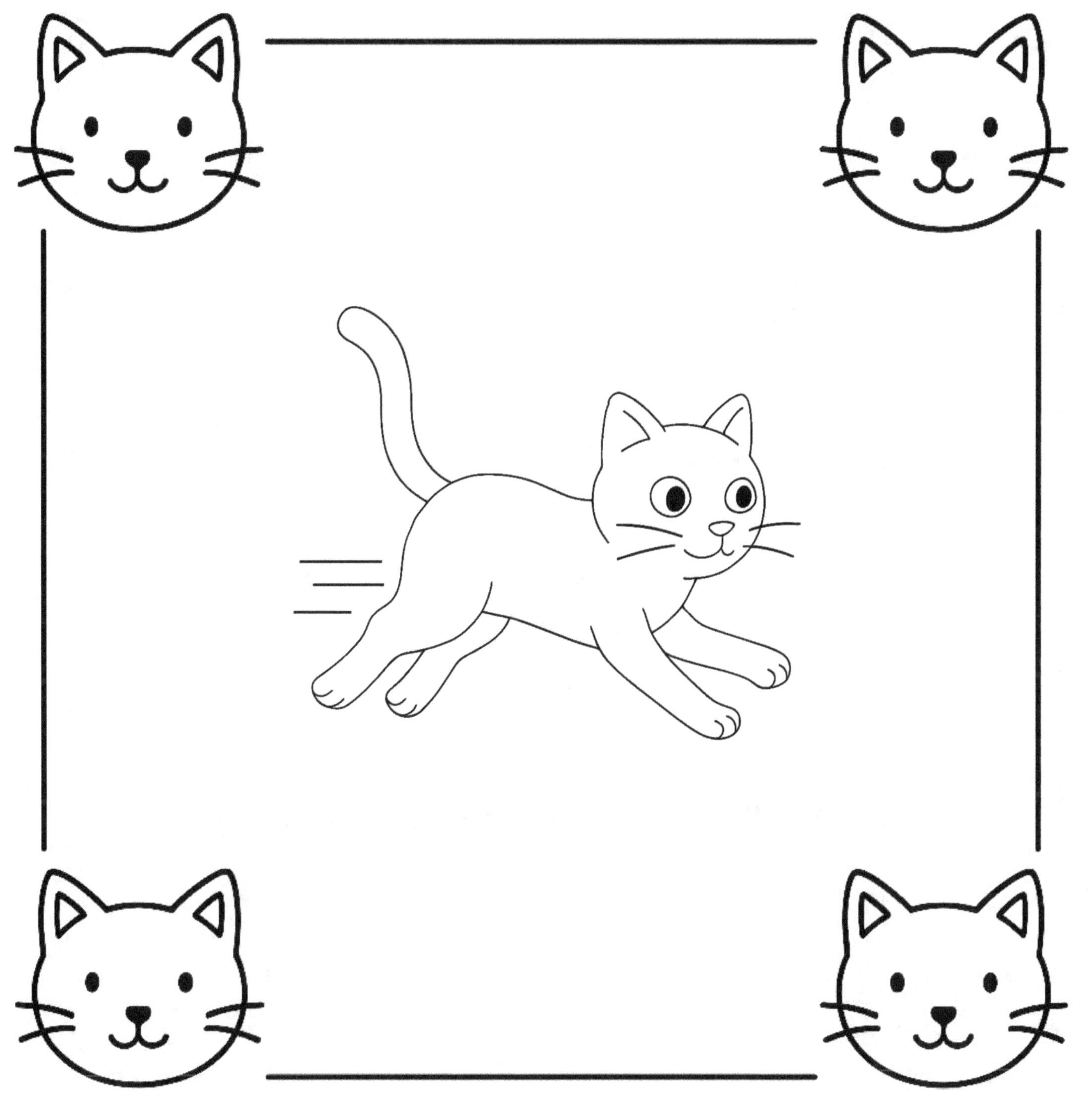

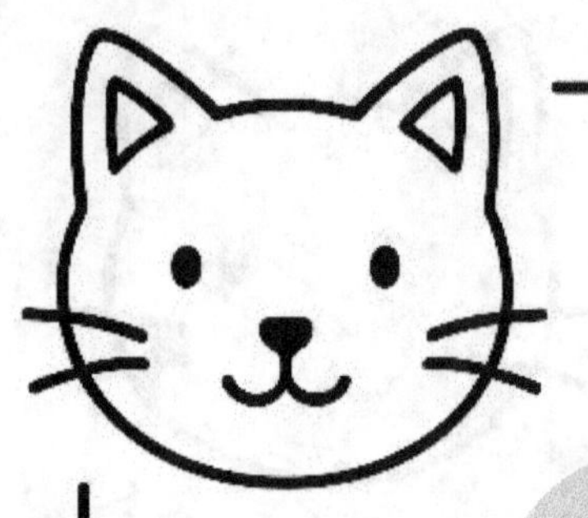
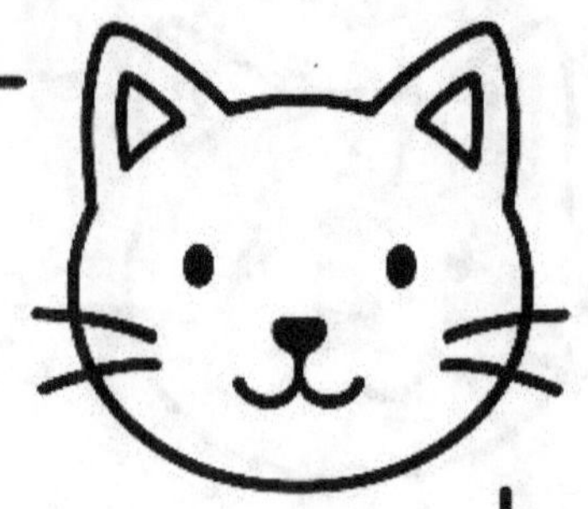

CATS WALK ON THEIR TOES.

Los gatos caminan de puntillas.

Category 2: Learning and Growing

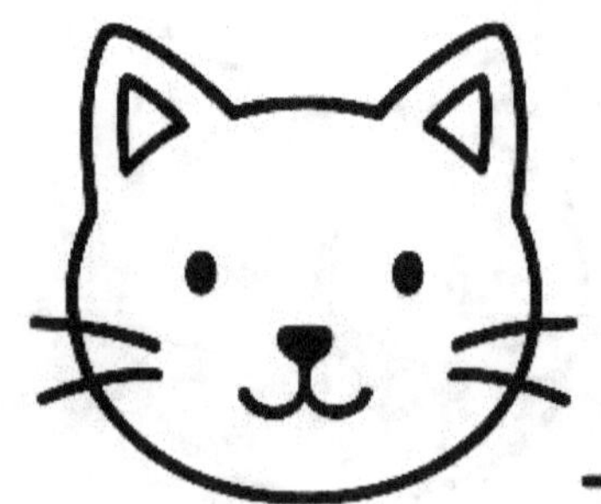
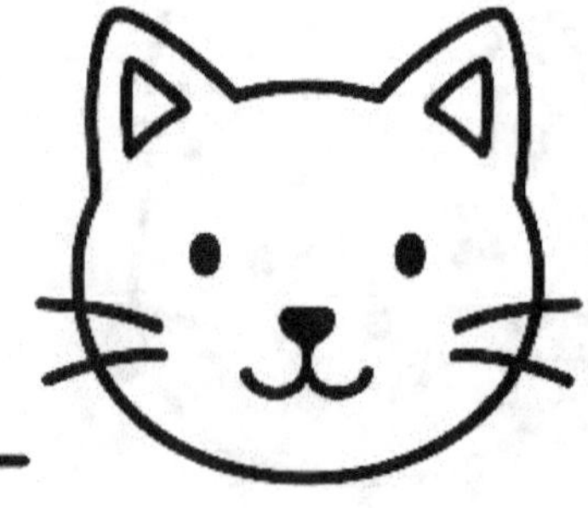

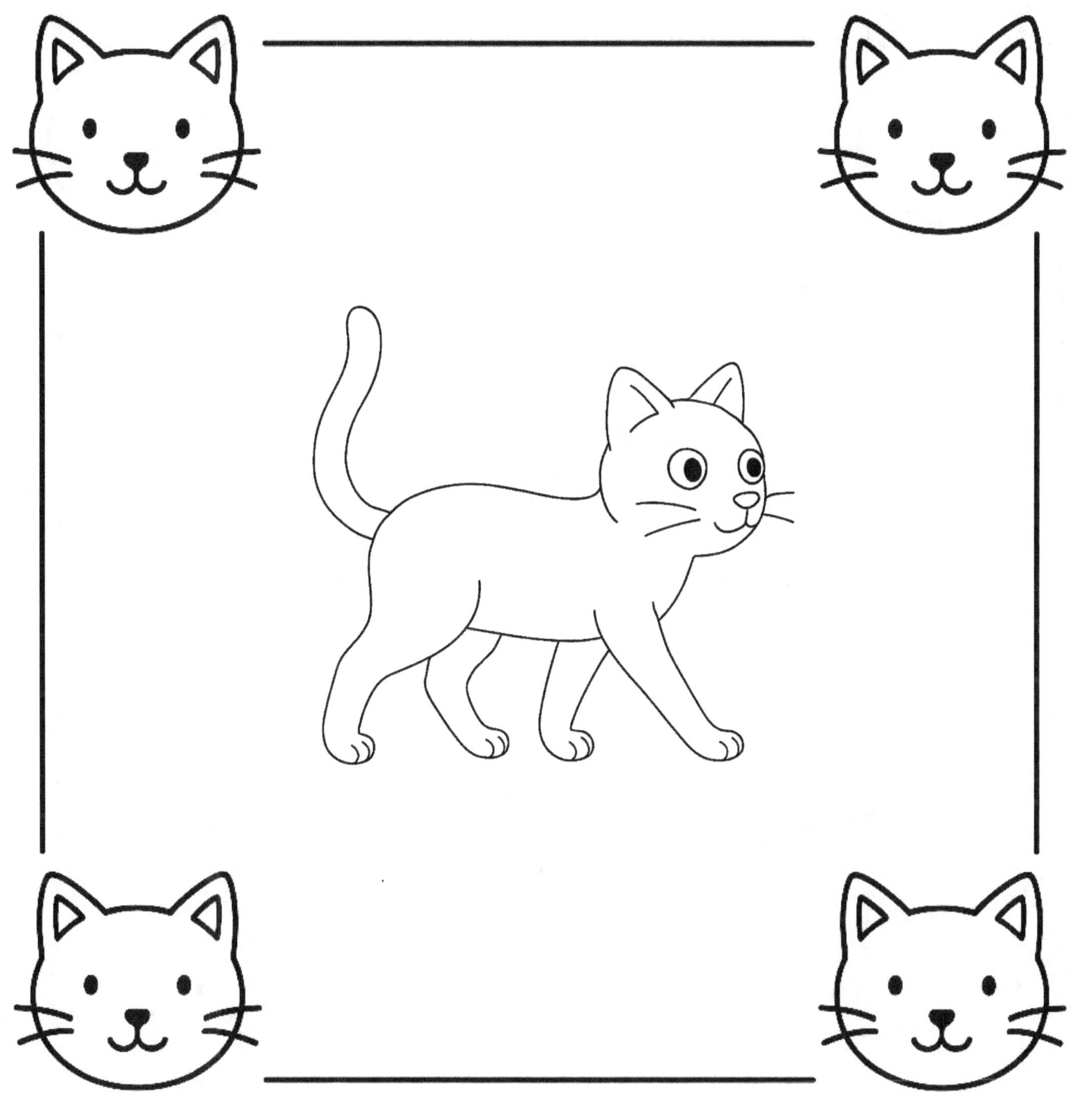

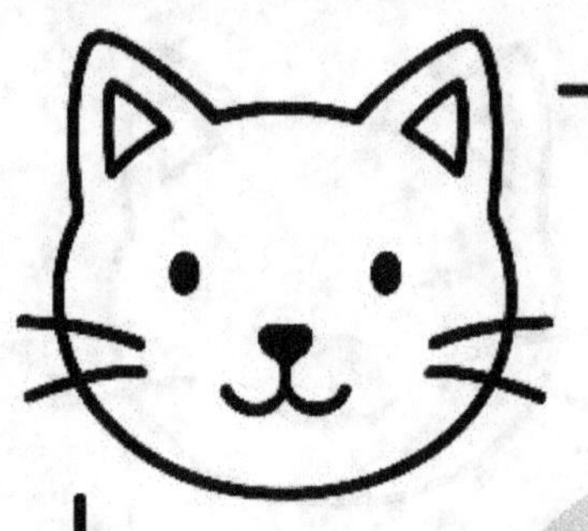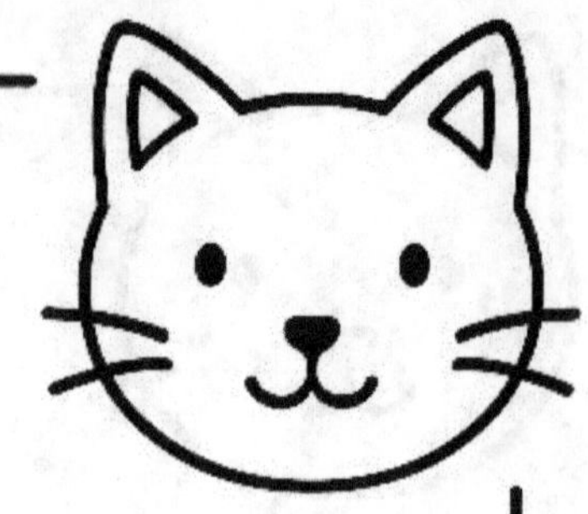

Fact #21

CATS STRETCH AFTER EVERY NAP.

Los gatos se estiran después de cada siesta

Category 3: Behavior and Movement

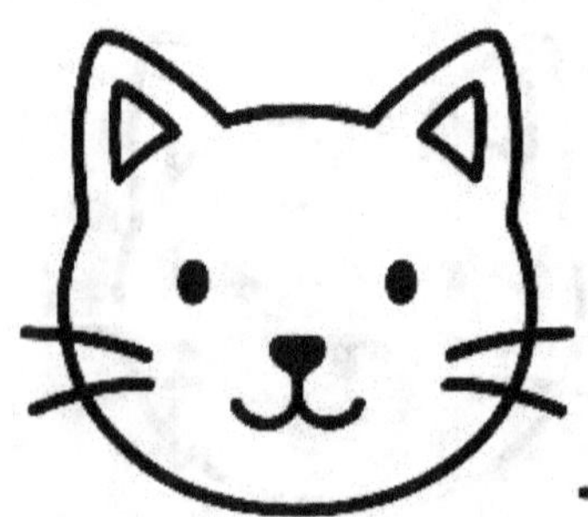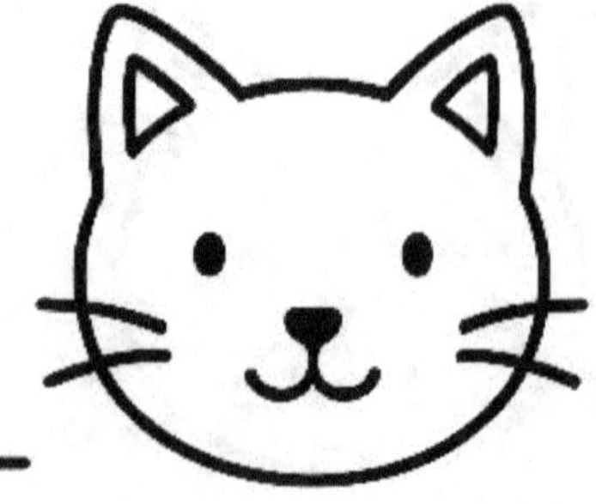

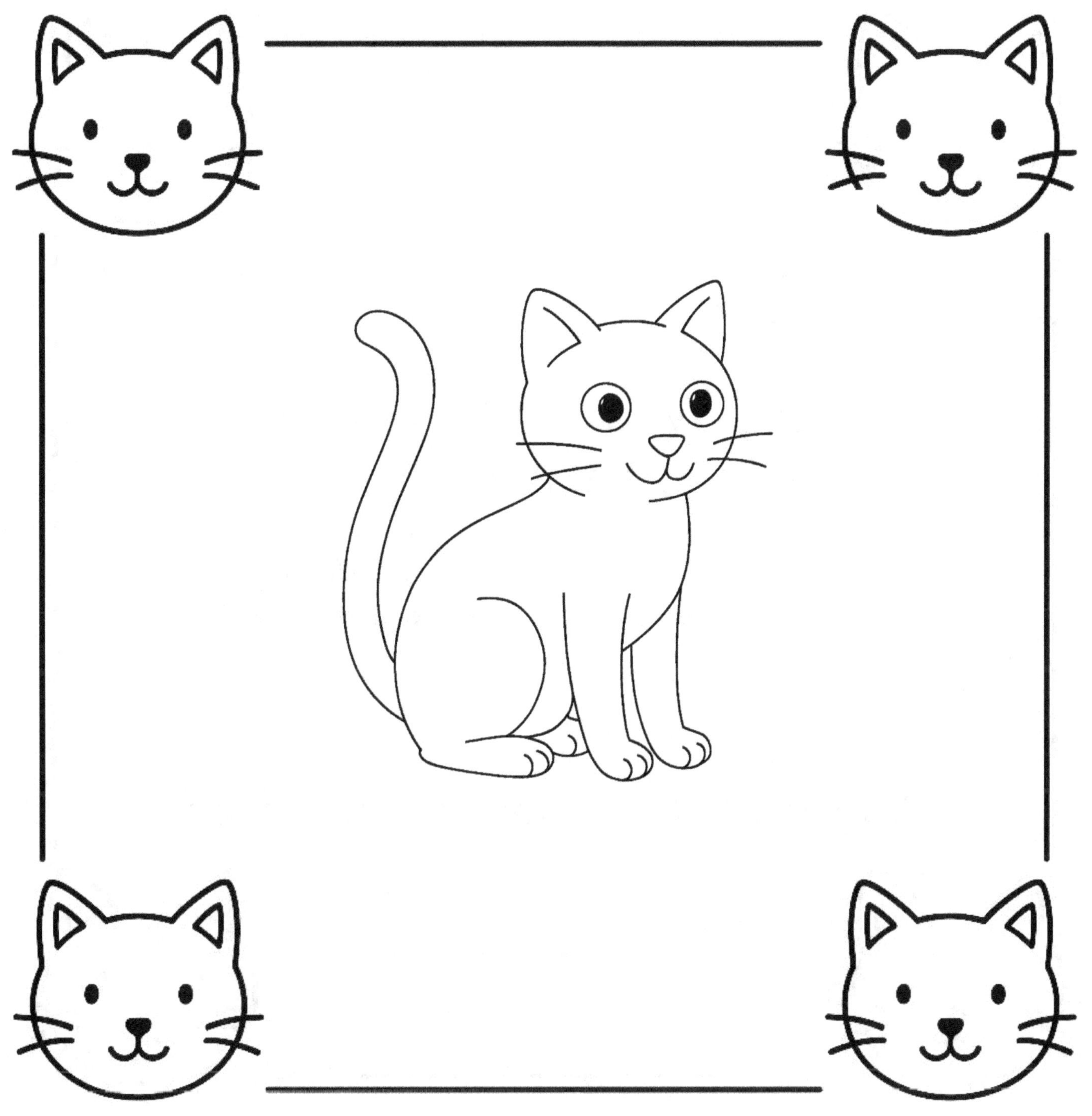

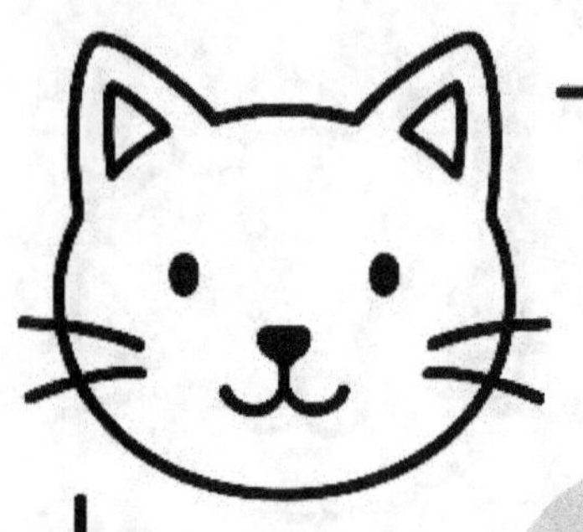
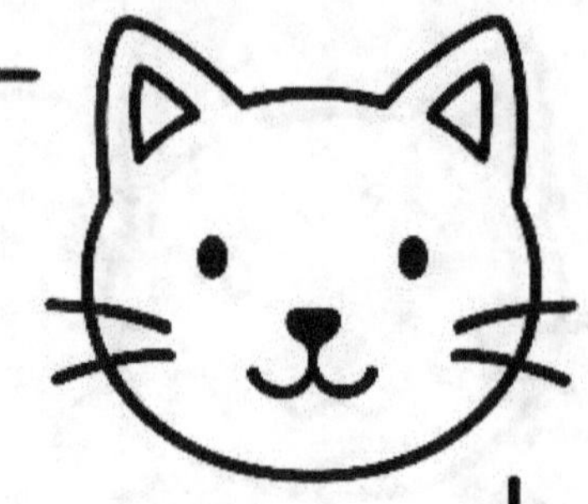

CATS LOVE TO HIDE IN BOXES AND BAGS.

A los gatos les encanta esconderse en cajas y bolsas.

Category 3: Behavior and Movement

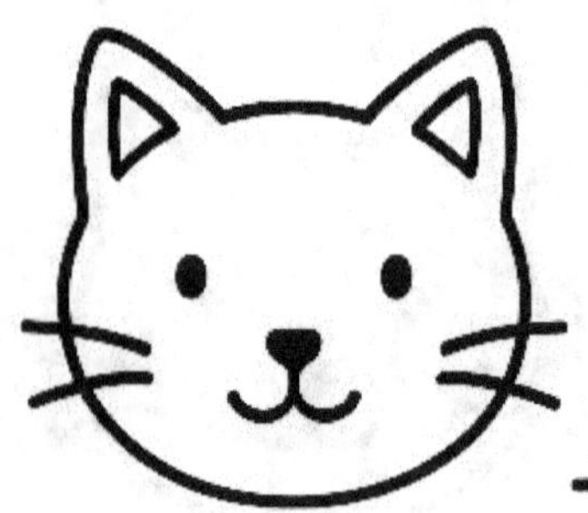
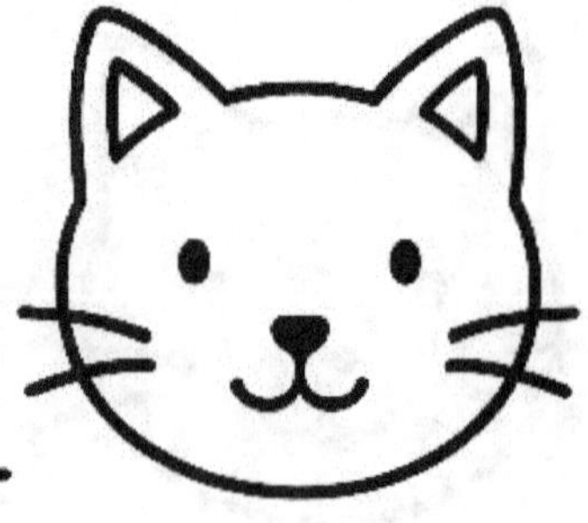

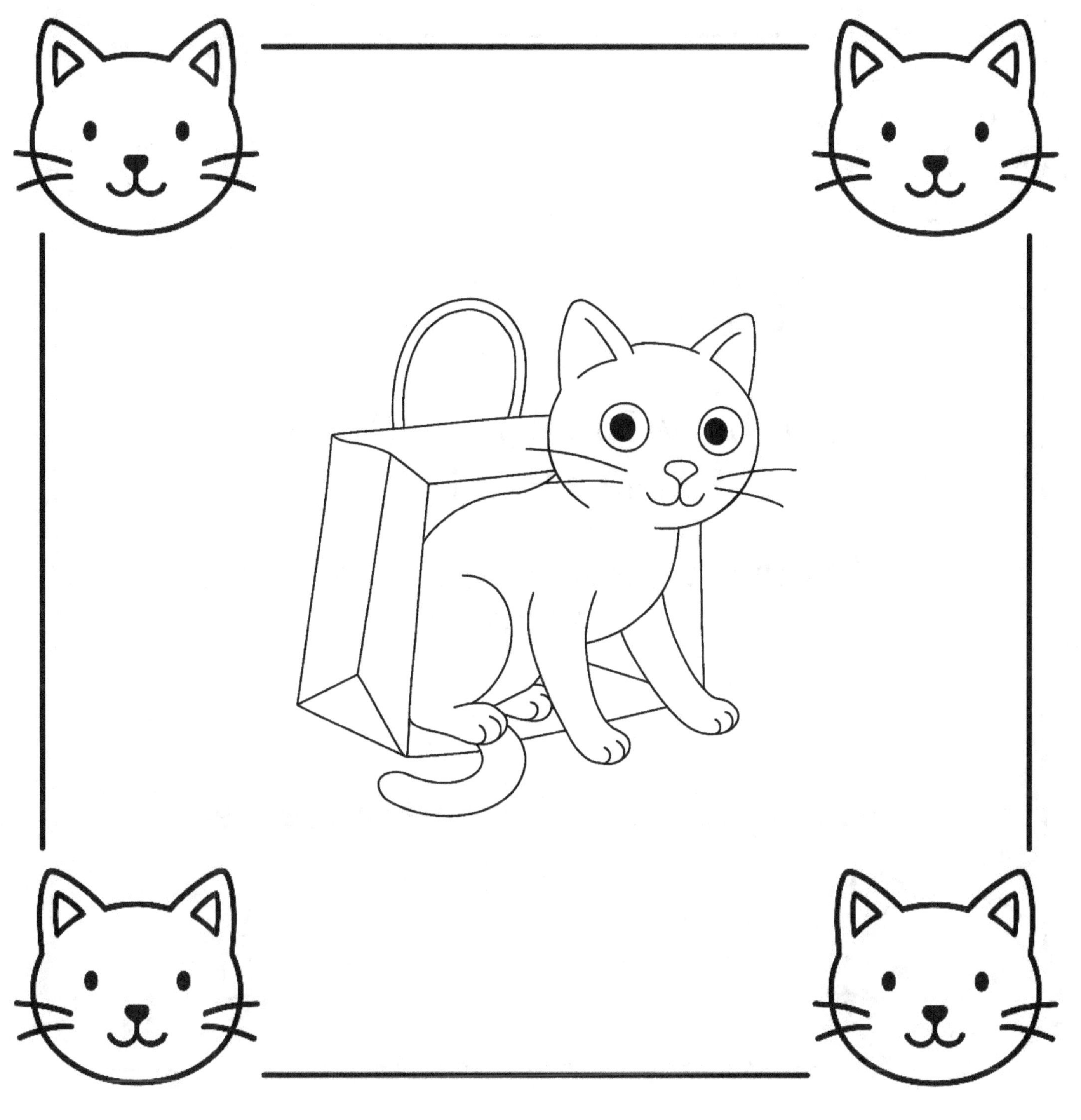

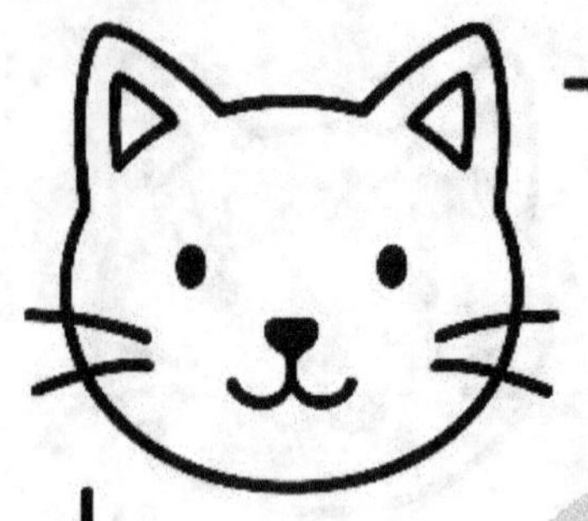
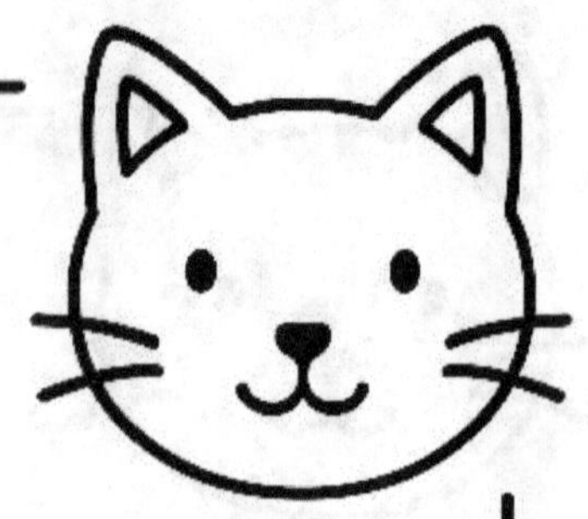

SOME CATS LIKE TO DRINK FROM THE SINK!

¡A algunos gatos les gusta beber del grifo!

Category 3: Behavior and Movement

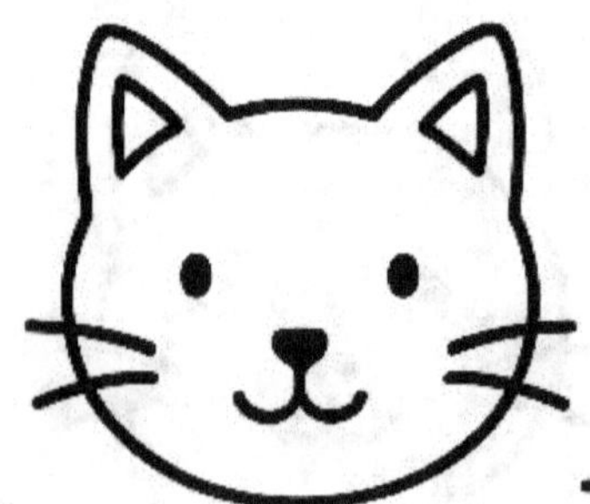
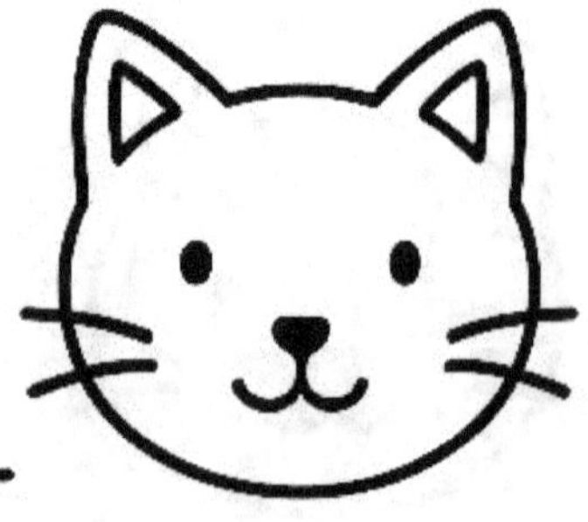

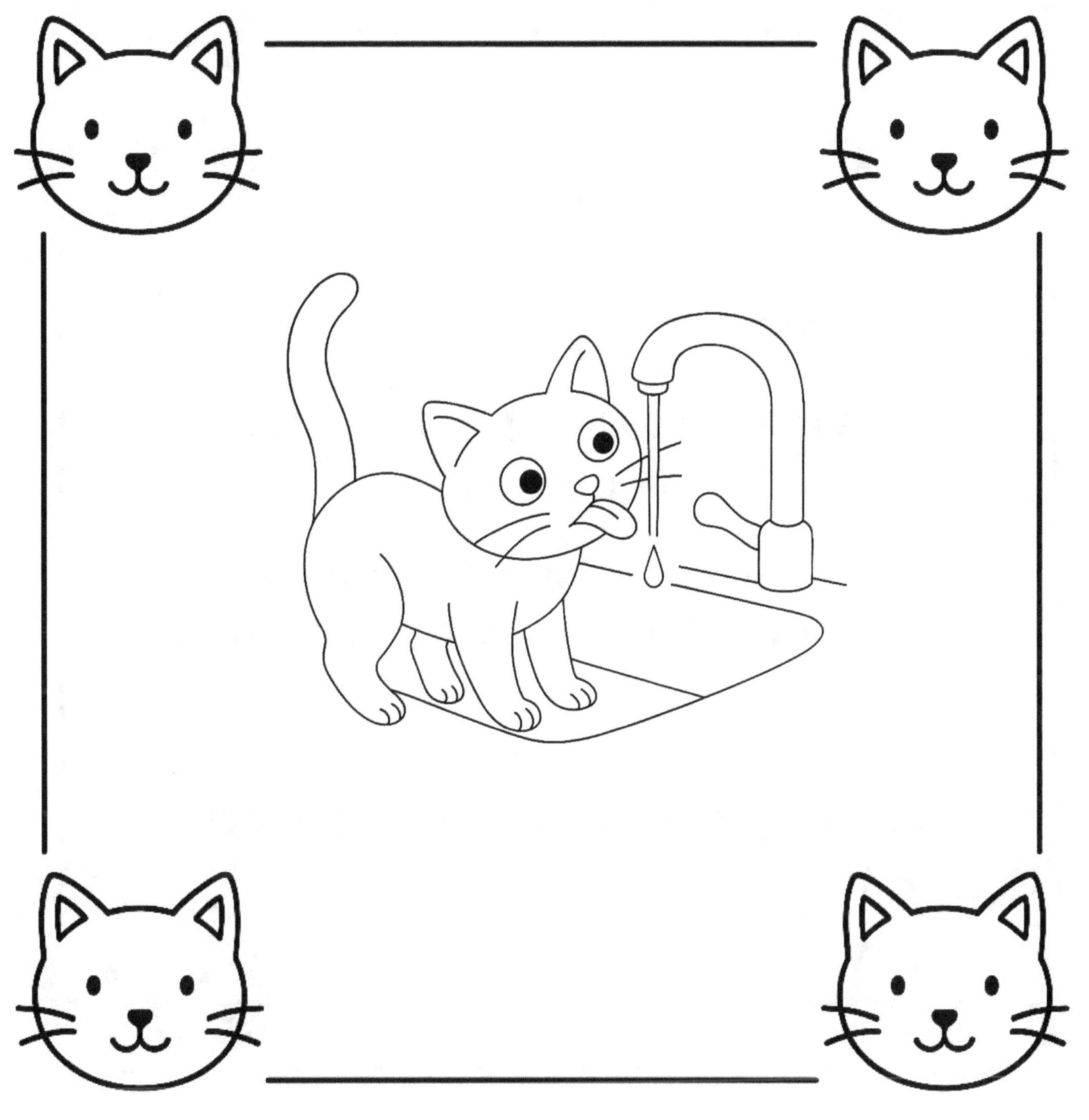

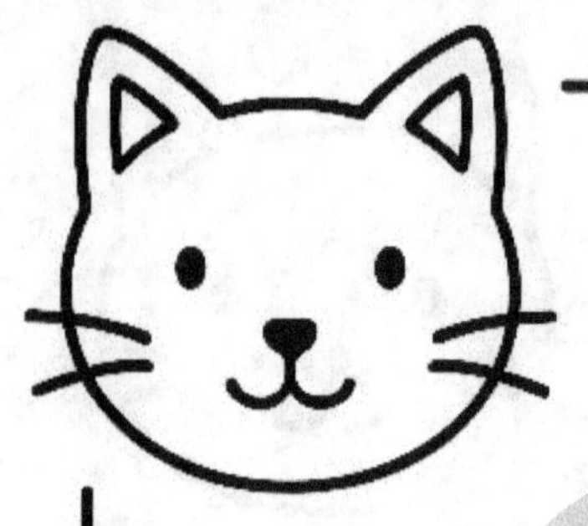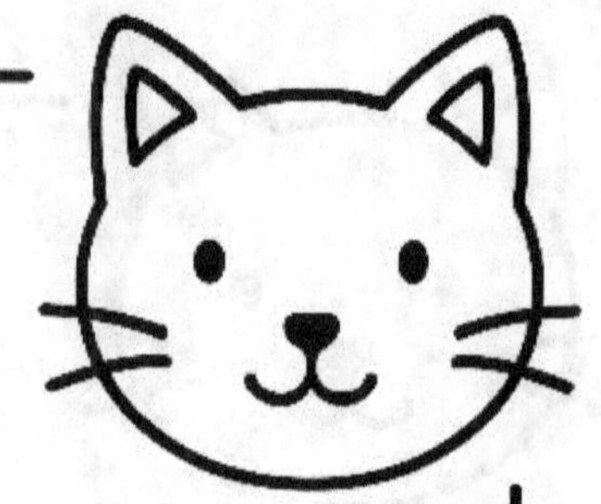

CATS CAN RUN UP TO 30 MILES PER HOUR.

Los gatos pueden correr hasta 48 kilómetros por hora.

Category 3: Behavior and Movement

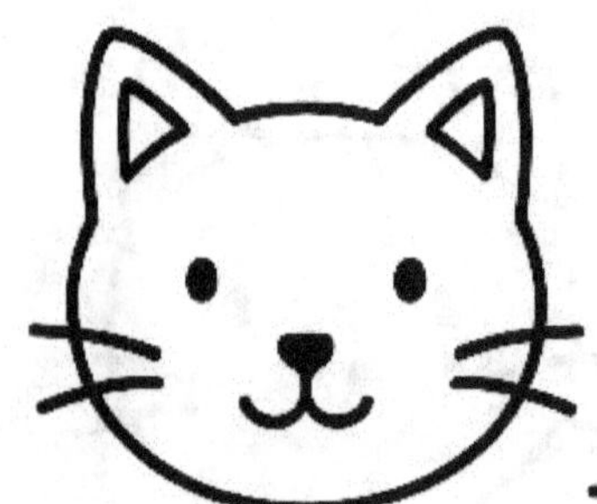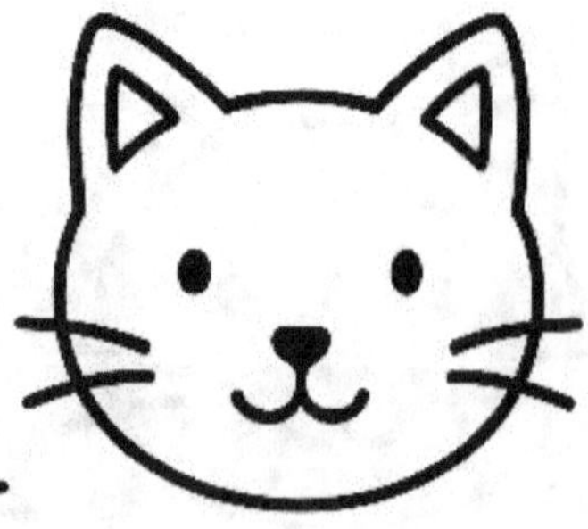

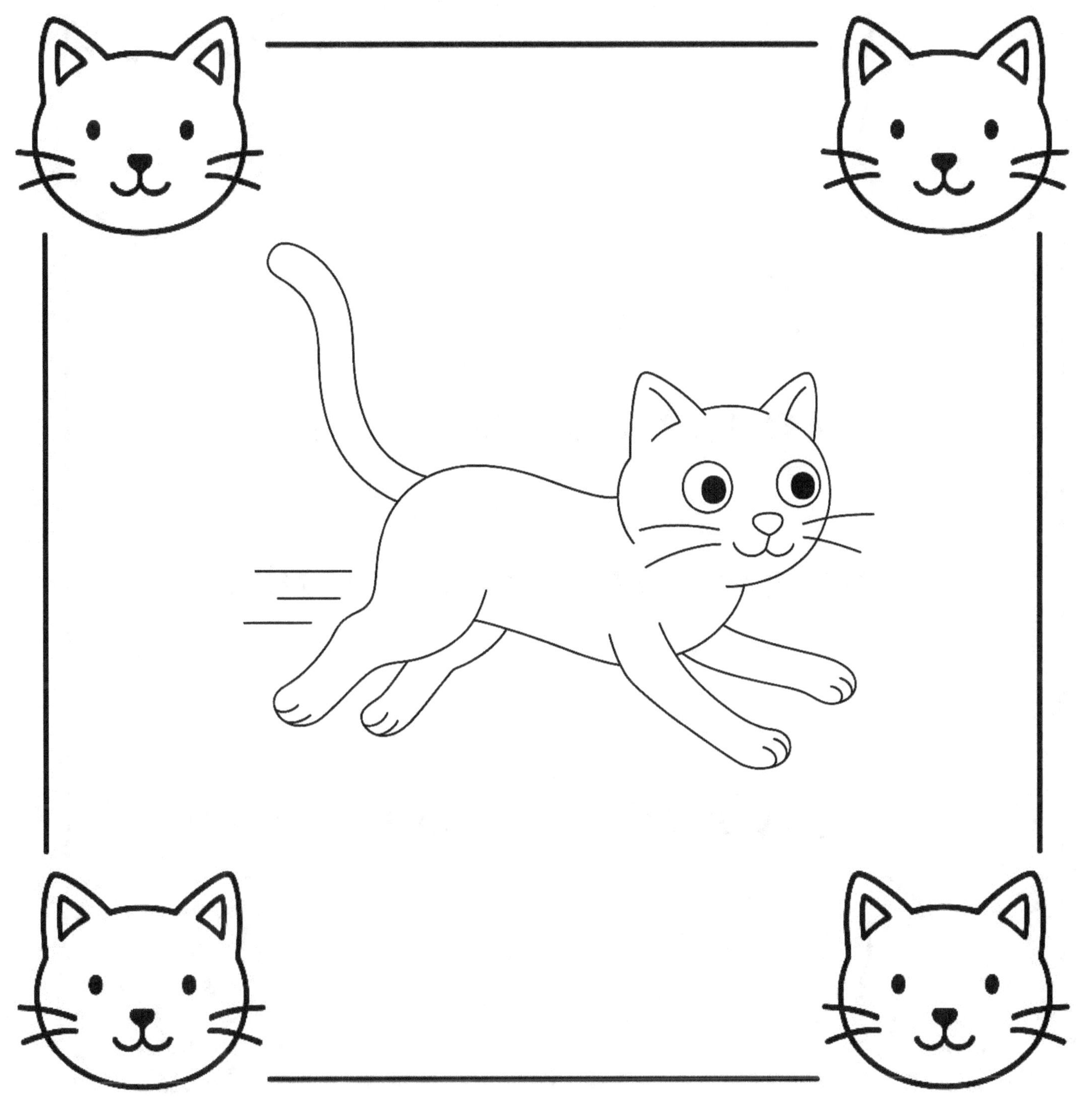

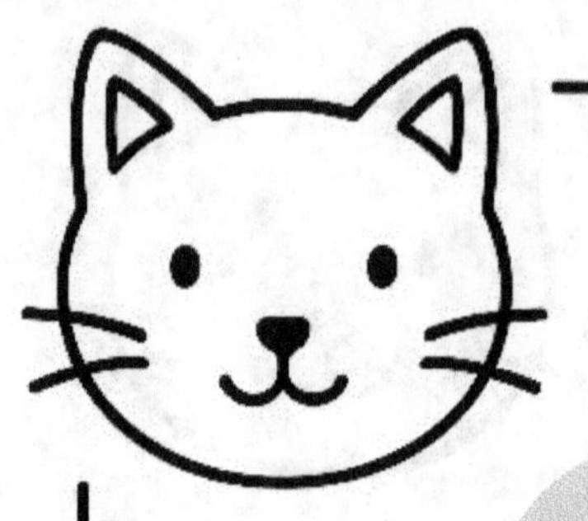
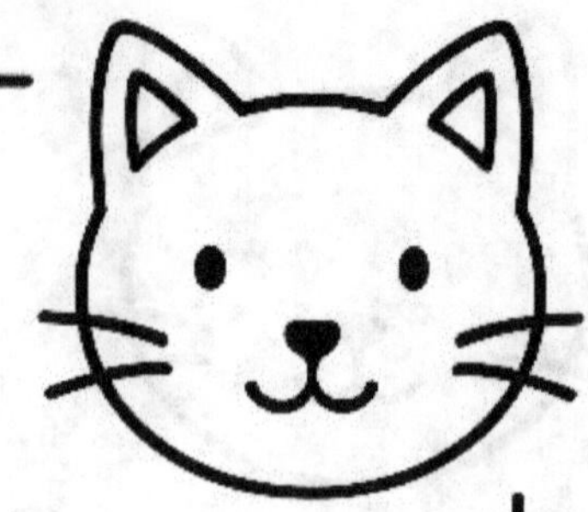

Fact #25

CATS WALK ON THEIR TOES.

Los gatos caminan de puntillas.

Category 3: Behavior and Movement

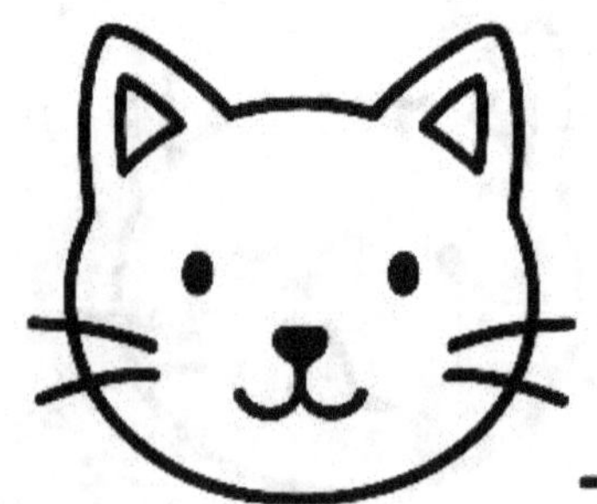
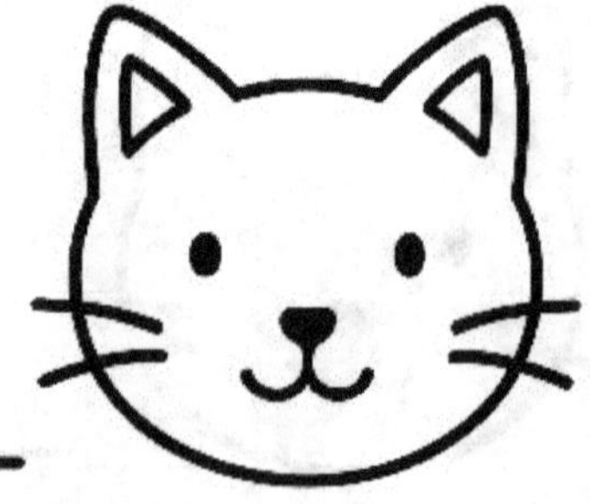

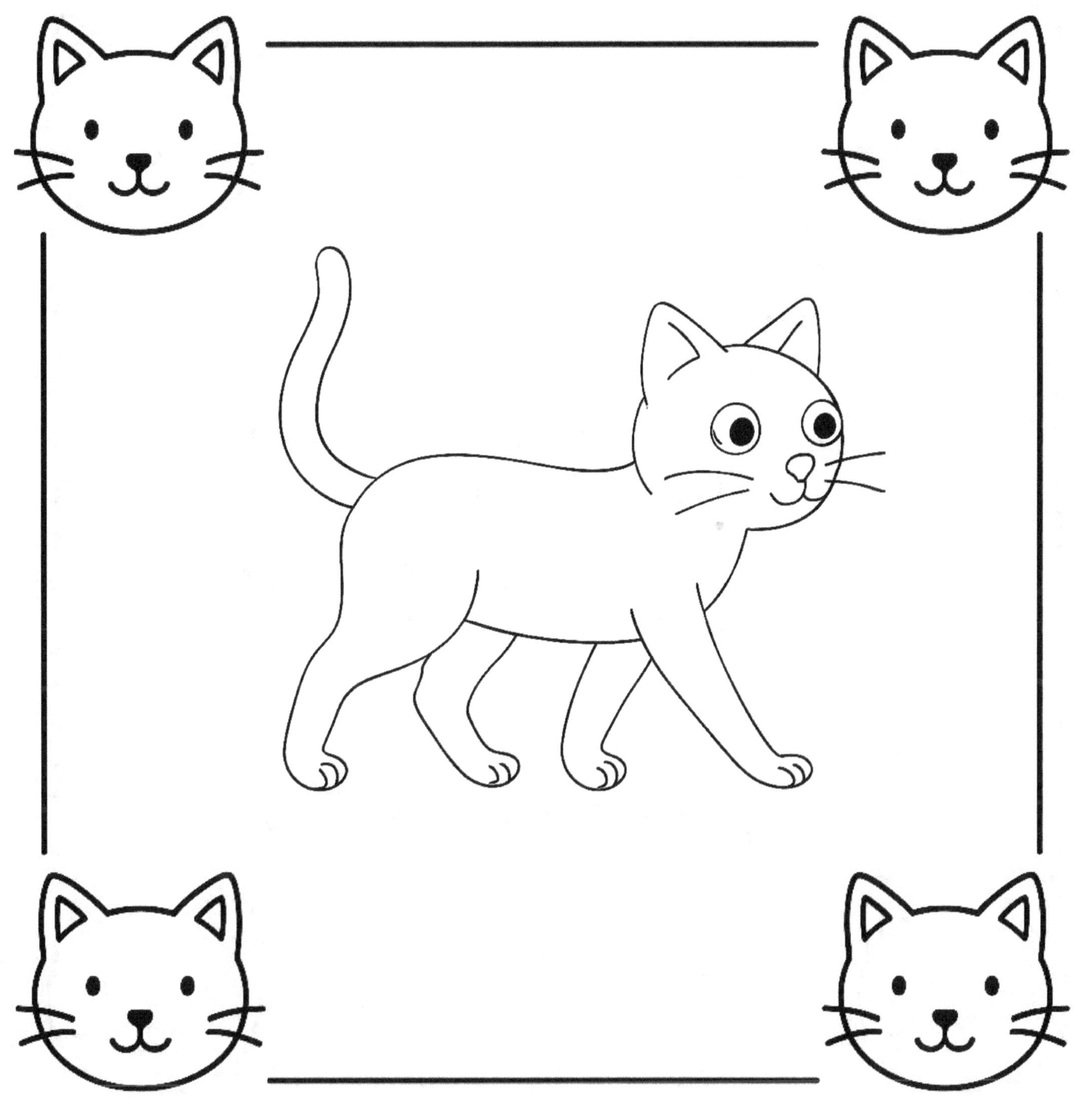

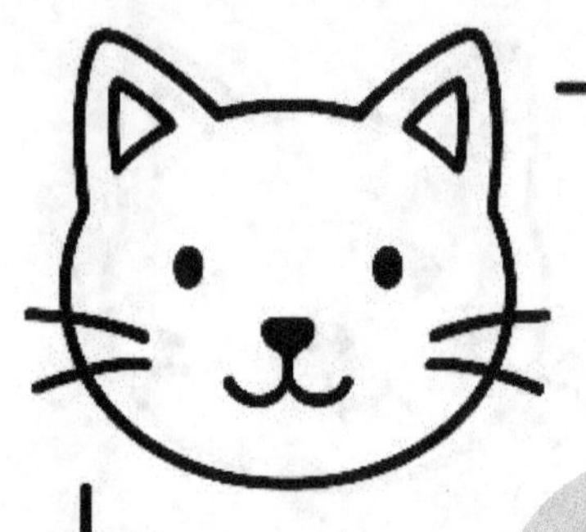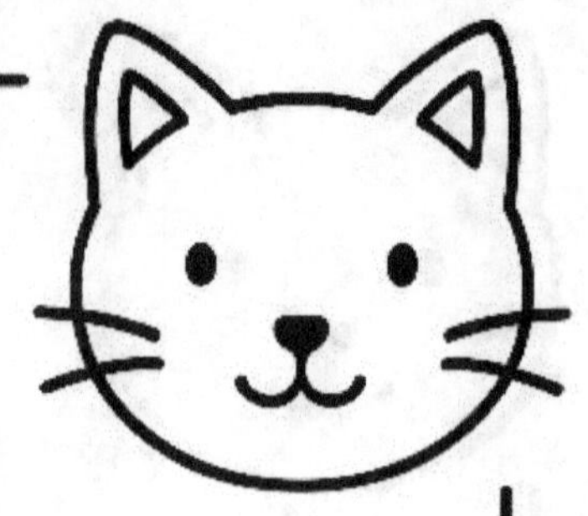

CATS CAN HAVE SHORT, LONG, OR CURLY FUR.

Los gatos pueden tener pelaje corto, largo o rizado.

Category 4: Fur, Eyes & Body

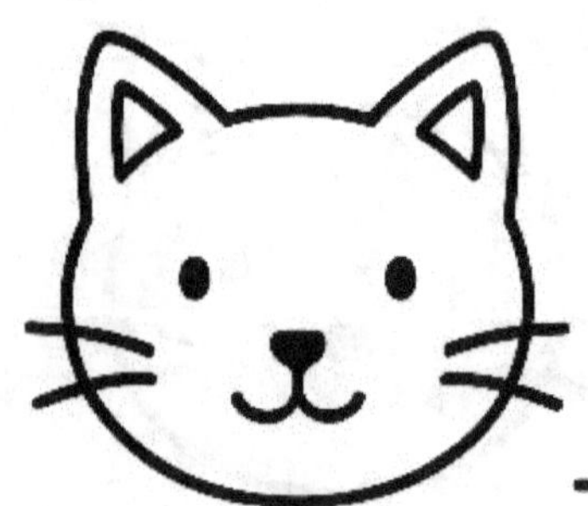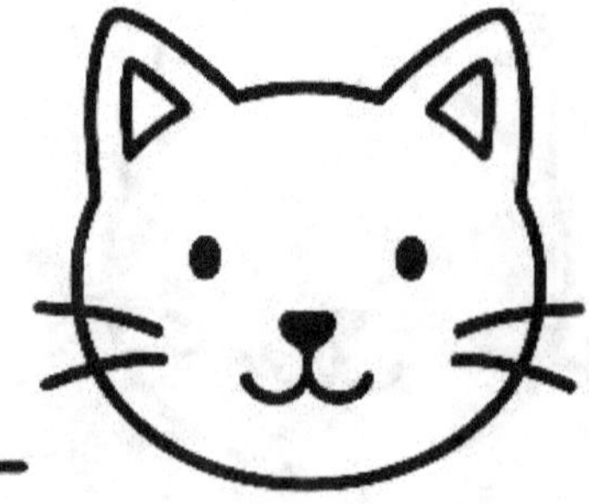

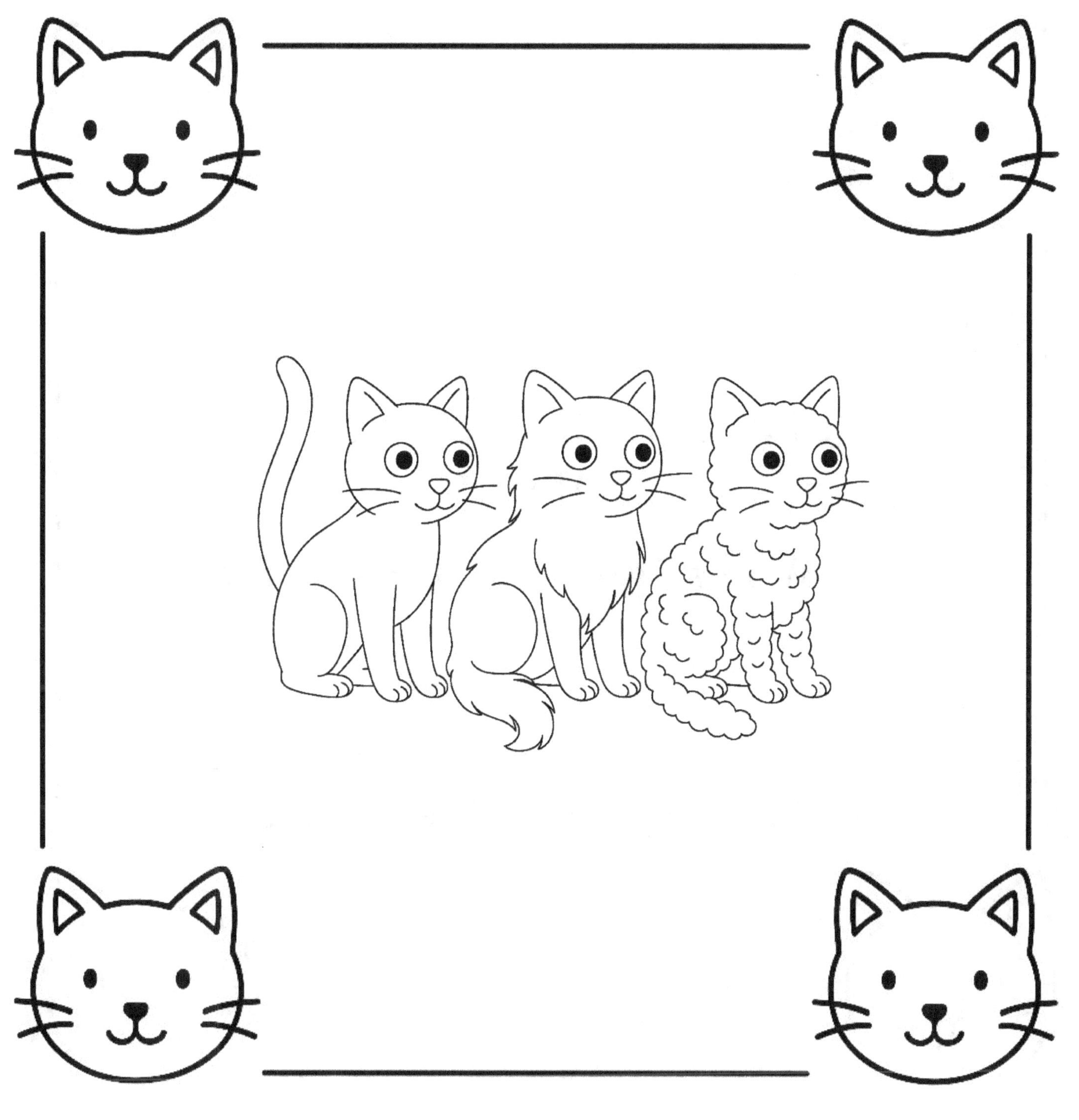

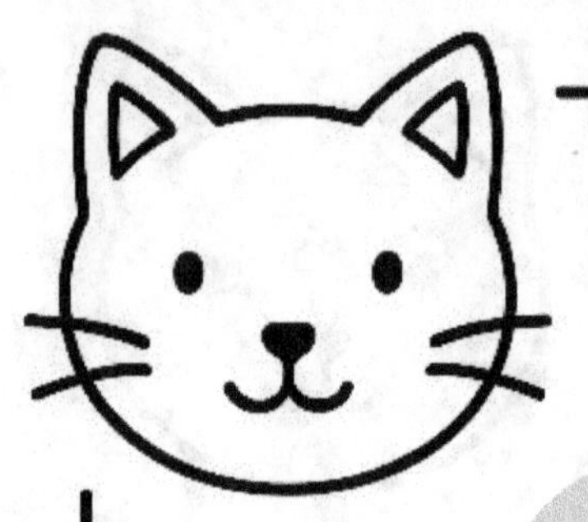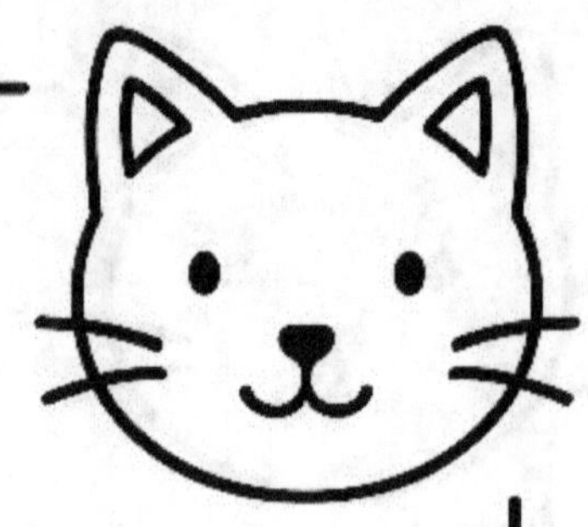

SOME CATS HAVE NO FUR AT ALL!

¡Algunos gatos no tienen nada de pelaje!

Category 4: Fur, Eyes & Body

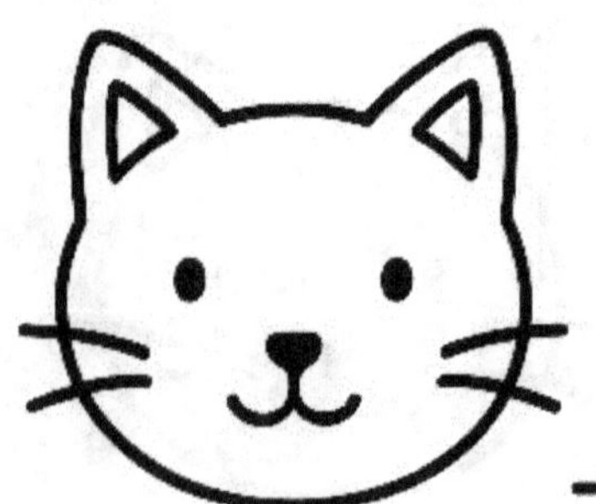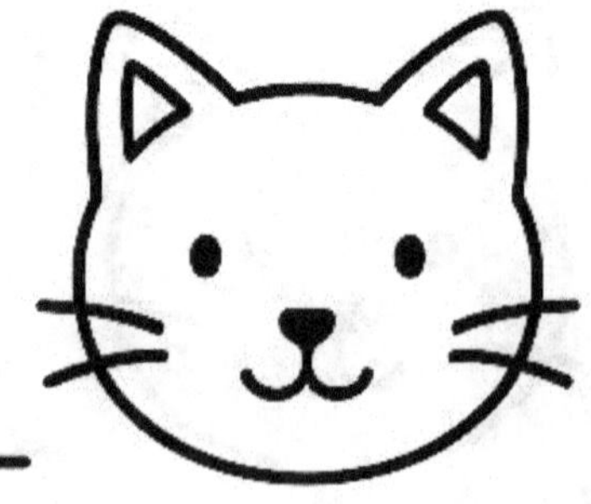

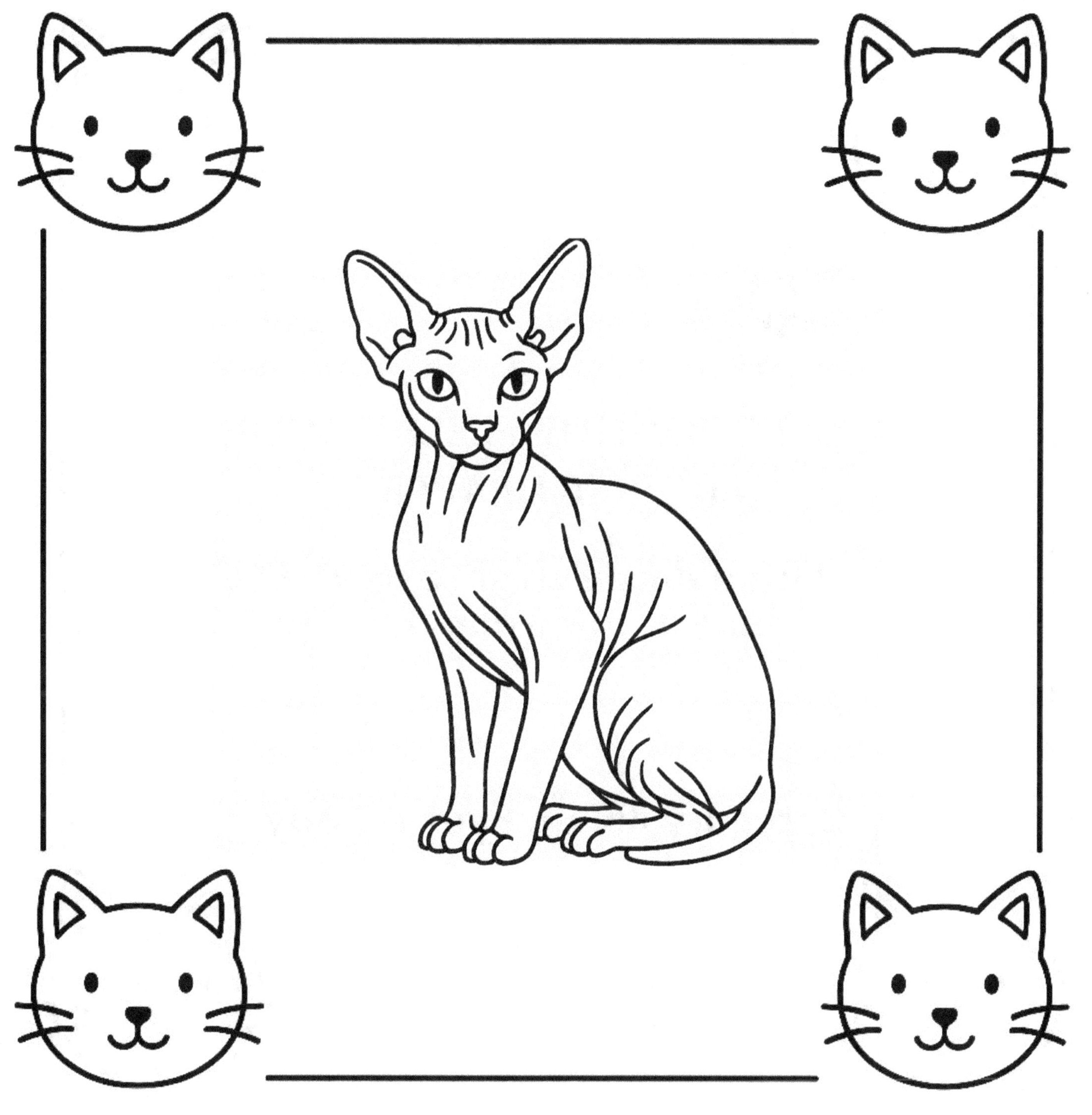

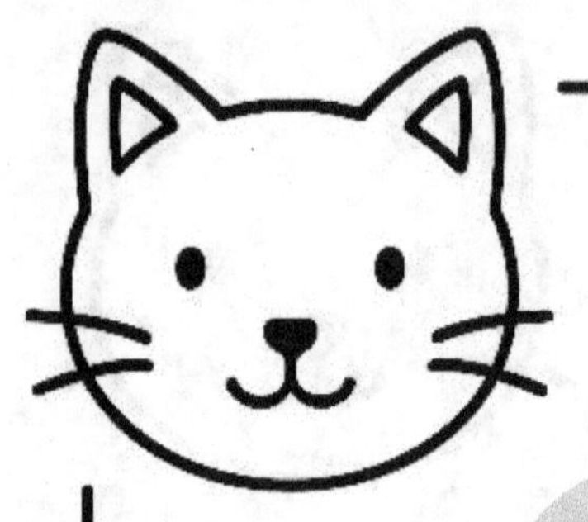
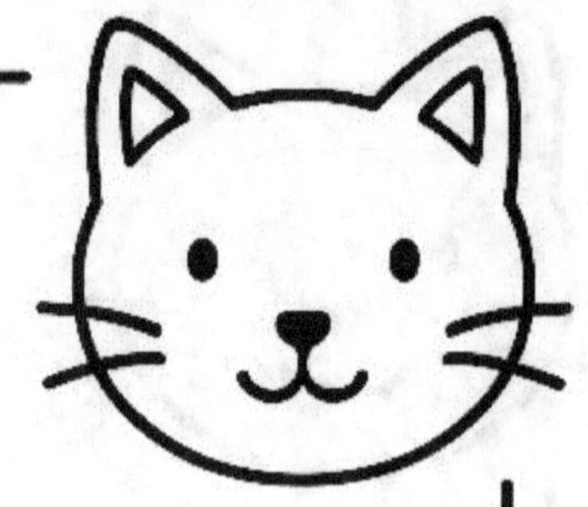

A CAT'S TONGUE FEELS ROUGH LIKE SANDPAPER.

La lengua de un gato se siente áspera como papel de lija.

Category 4: Fur, Eyes & Body

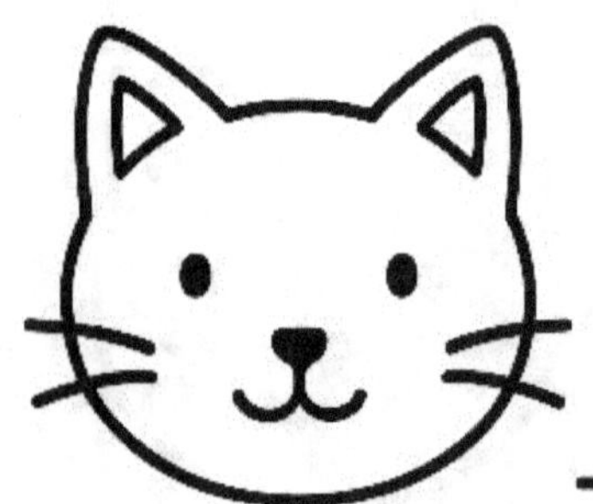
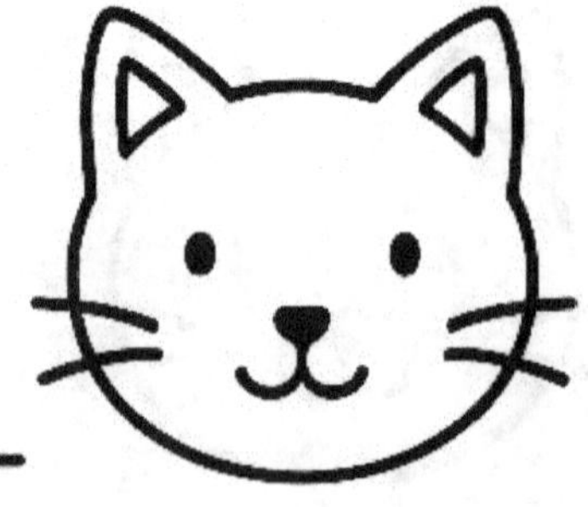

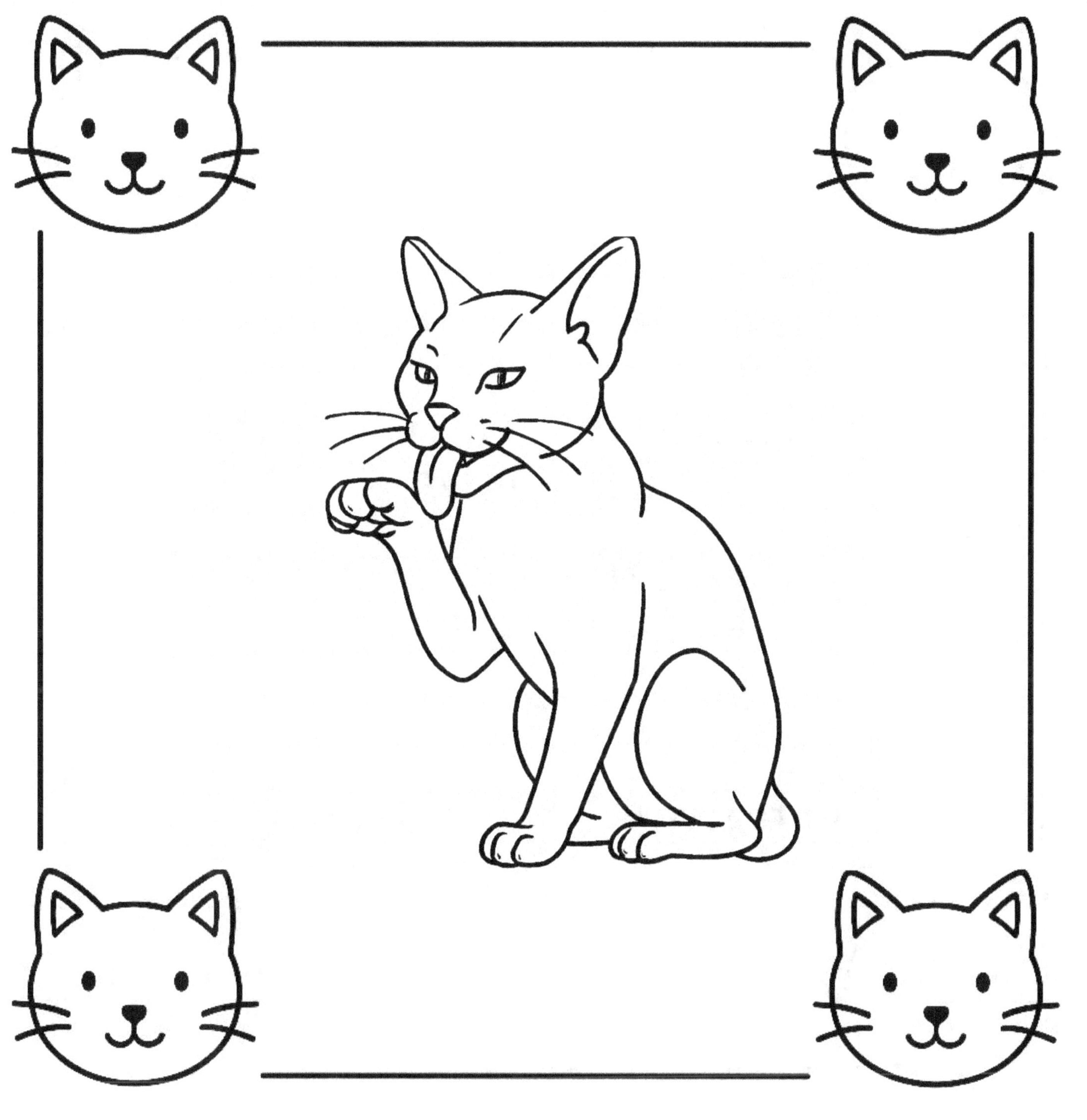

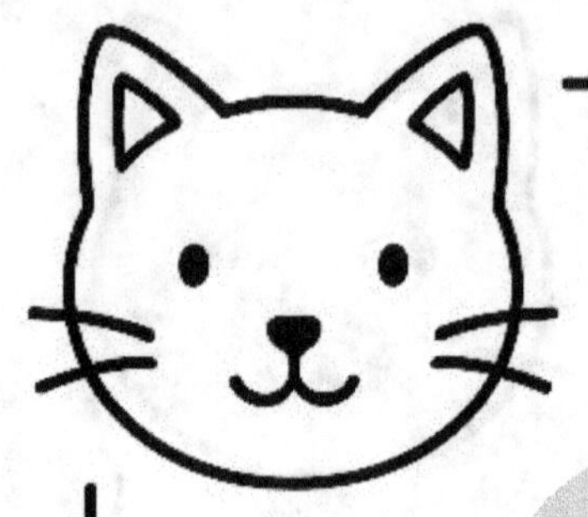
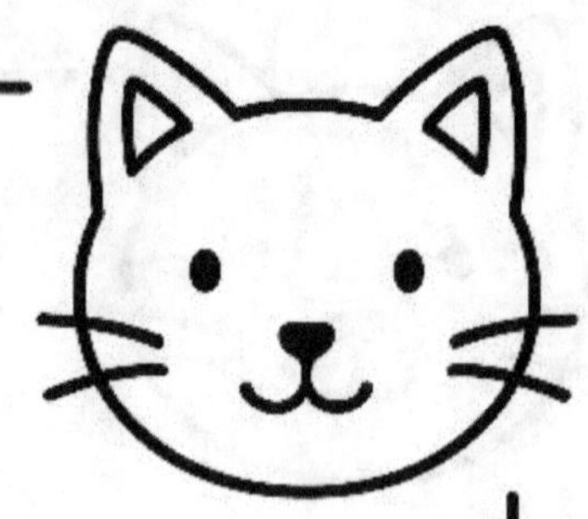

Fact #29

CATS HAVE FIVE TOES ON THEIR FRONT PAWS.

Los gatos tienen cinco dedos en las patas delanteras.

Category 4: Fur, Eyes & Body

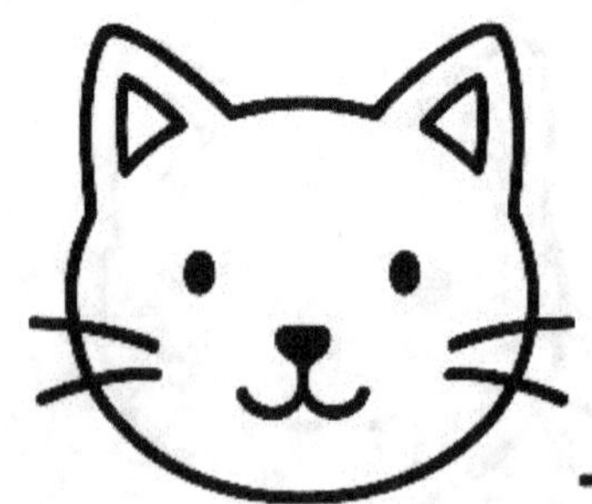
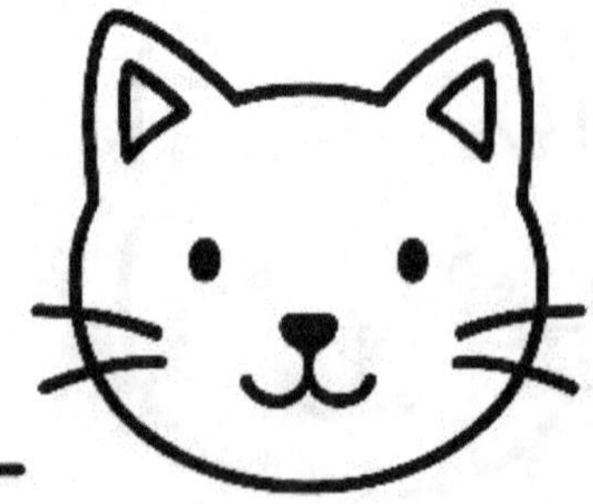

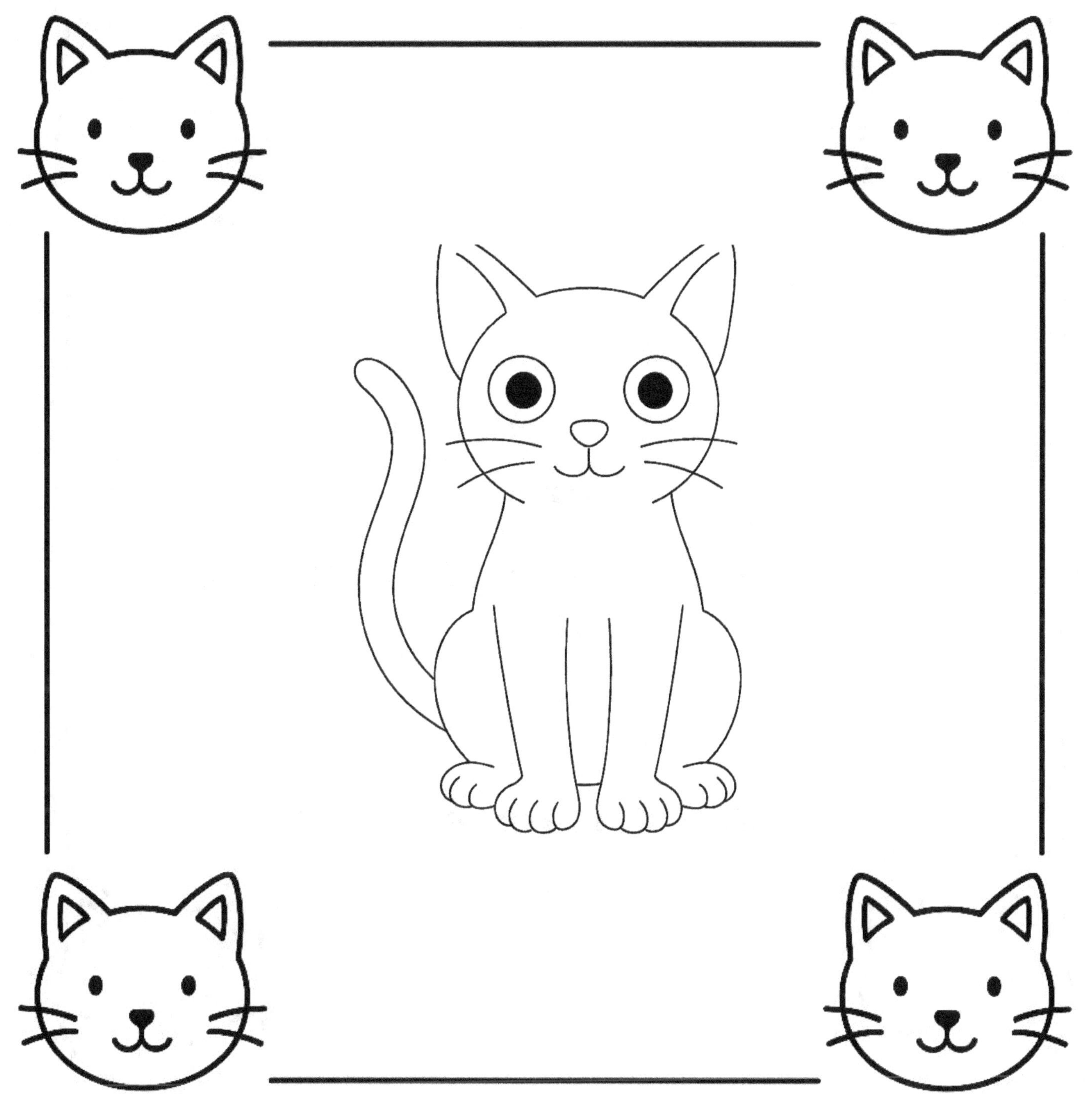

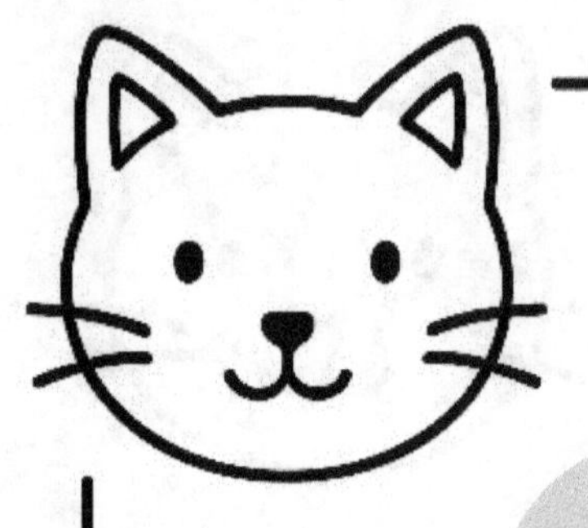
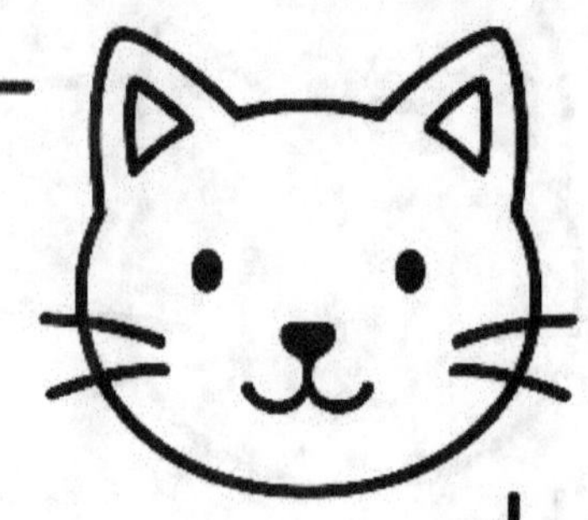

A CAT'S EYES SHINE IN THE DARK.

Los ojos de los gatos brillan en la oscuridad.

Category 4: Fur, Eyes & Body

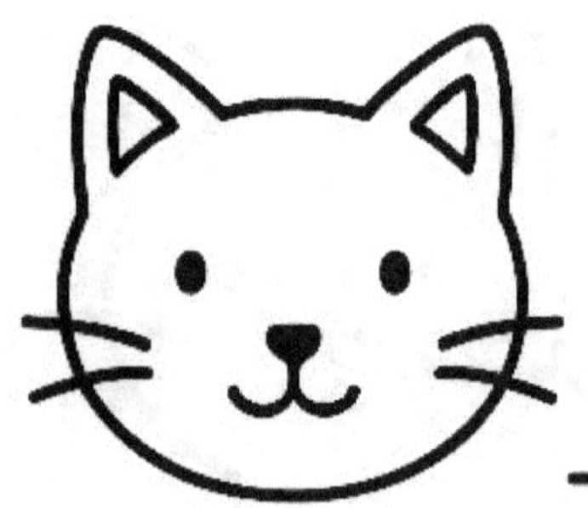
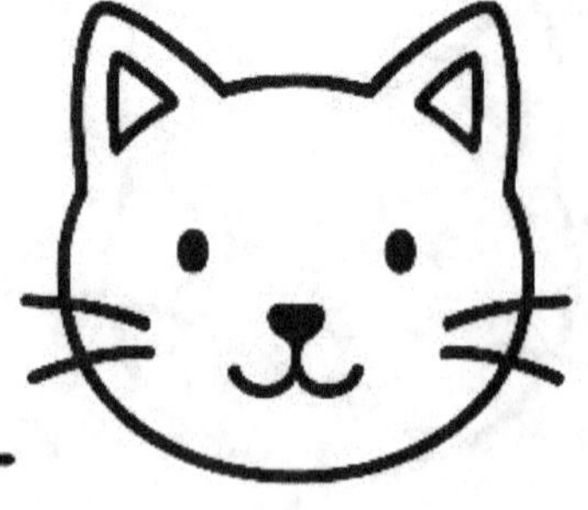

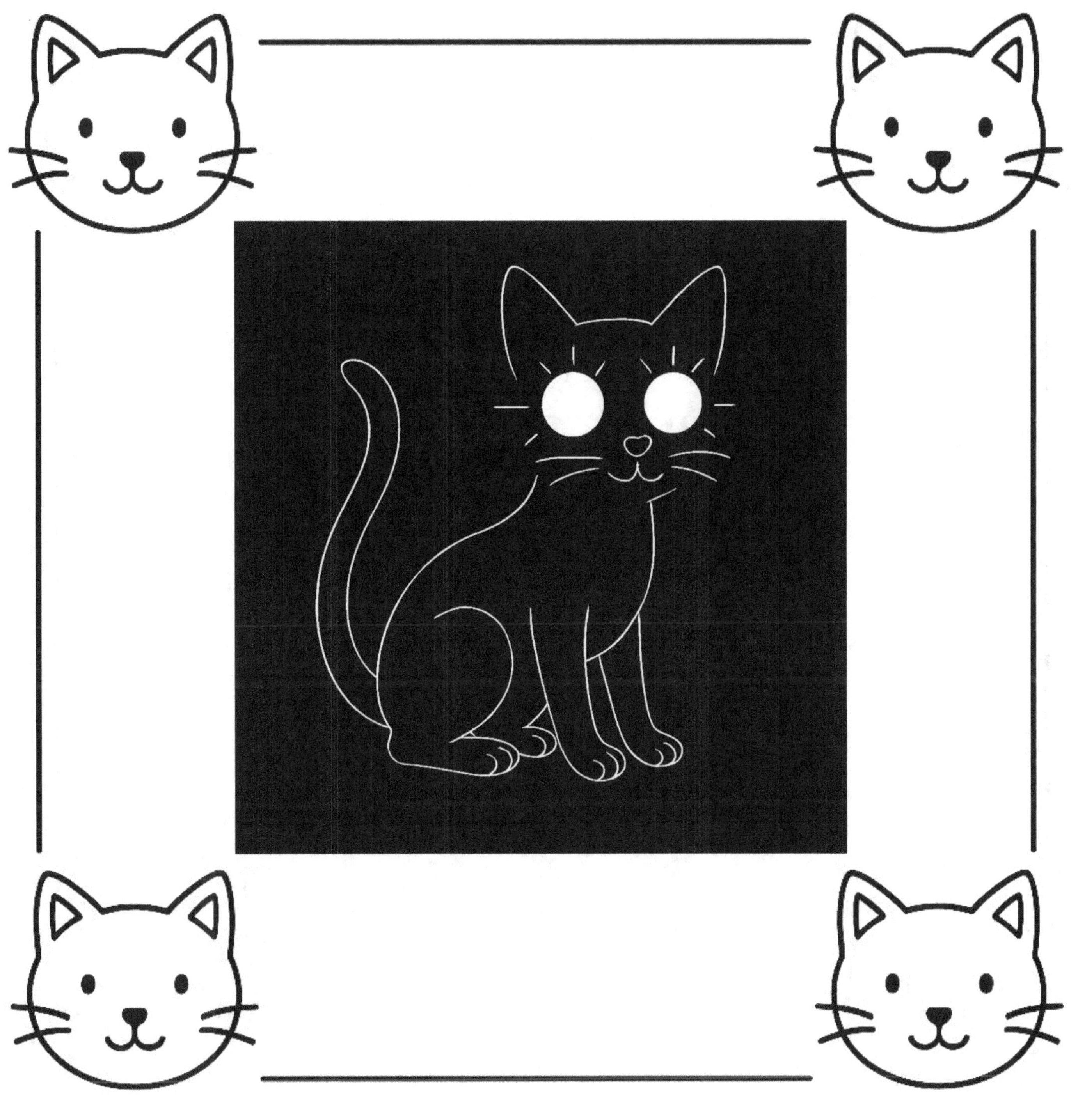

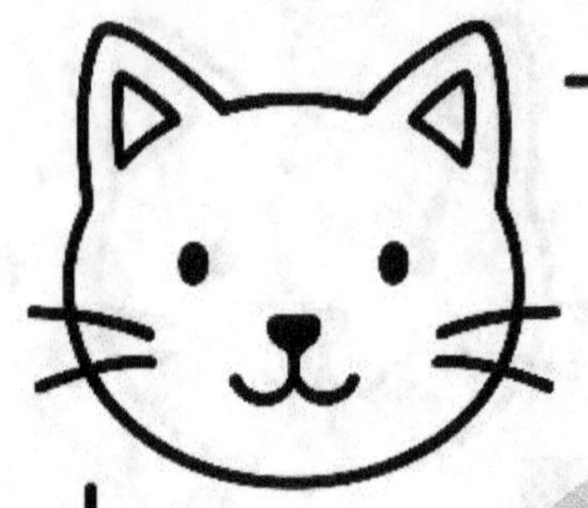
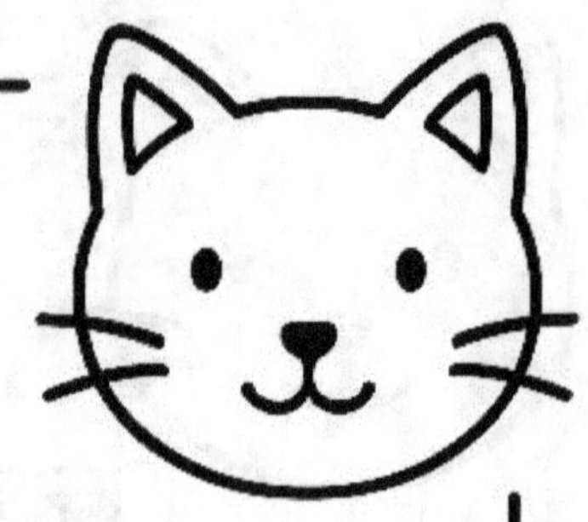

THE MAINE COON IS ONE OF THE BIGGEST CAT BREEDS.

El Maine Coon es una de las razas de gatos más grandes.

Category 5: Breeds & Types

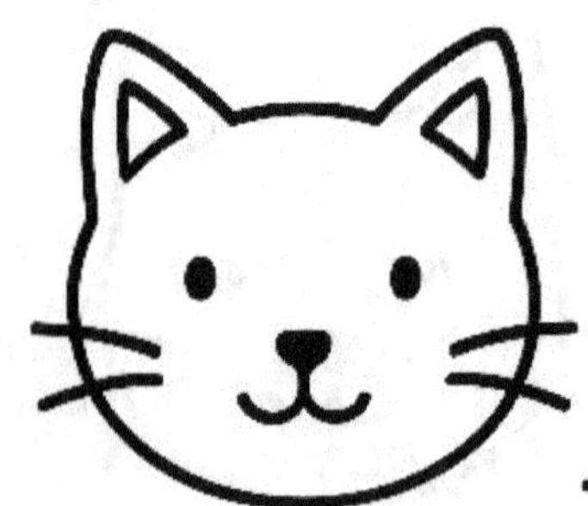
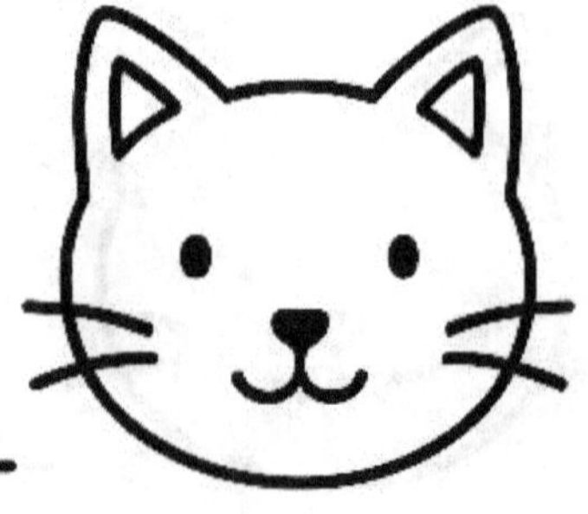

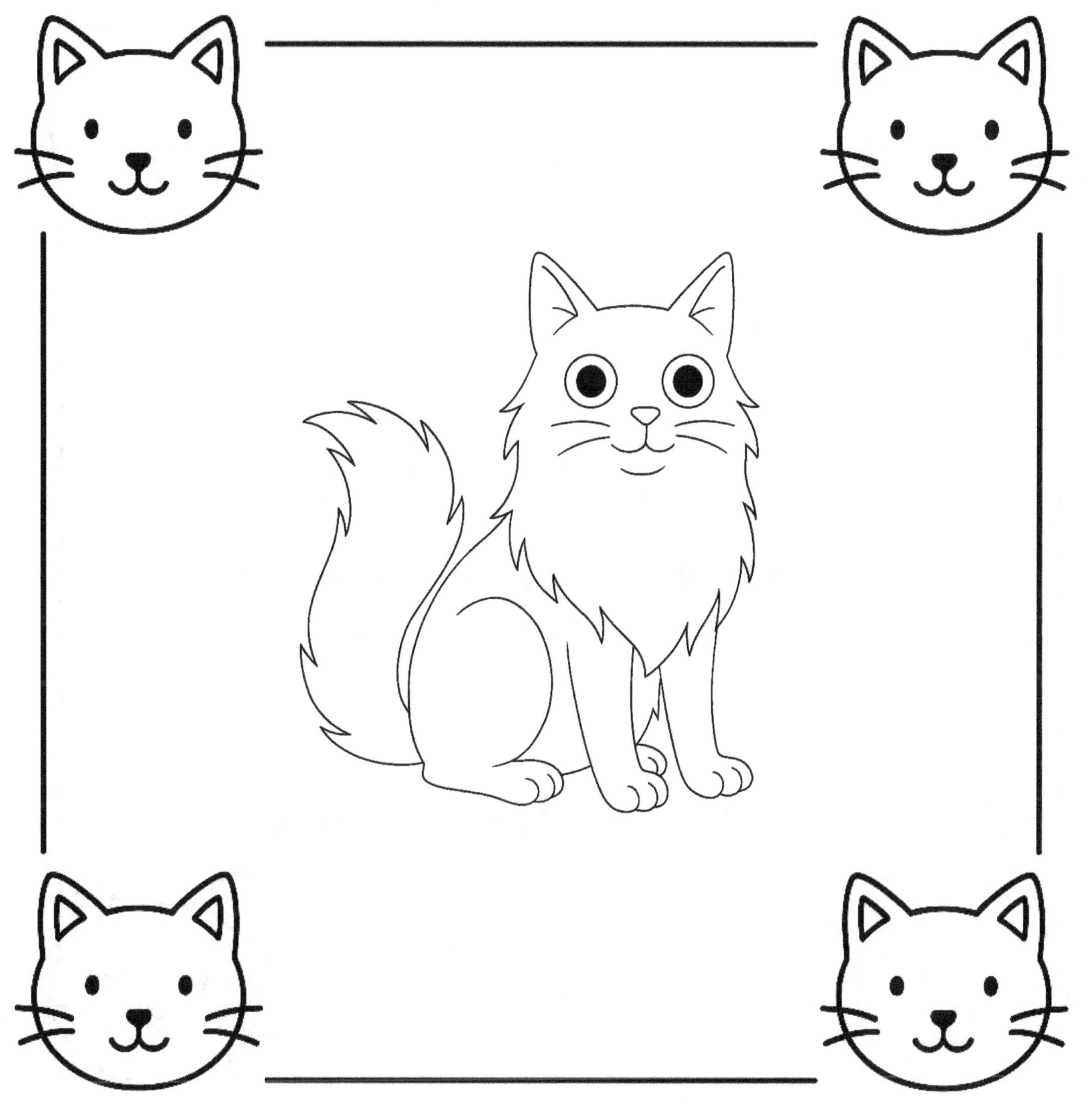

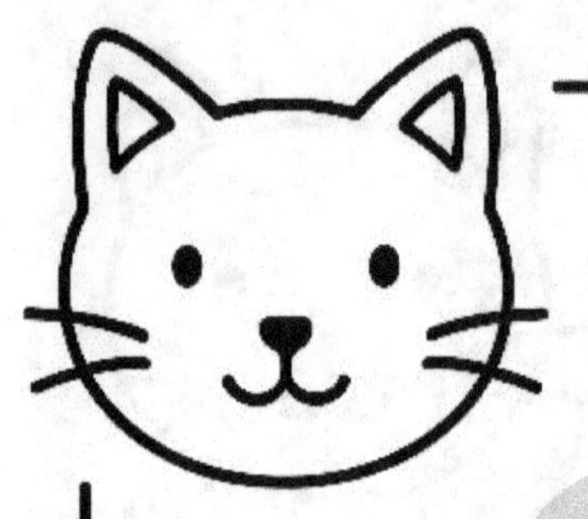 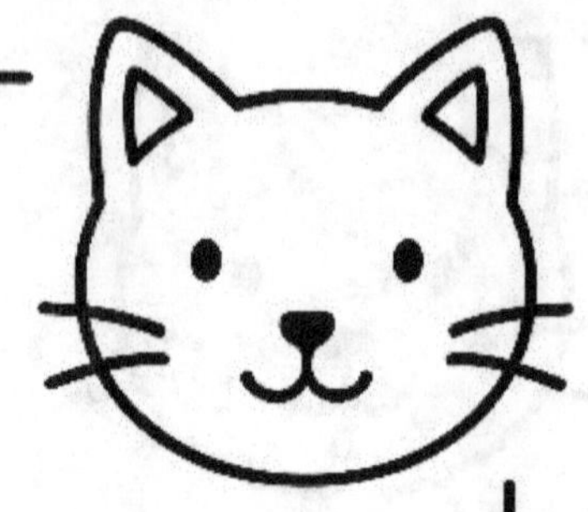

THE SIAMESE CAT IS KNOWN FOR ITS LOUD MEOW.

El gato siamés es conocido por su maullido fuerte.

Category 5: Breeds & Types

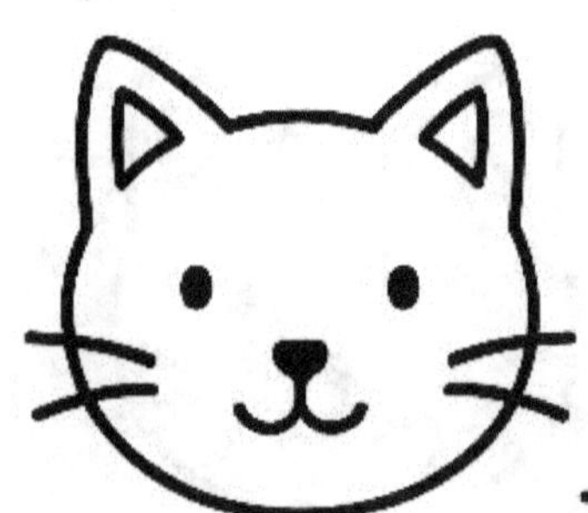 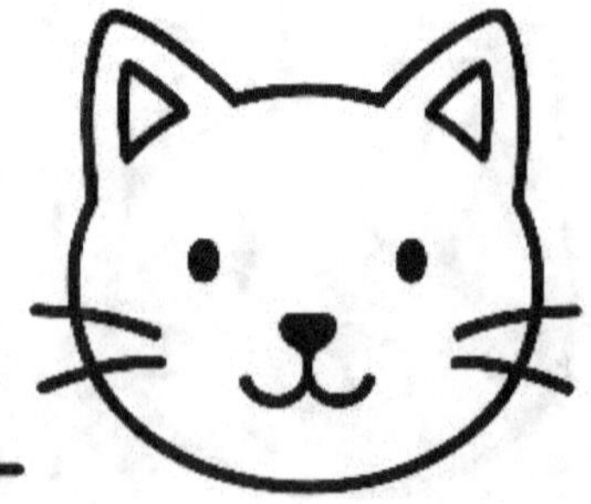

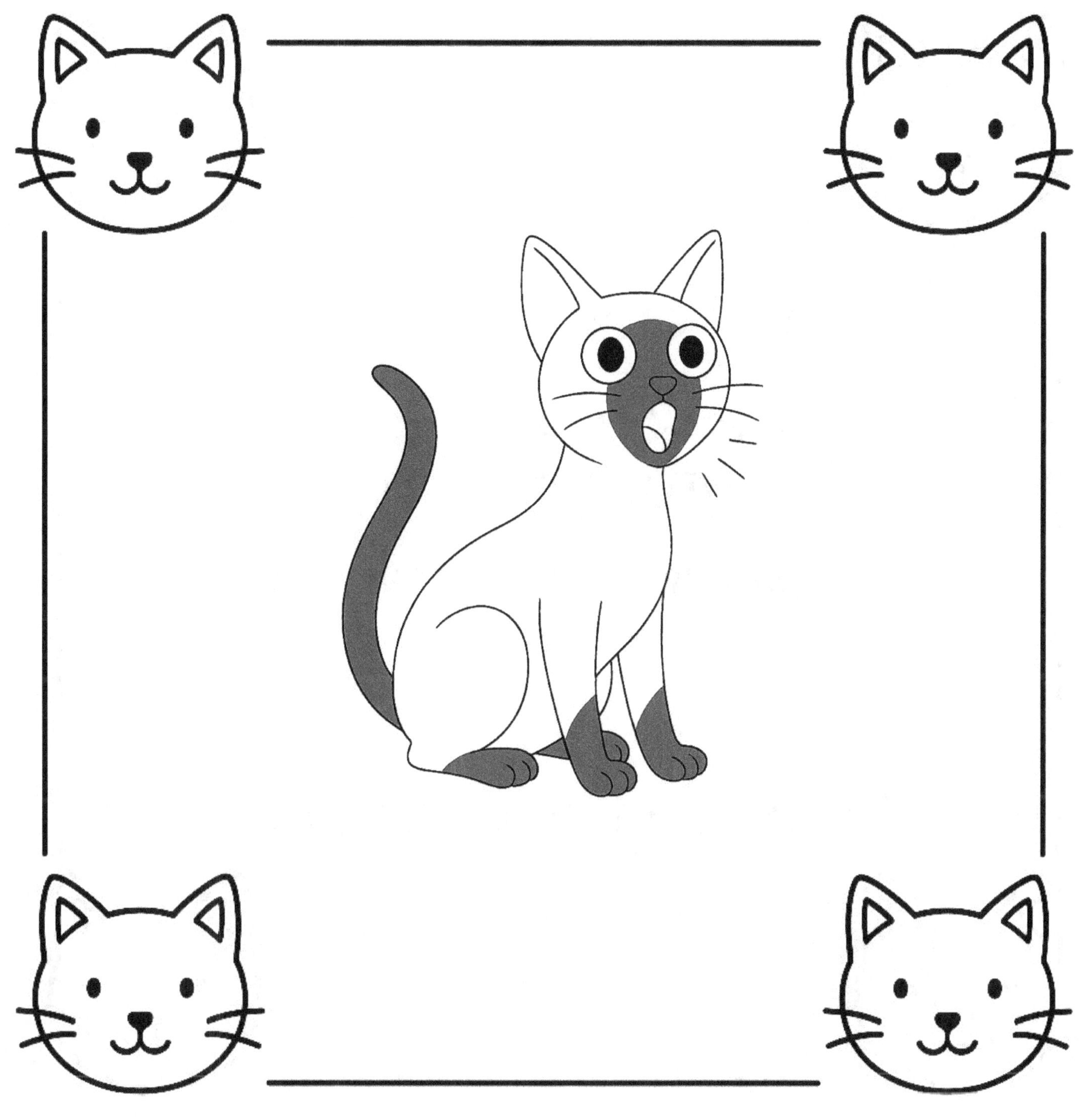

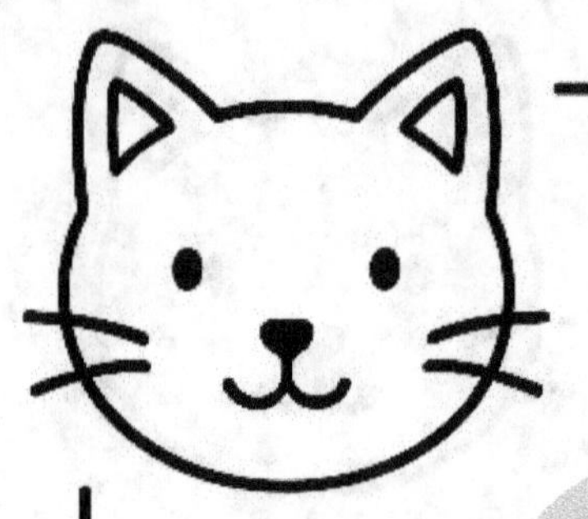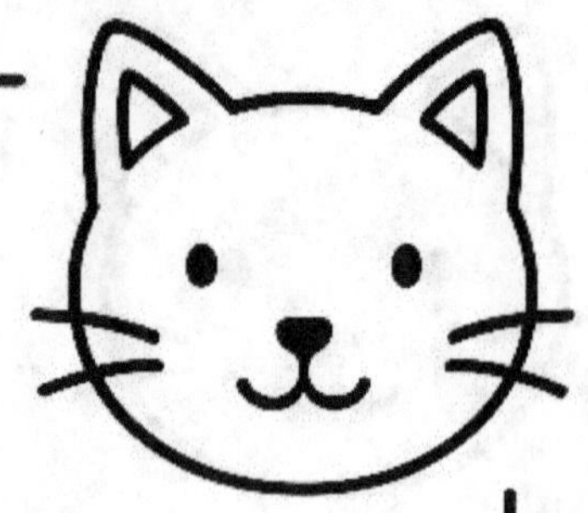

THE SPHYNX IS A HAIRLESS CAT WITH SOFT SKIN.

El Sphynx es un gato sin pelo con piel suave.

Category 5: Breeds & Types

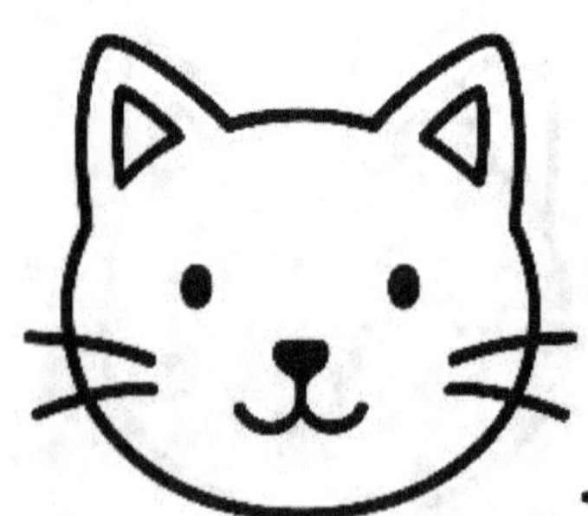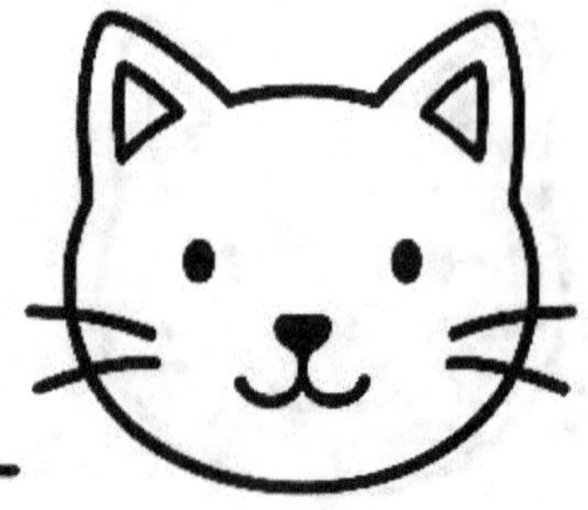

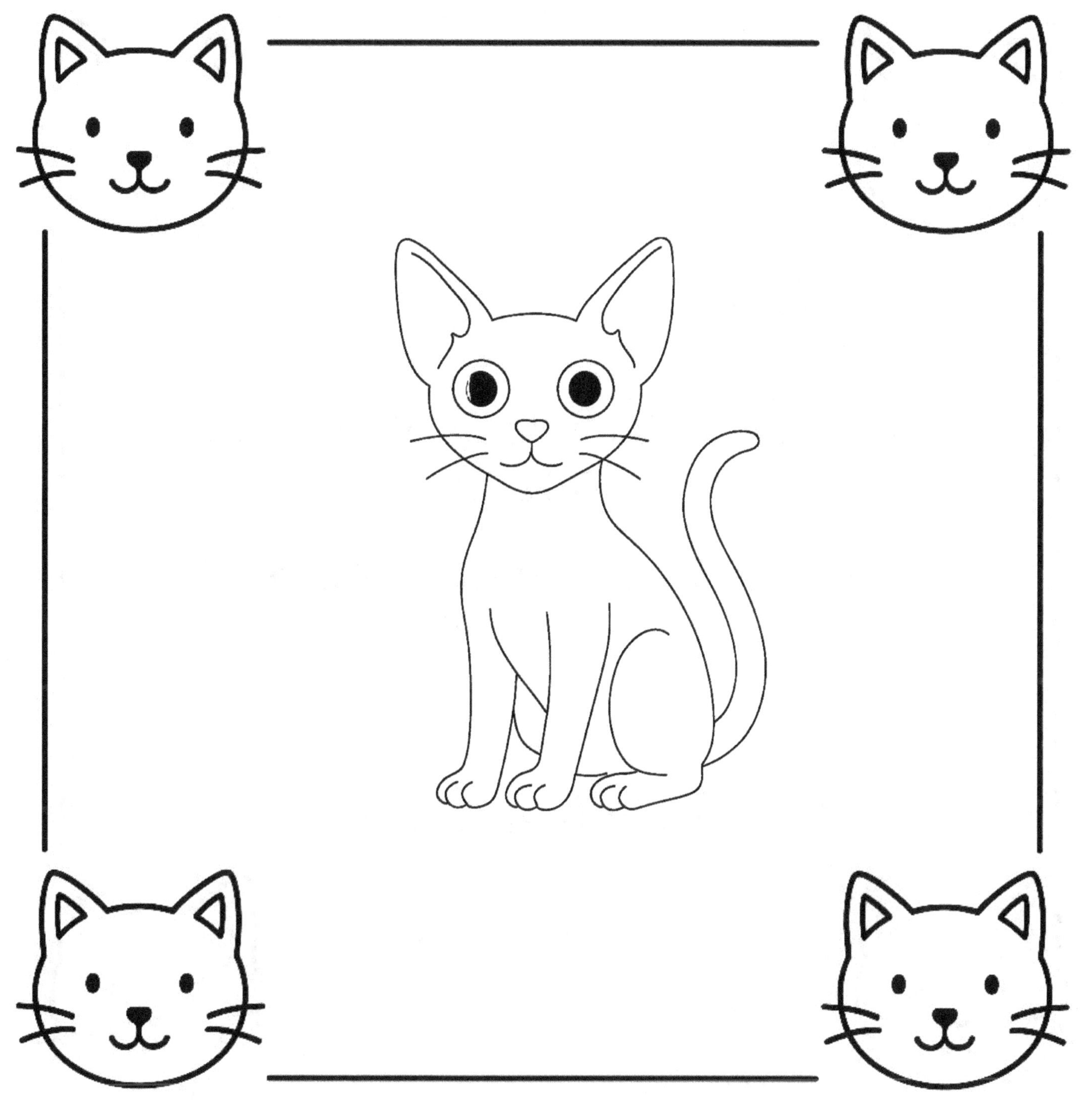

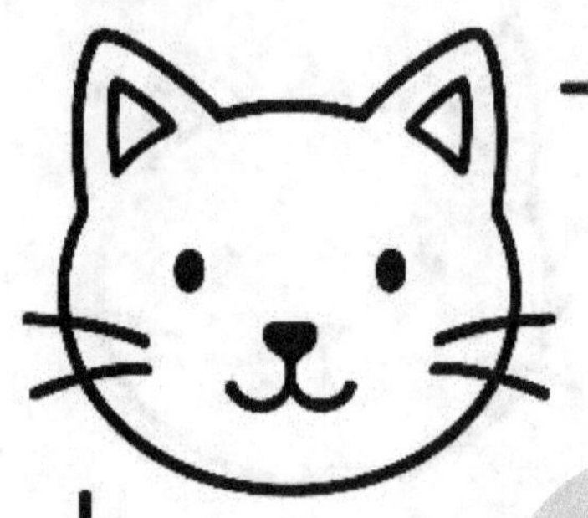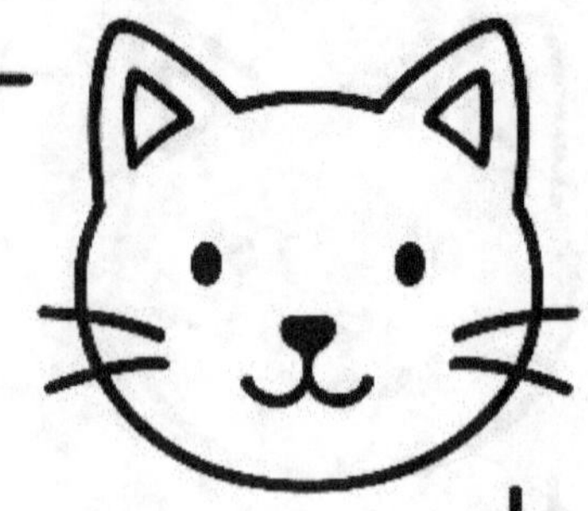

THE RAGDOLL CAT LOVES TO BE CUDDLED.

Al gato Ragdoll le encanta que lo abracen.

Category 5: Breeds & Types

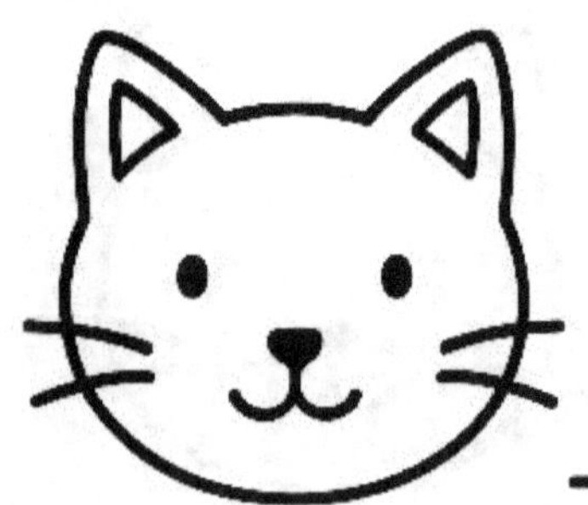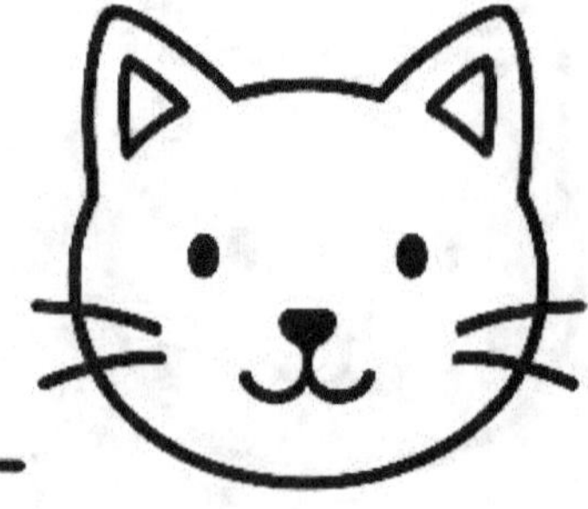

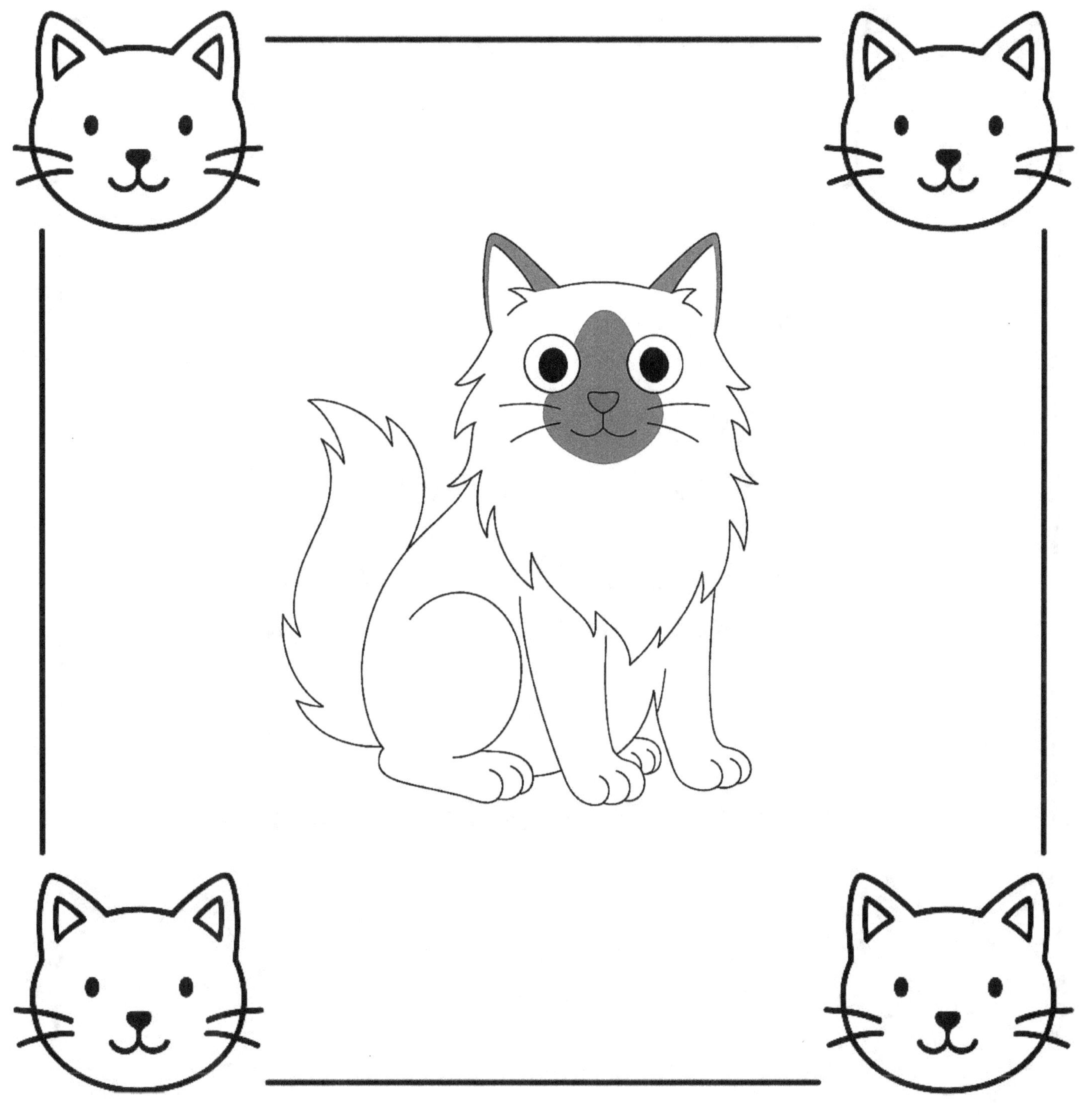

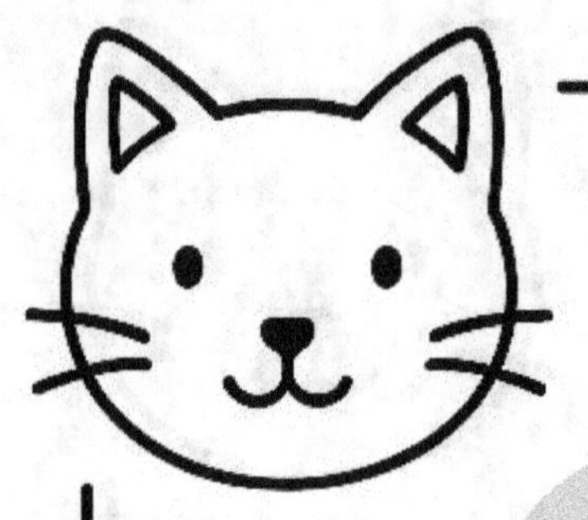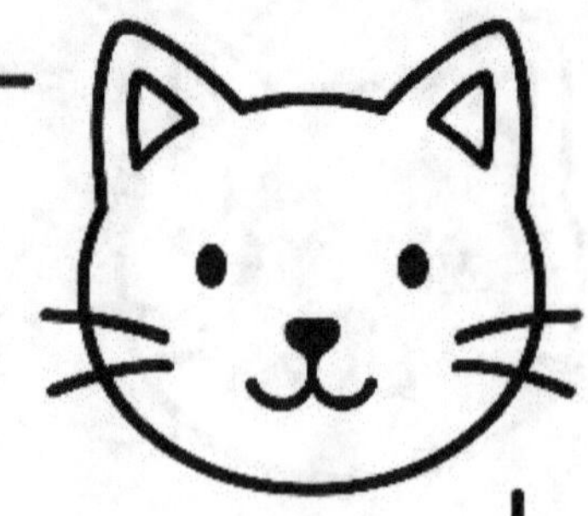

TABBY CATS HAVE STRIPES, SPOTS, OR SWIRLS.

Los gatos atigrados tienen rayas, manchas o remolinos.

Category 5: Breeds & Types

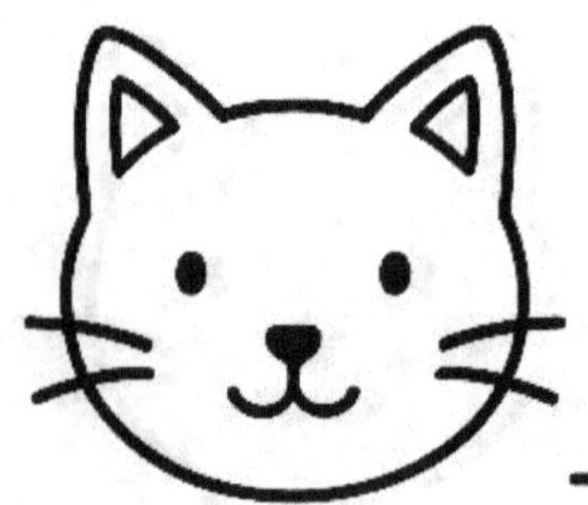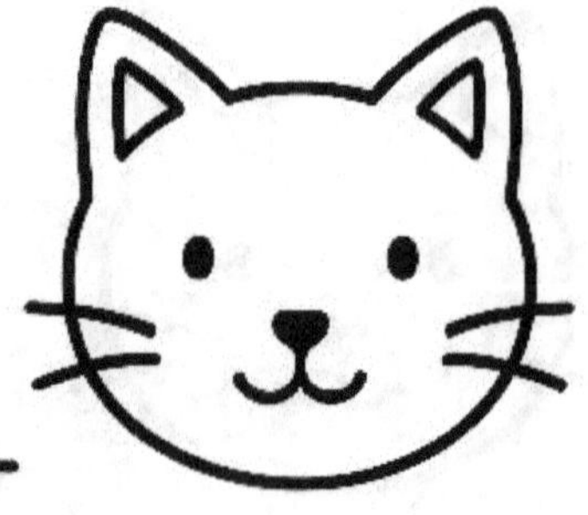

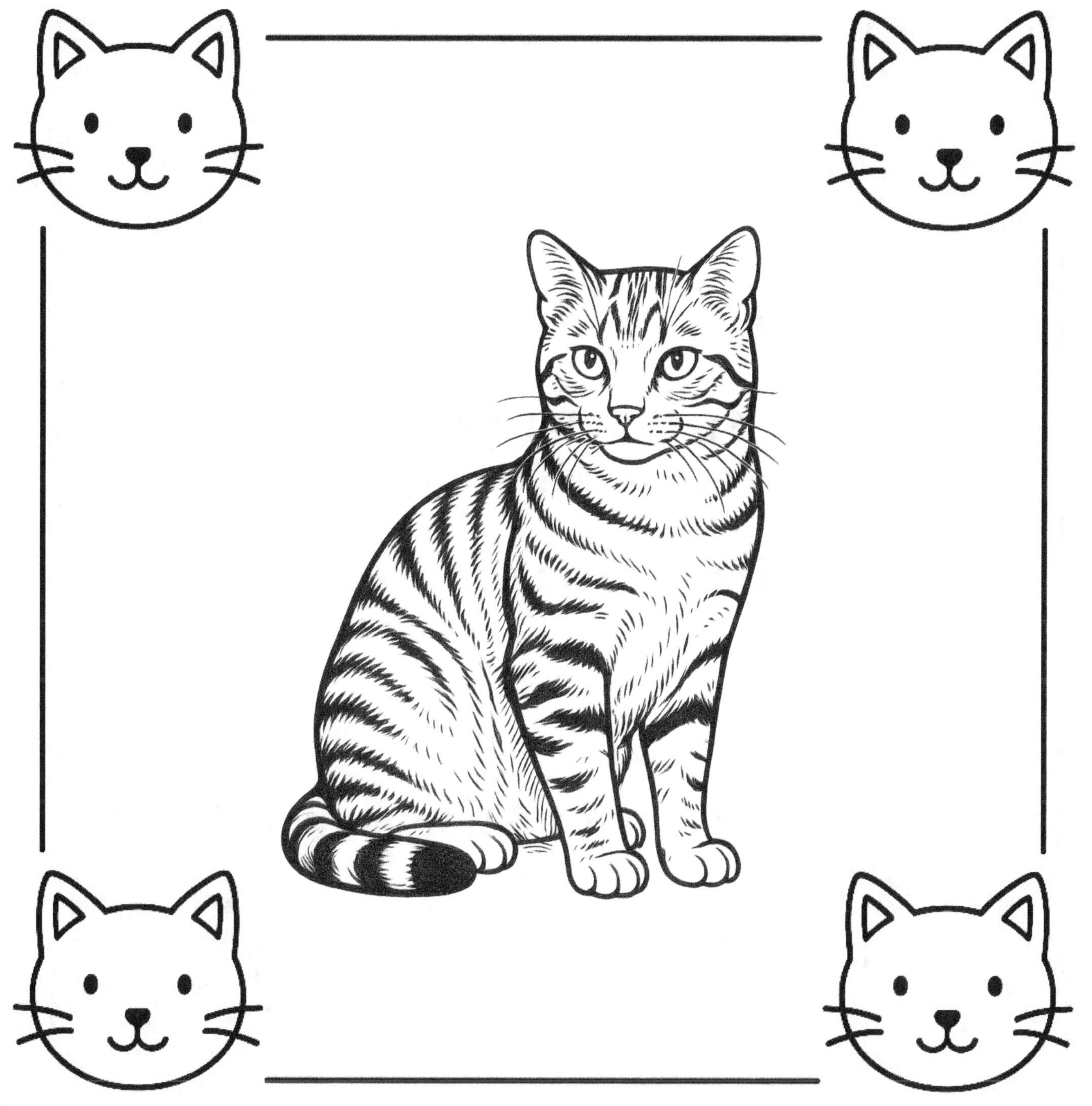

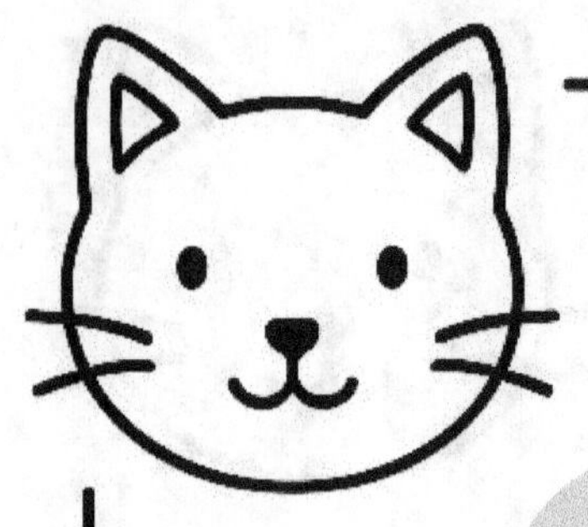
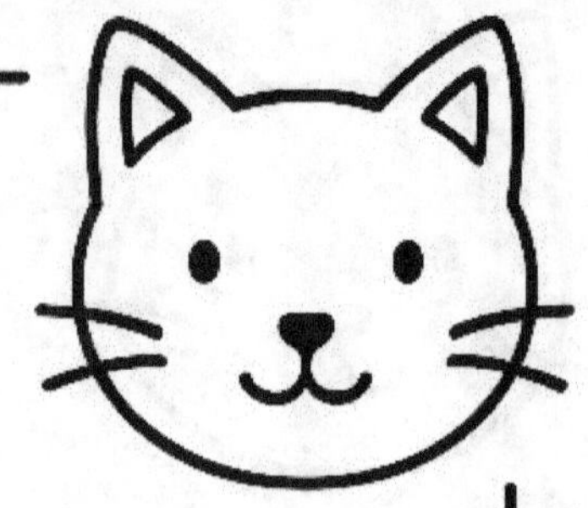

CATS USE THEIR EARS TO SHOW HOW THEY FEEL.

Los gatos usan sus orejas para mostrar cómo se sienten.

Category 6: Sounds & Communication

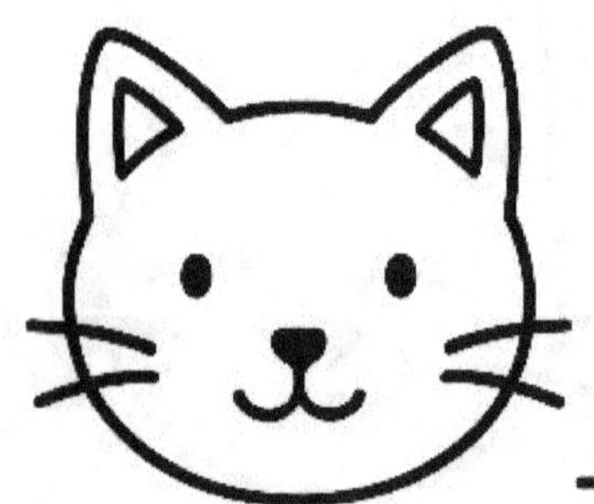
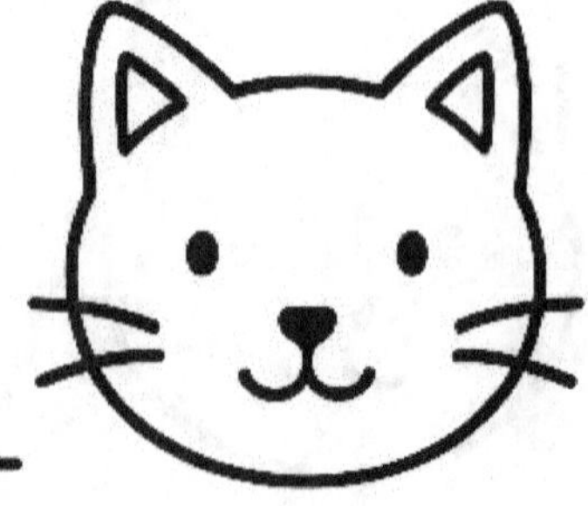

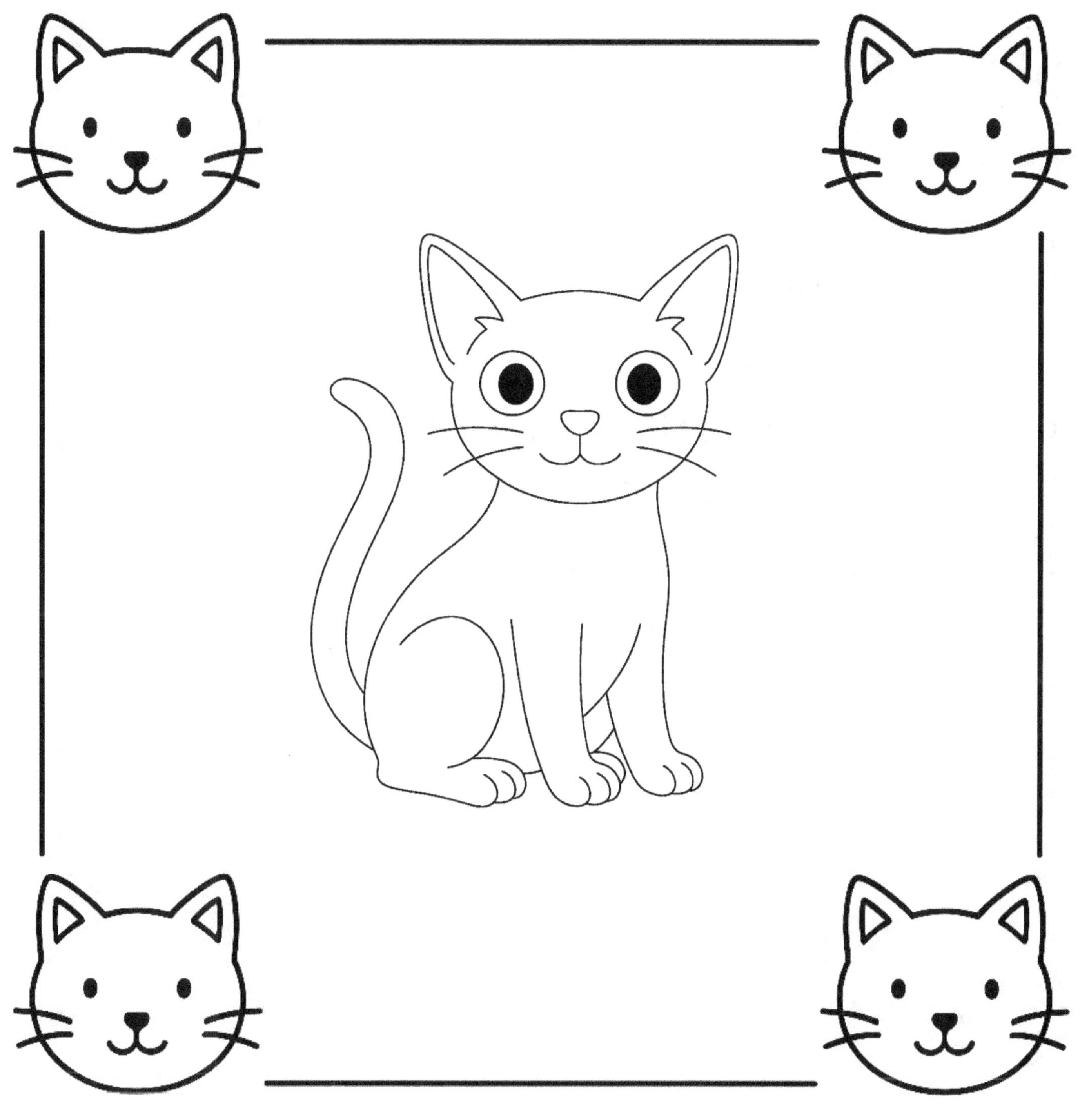

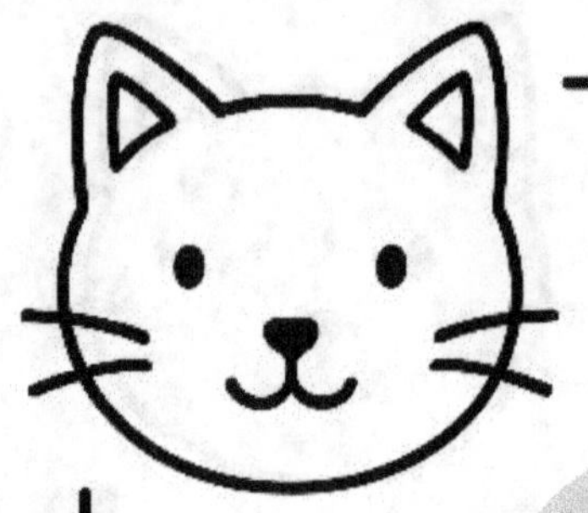
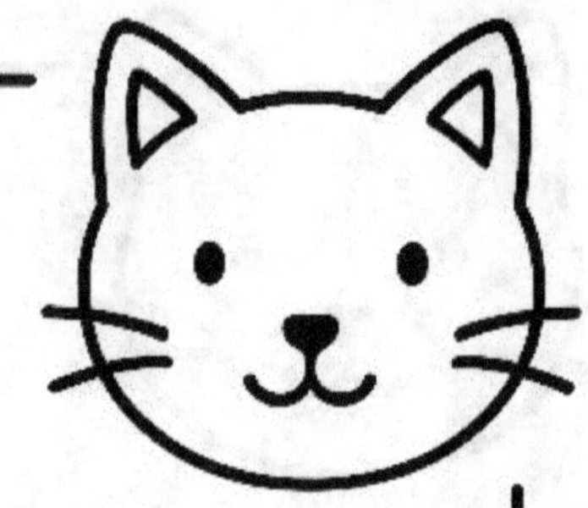

A FLICKING TAIL CAN MEAN A CAT IS ANNOYED.

Una cola moviéndose rápido puede significar que el gato está molesto.

Category 6: Sounds & Communication

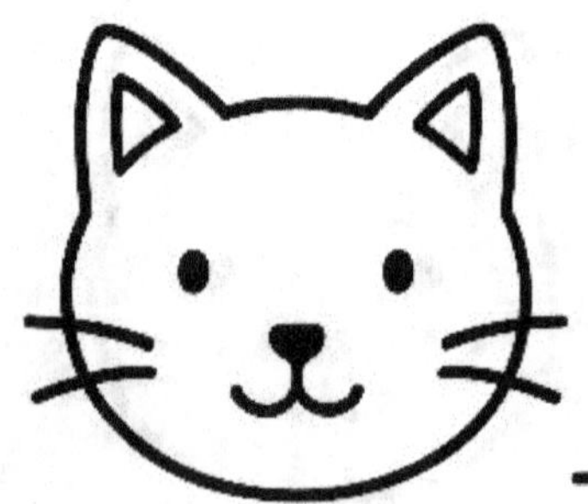
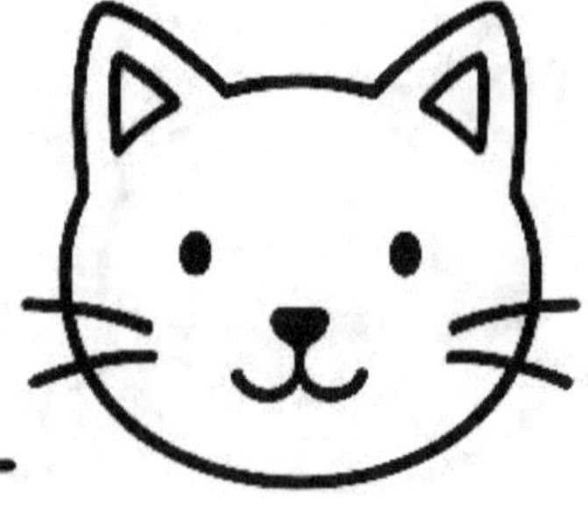

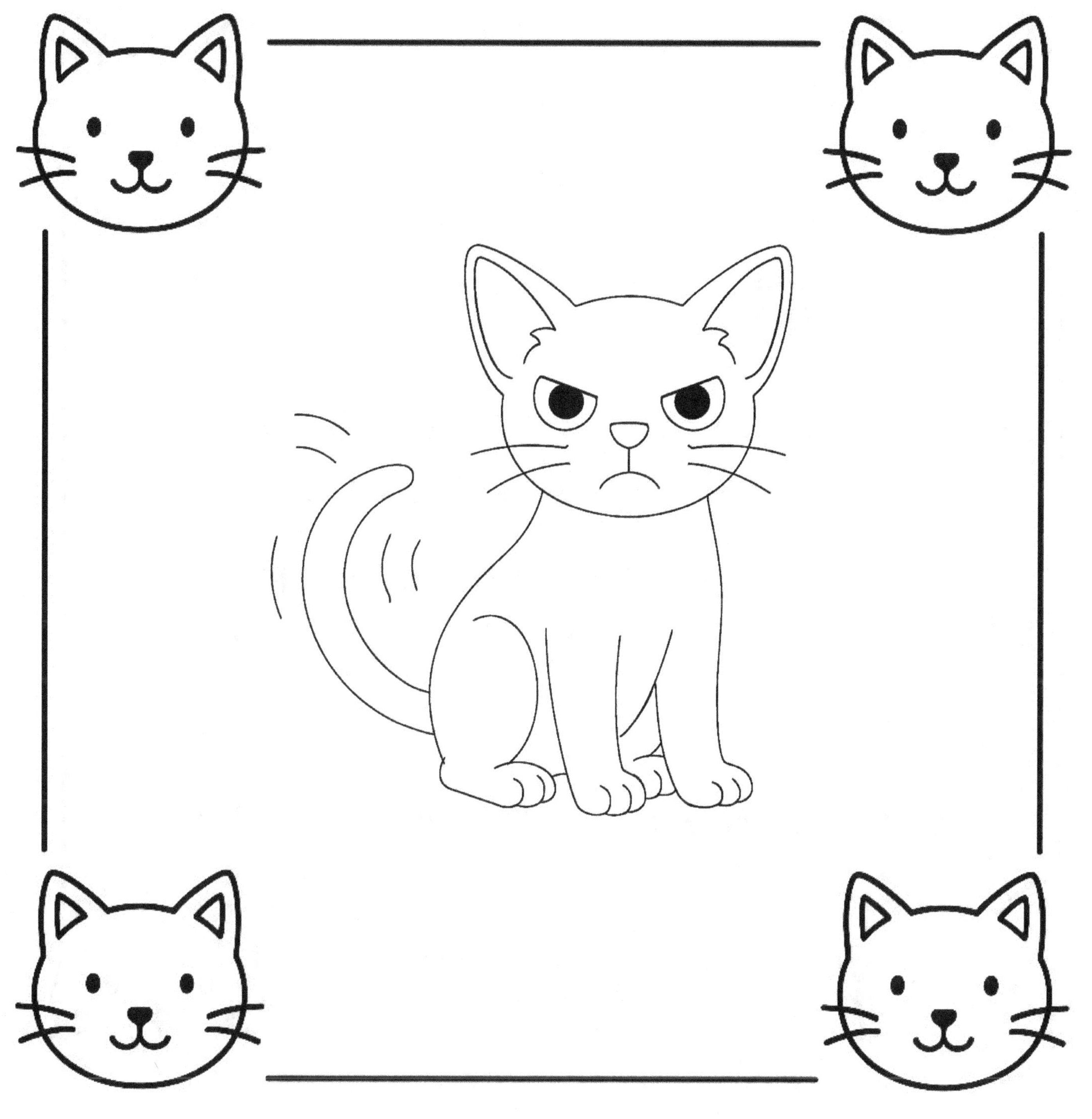

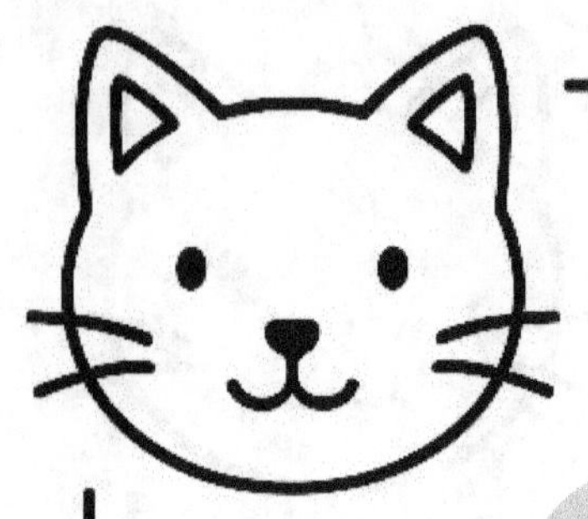 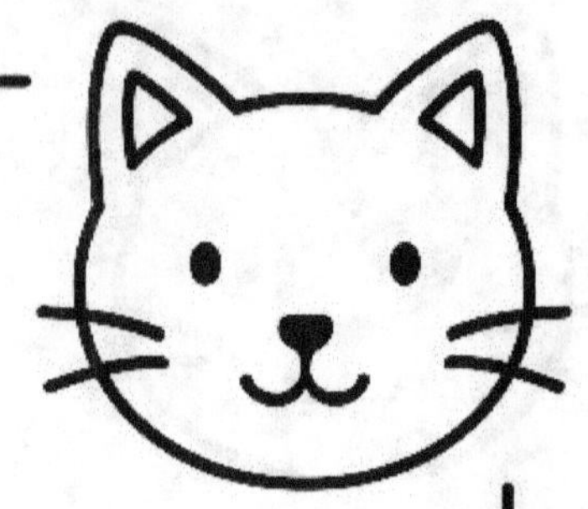

Fact #38

CATS MEOW MORE TO PEOPLE THAN TO OTHER CATS.

Los gatos maúllan más a las personas que a otros gatos.

Category 6: Sounds & Communication

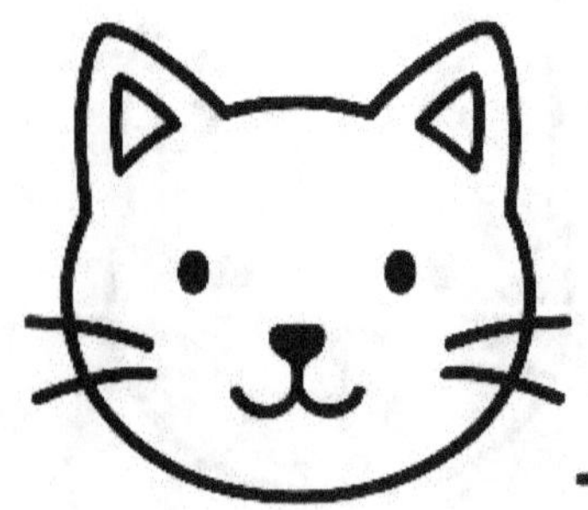 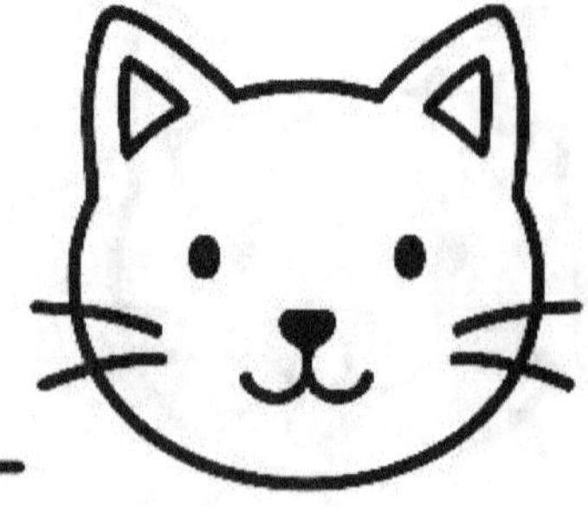

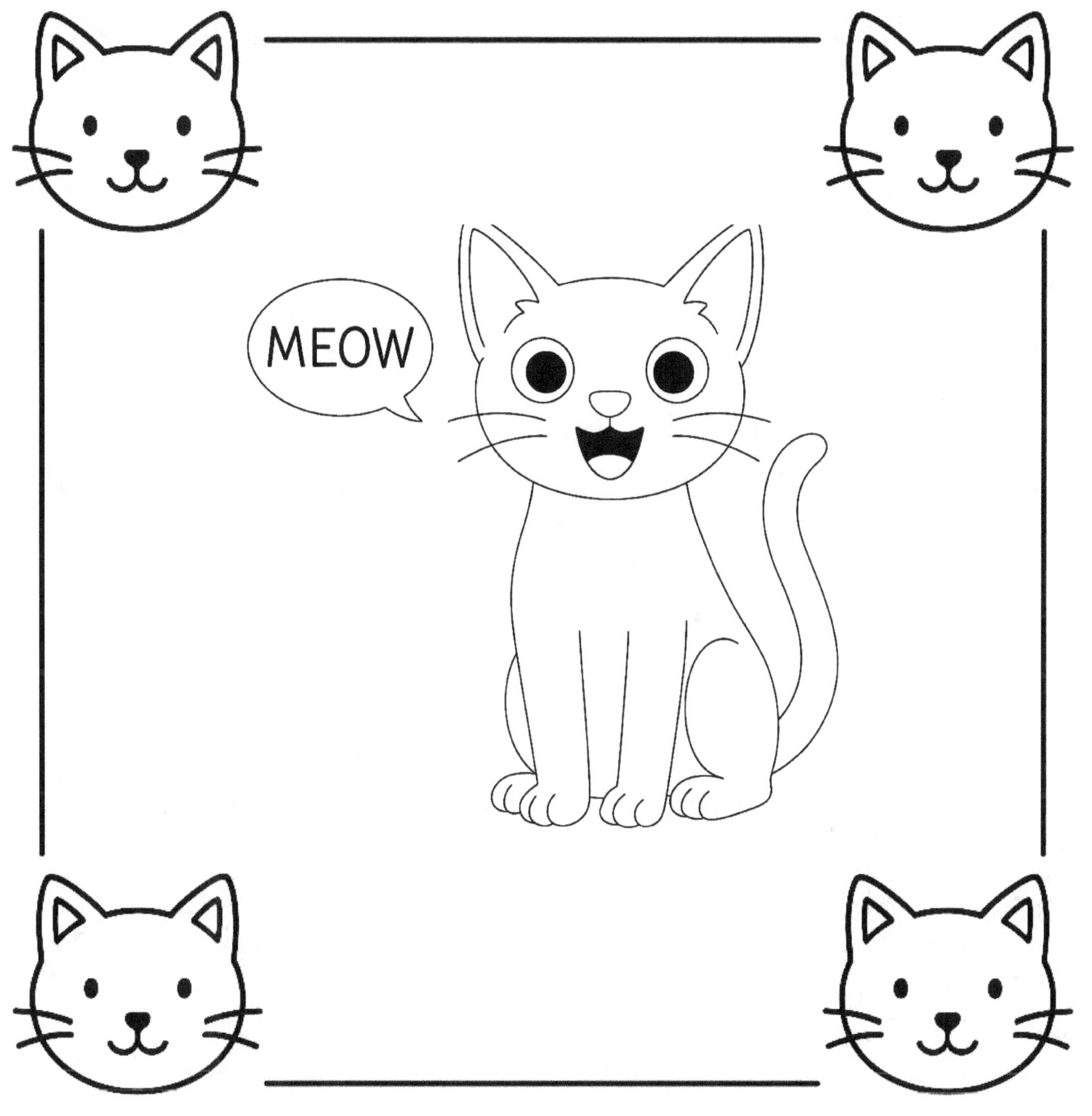
MEOW

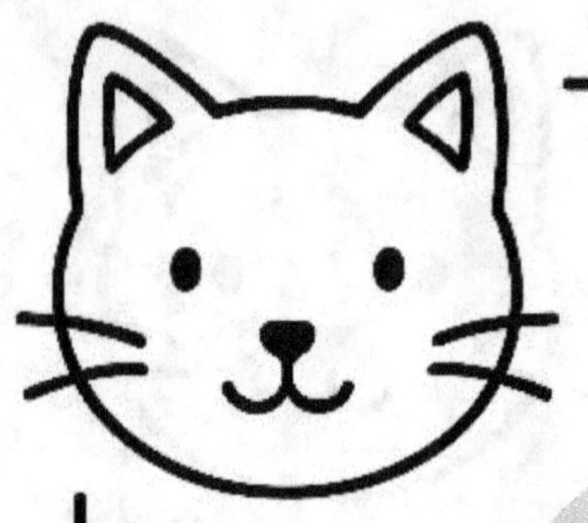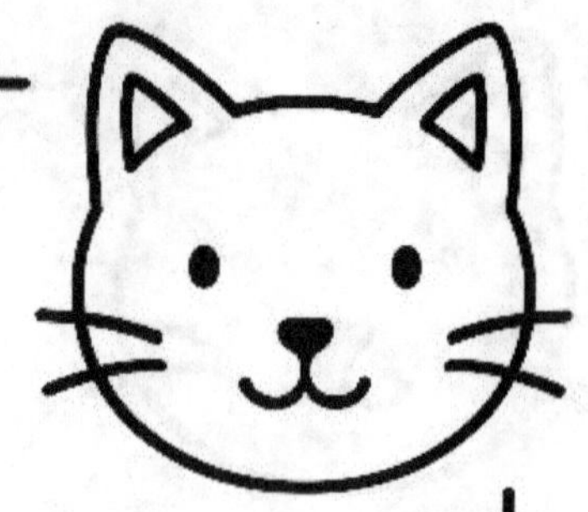

A SLOW BLINK FROM A CAT MEANS "I LOVE YOU."

Un parpadeo lento de un gato significa "te quiero".

Category 6: Sounds & Communication

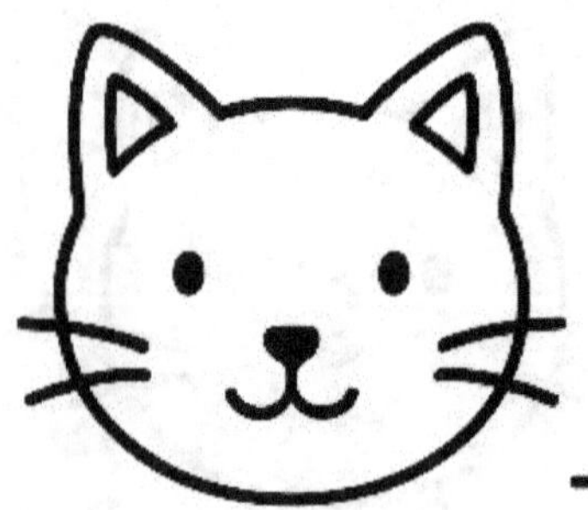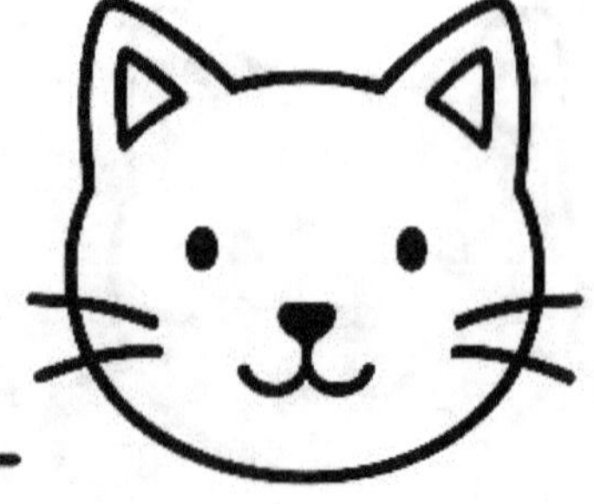

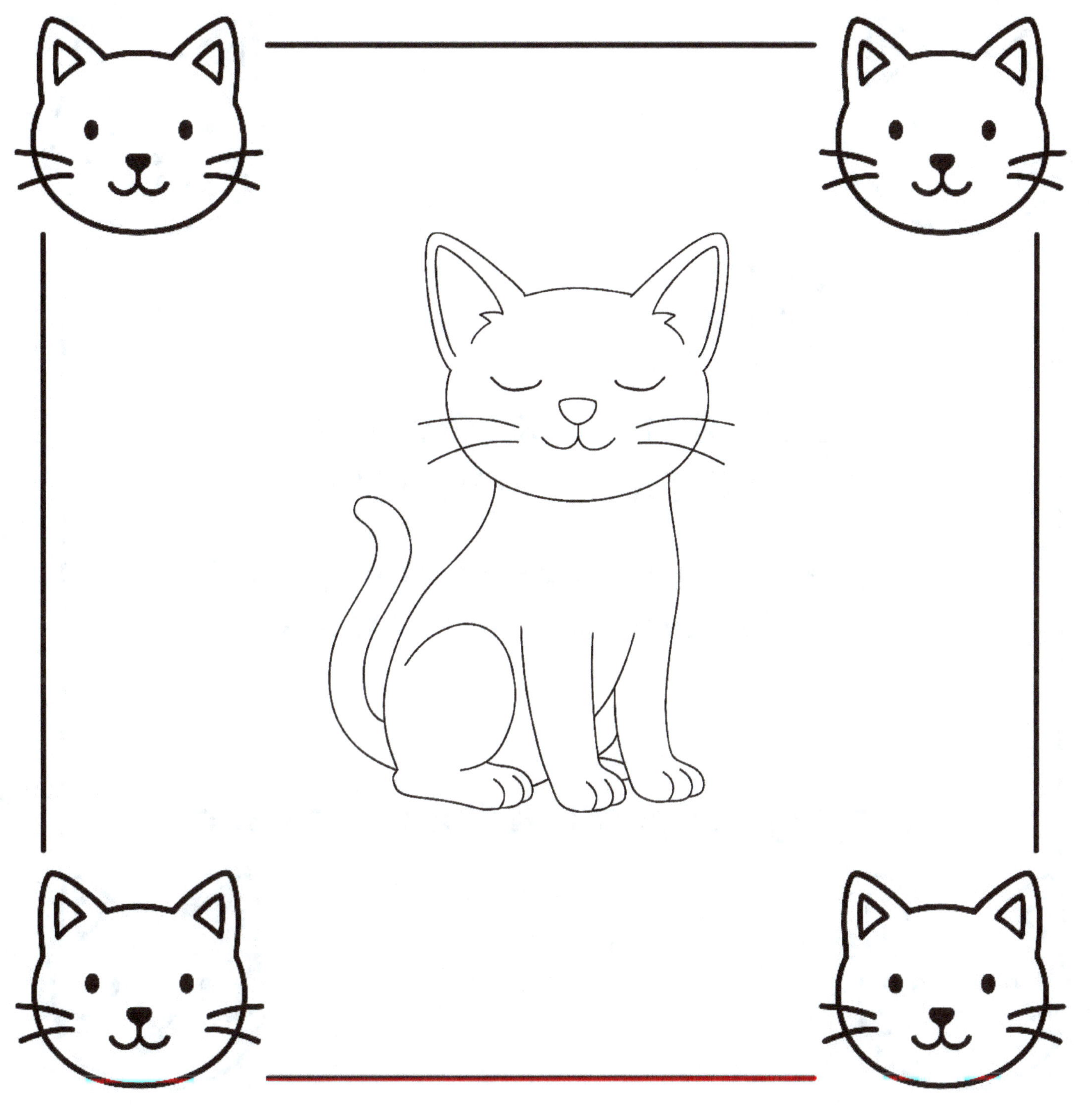

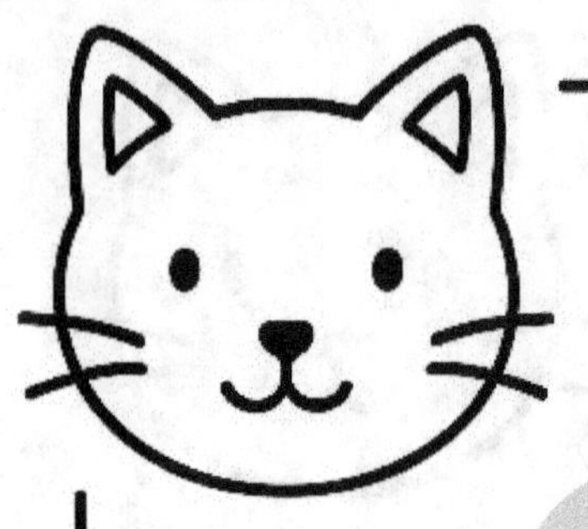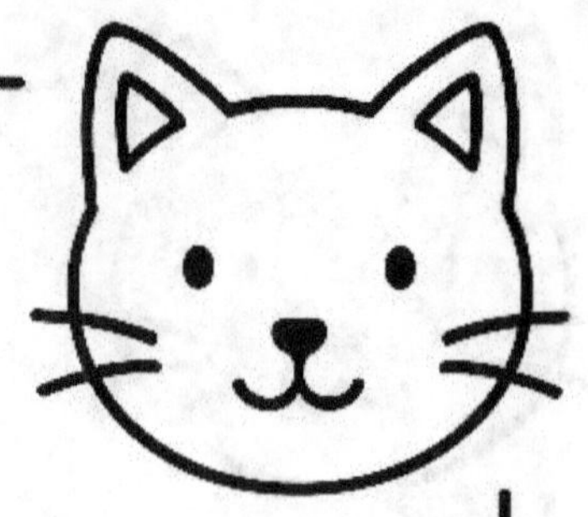

CATS CAN MAKE OVER 100 DIFFERENT SOUNDS!

¡Los gatos pueden hacer más de 100 sonidos diferentes!

Category 6: Sounds & Communication

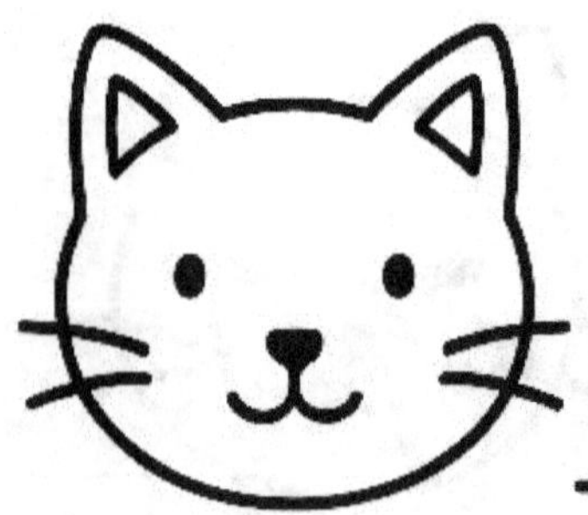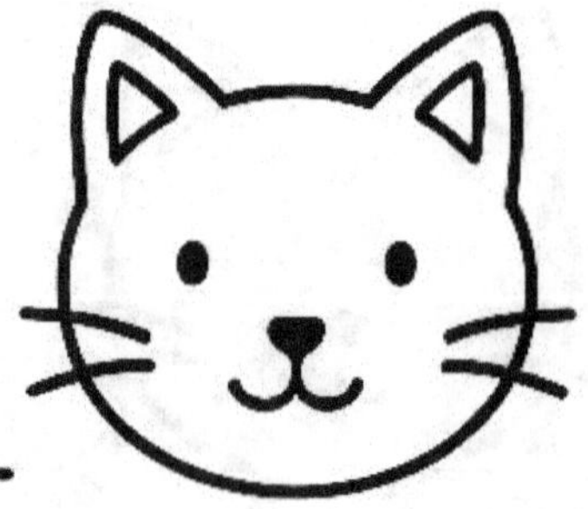

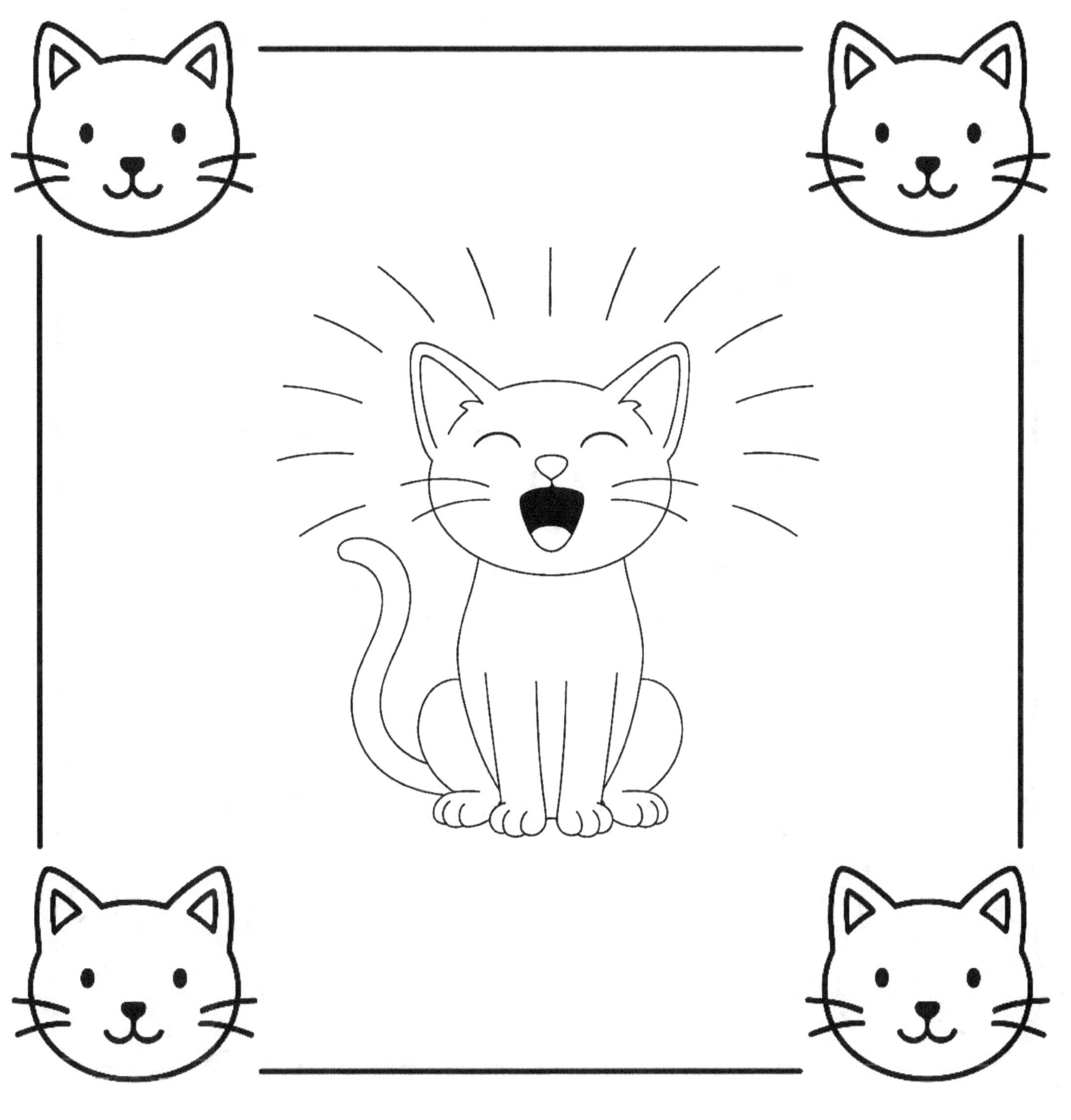

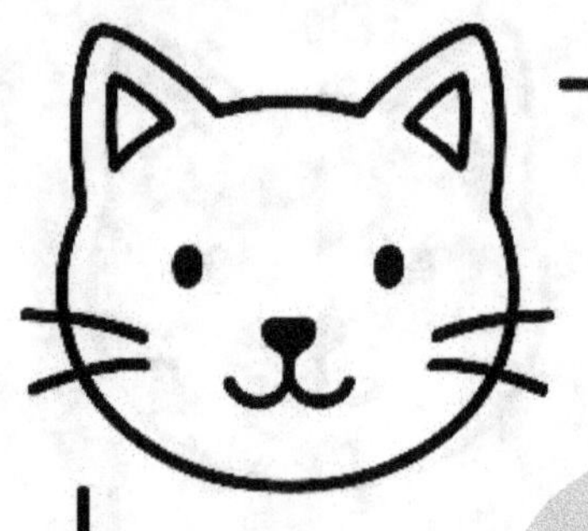
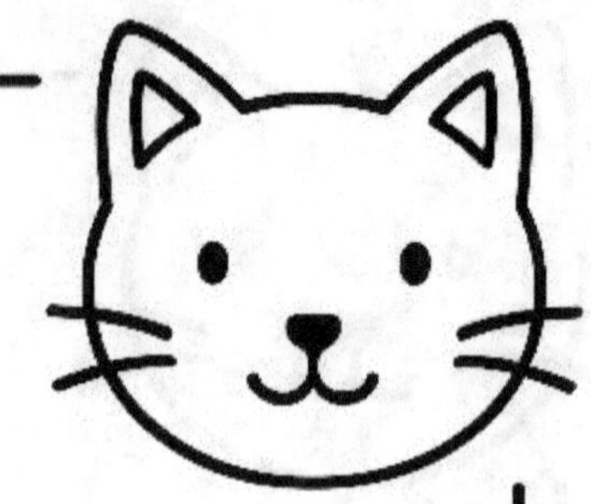

CATS HAVE BEEN KEPT AS PETS FOR THOUSANDS OF YEARS.

Los gatos han sido mascotas durante miles de años.

Category 7: Fun & Global Cat Facts

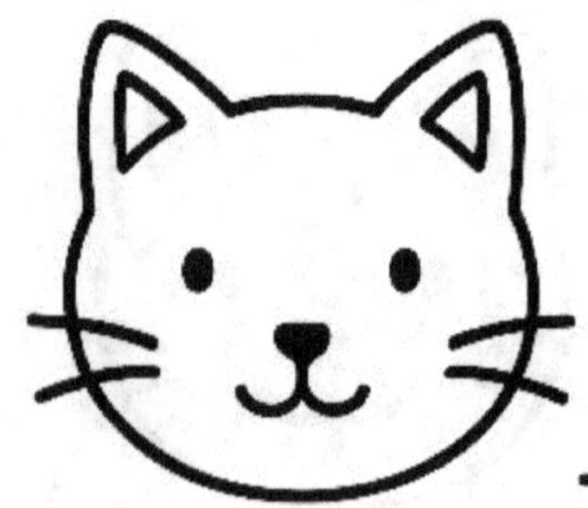
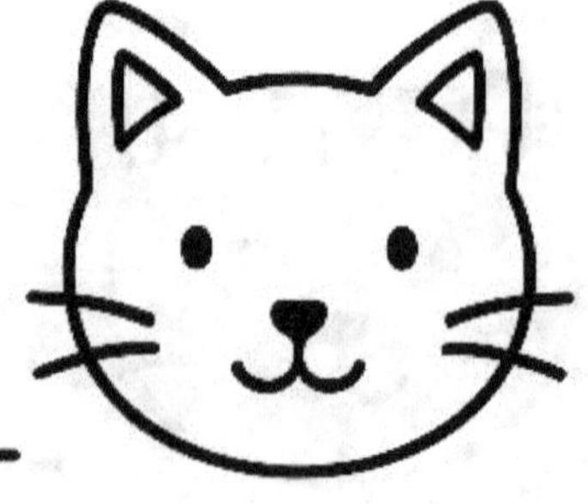

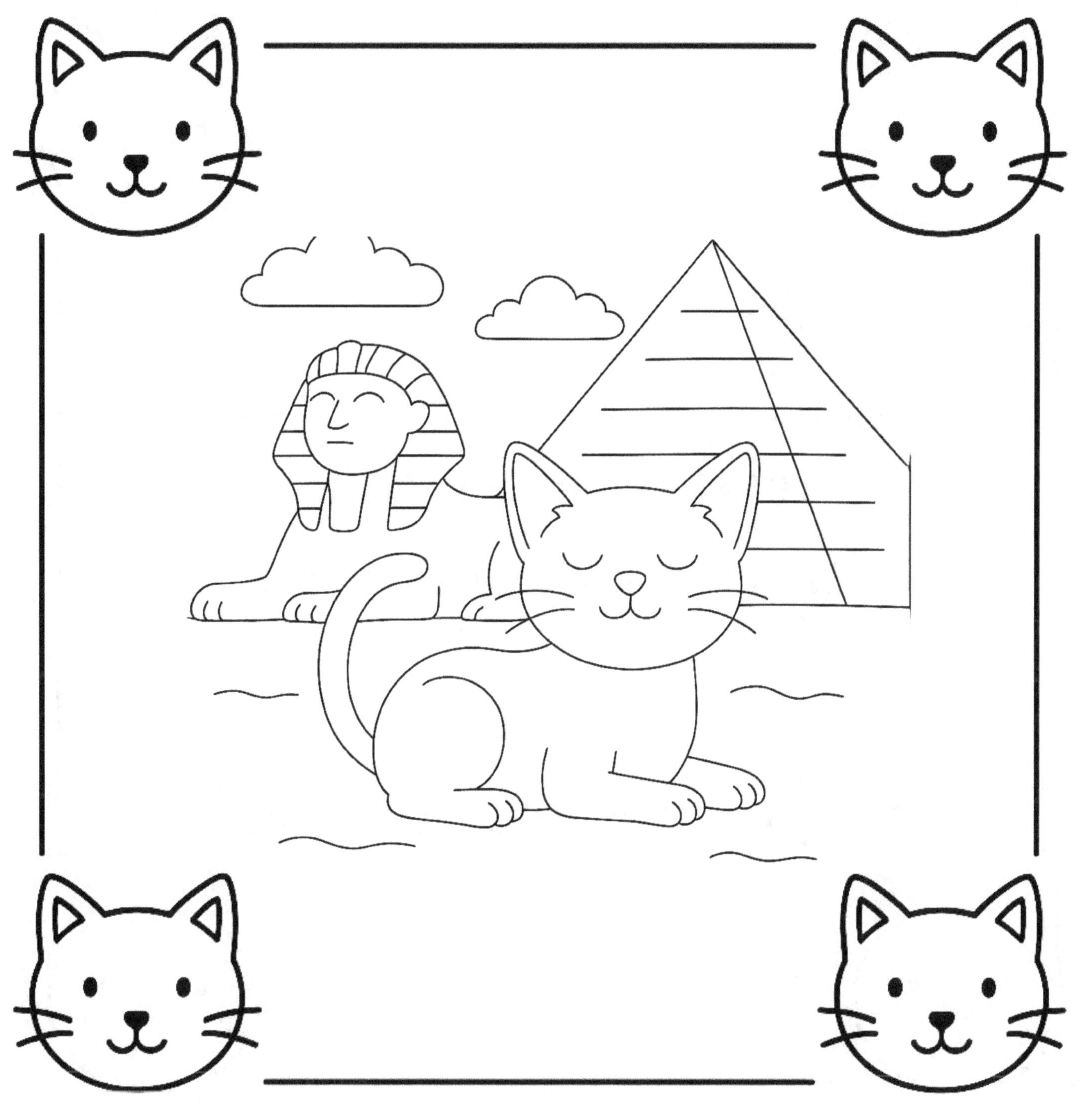

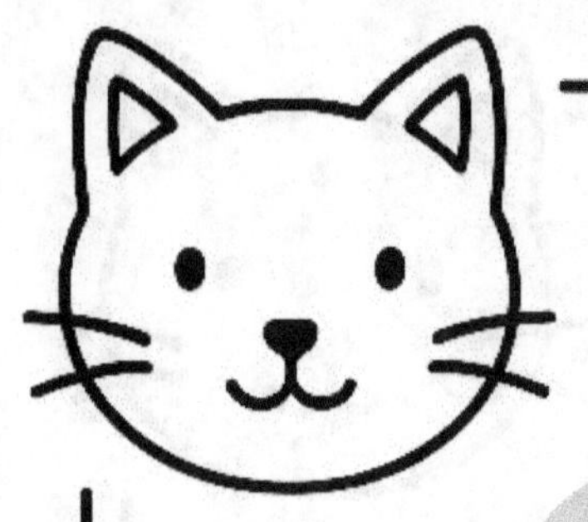
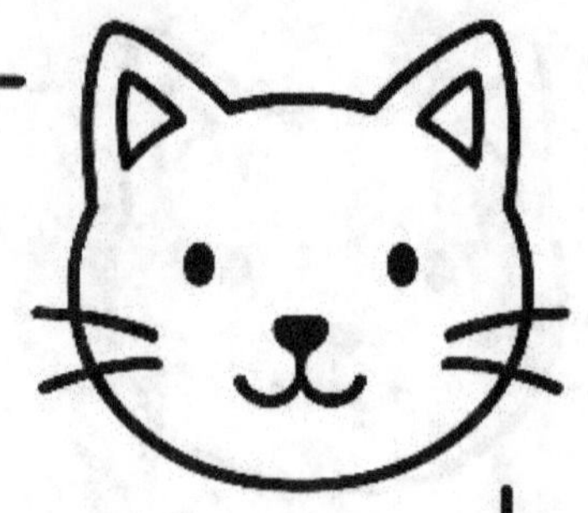

Fact #42

IN ANCIENT EGYPT, CATS WERE TREATED LIKE ROYALTY.

En el antiguo Egipto, los gatos eran tratados como reyes.

Category 7: Fun & Global Cat Facts

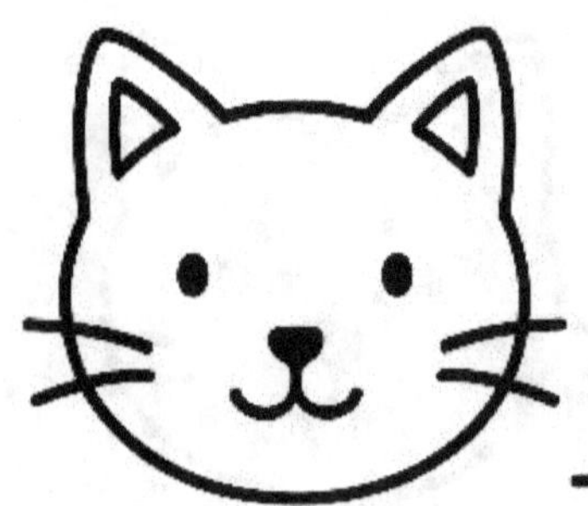
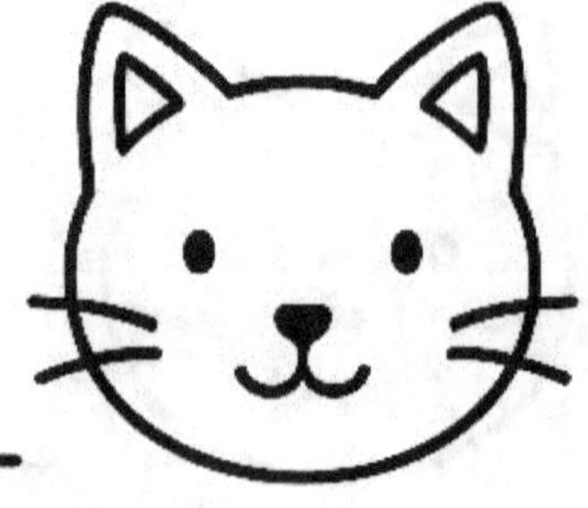

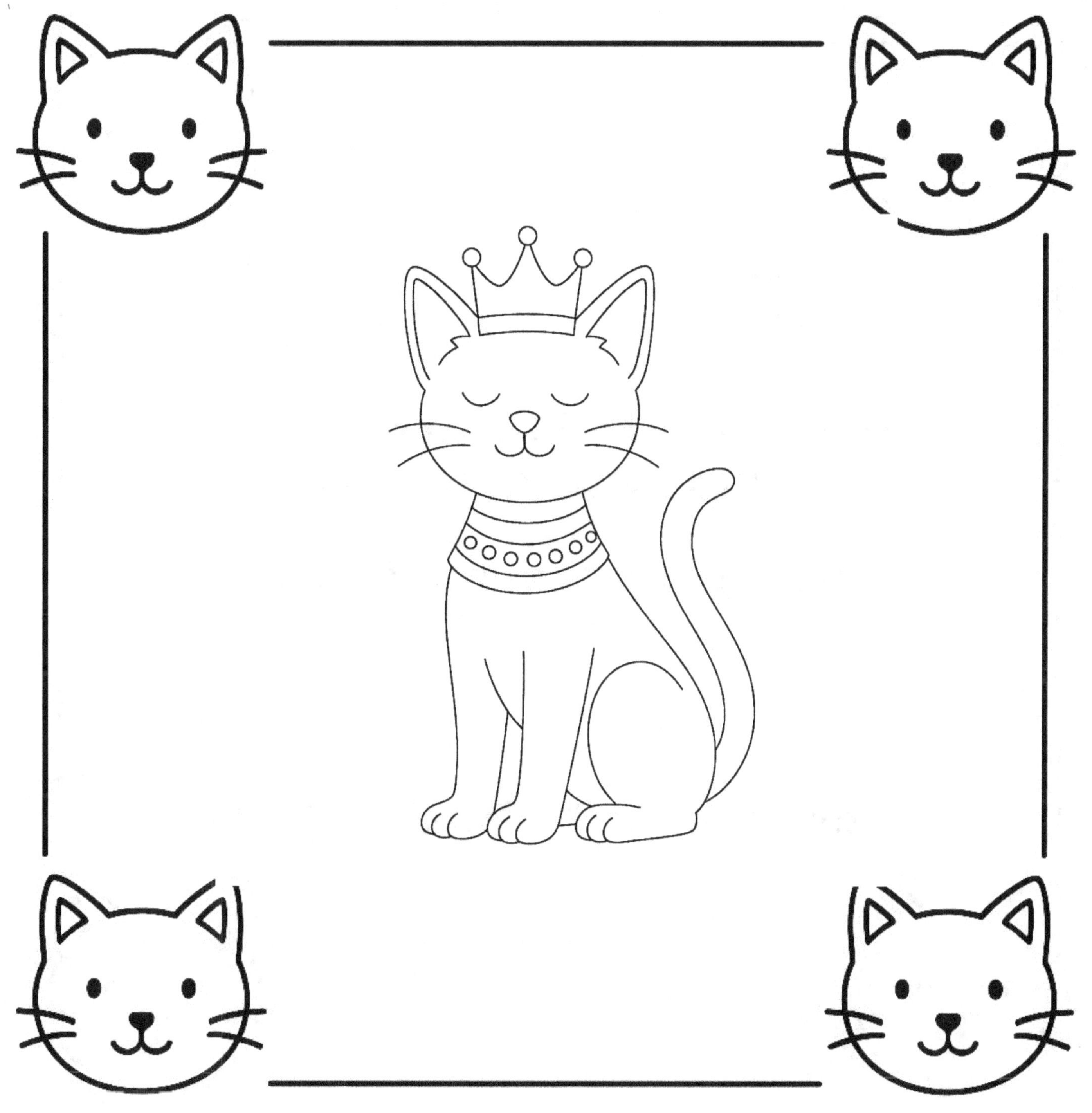

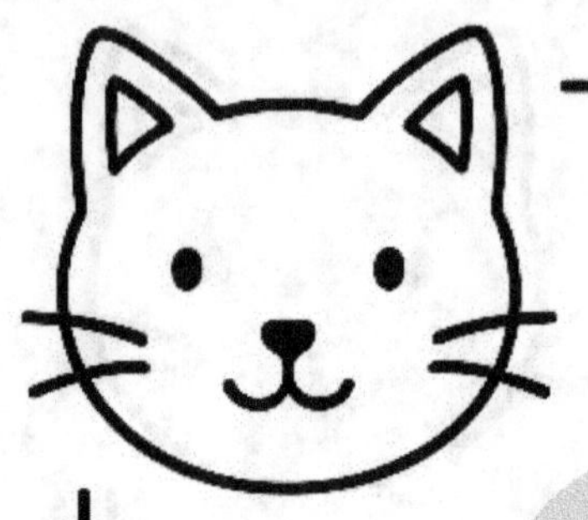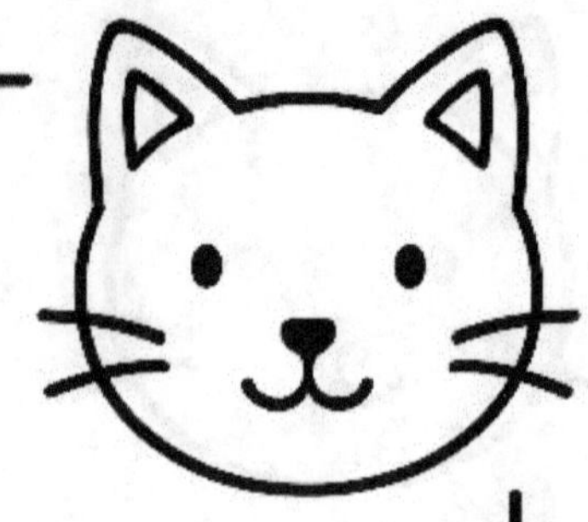

SOME CATS HAVE TRAVELED IN SHIPS AND AIRPLANES!

¡Algunos gatos han viajado en barcos y aviones!

Category 7: Fun & Global Cat Facts

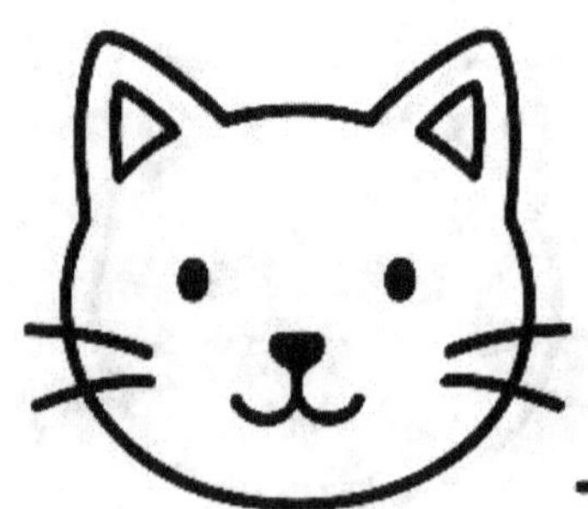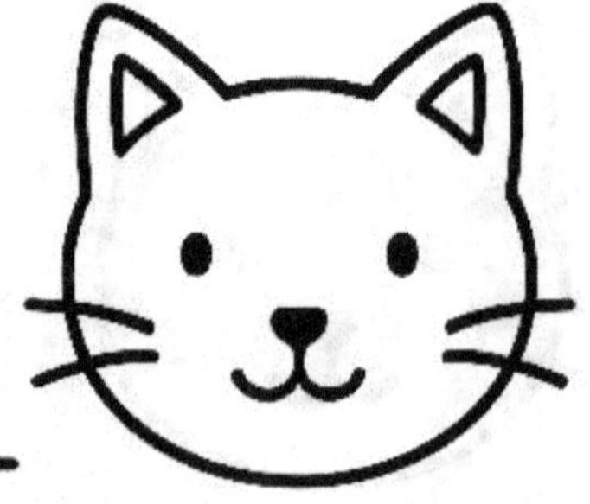

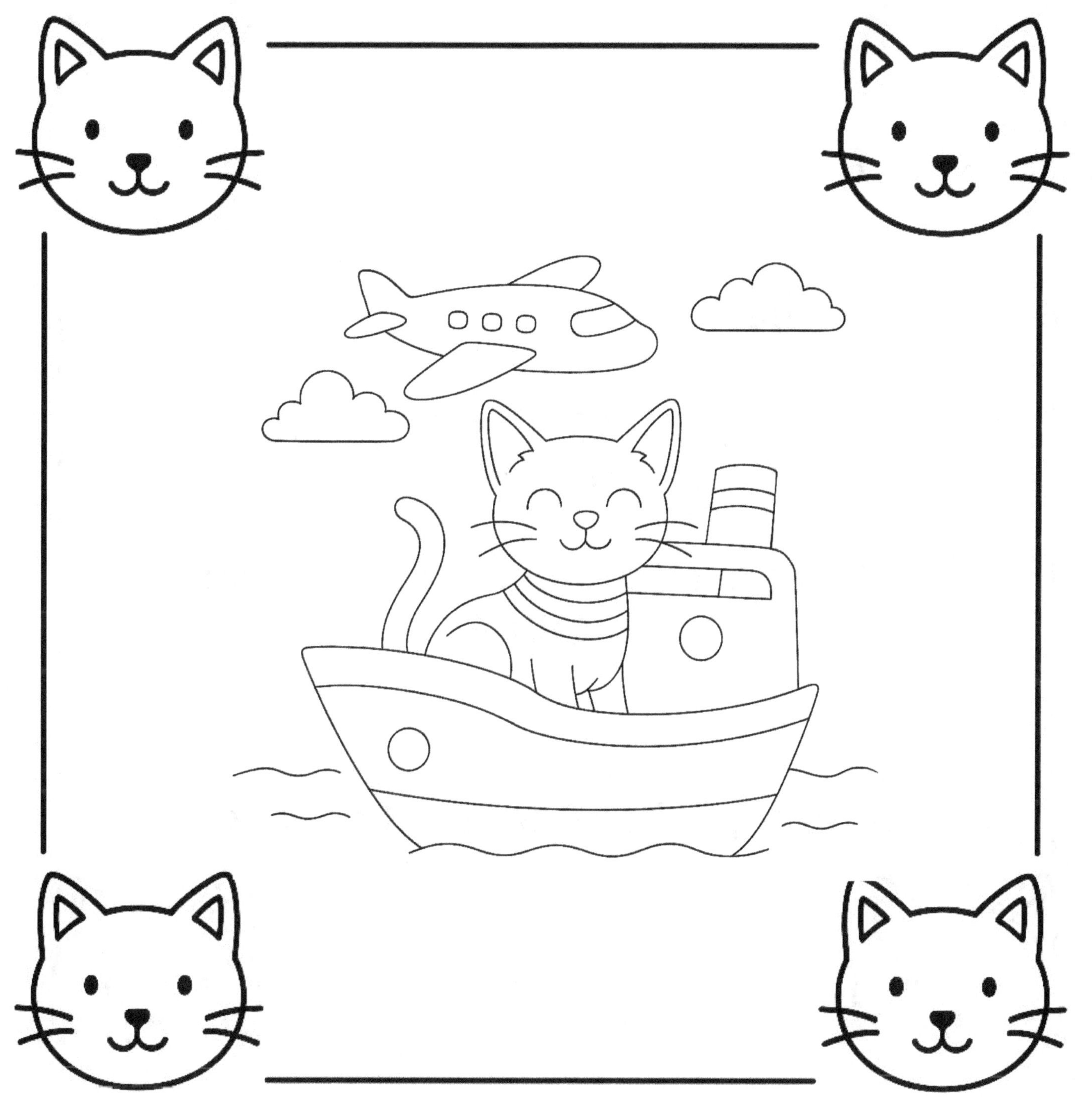

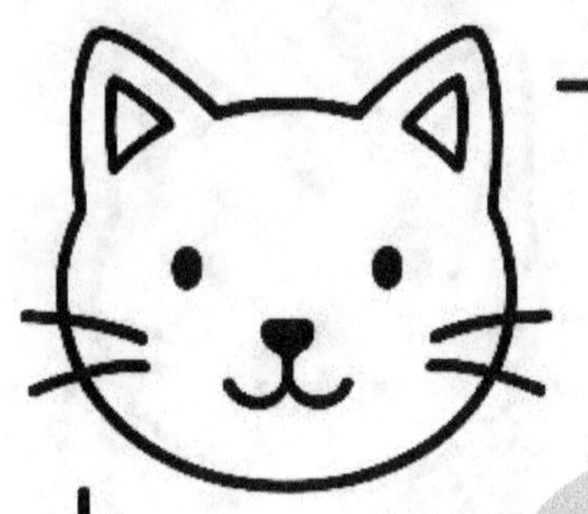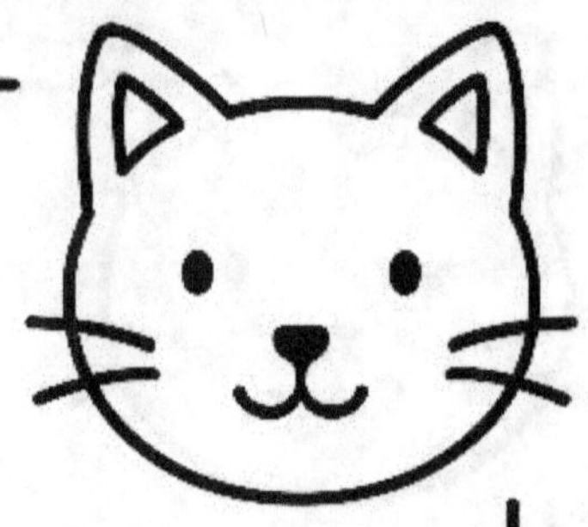

Fact #44

EVERY CAT HAS A UNIQUE NOSE PRINT.

Cada gato tiene una huella nasal única.

Category 7: Fun & Global Cat Facts

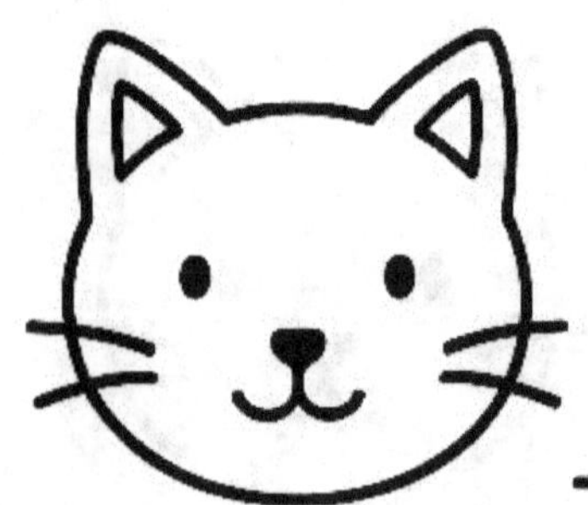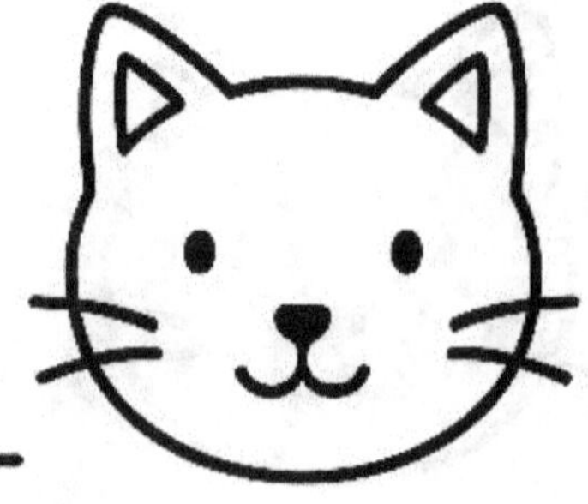

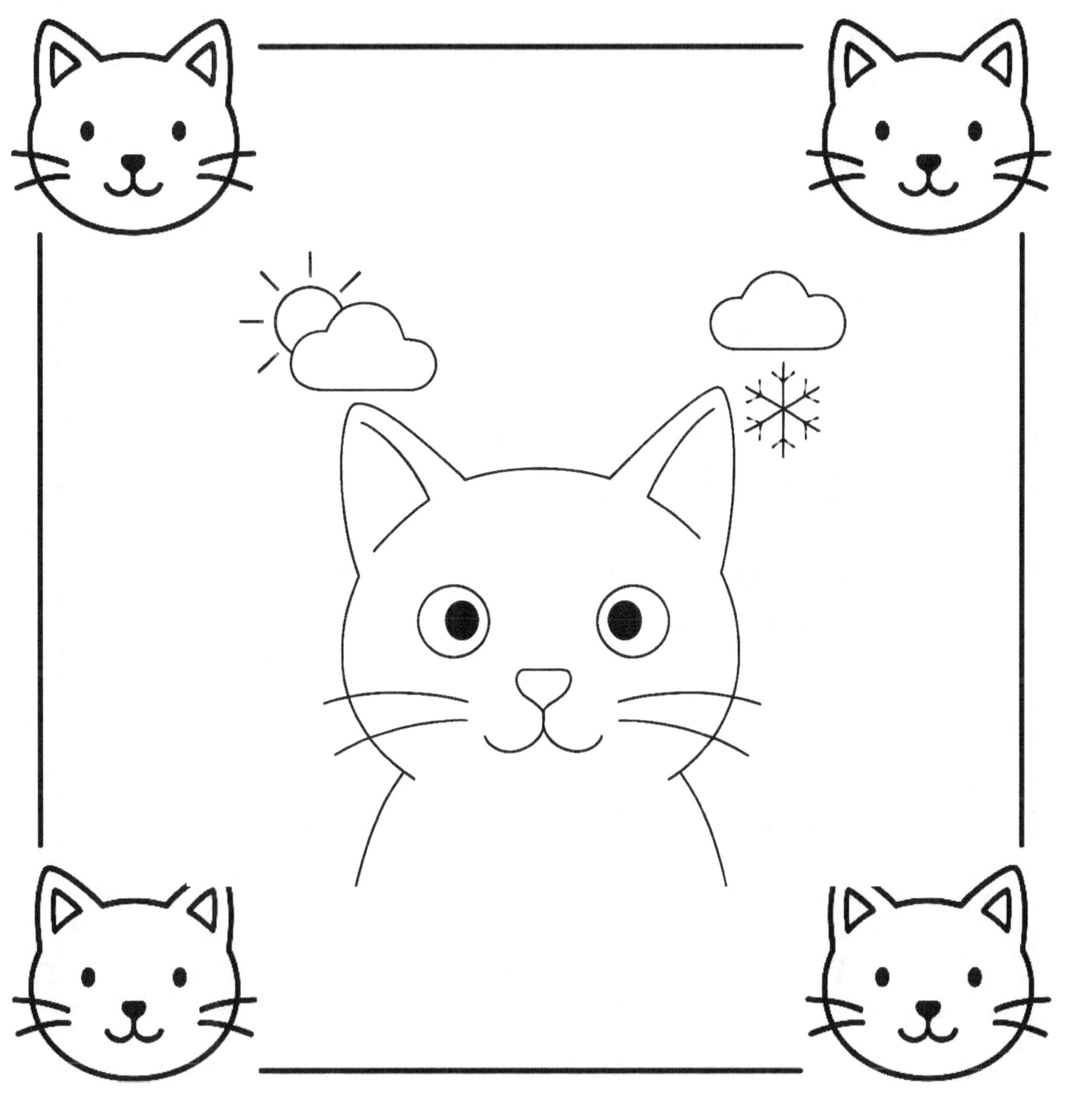

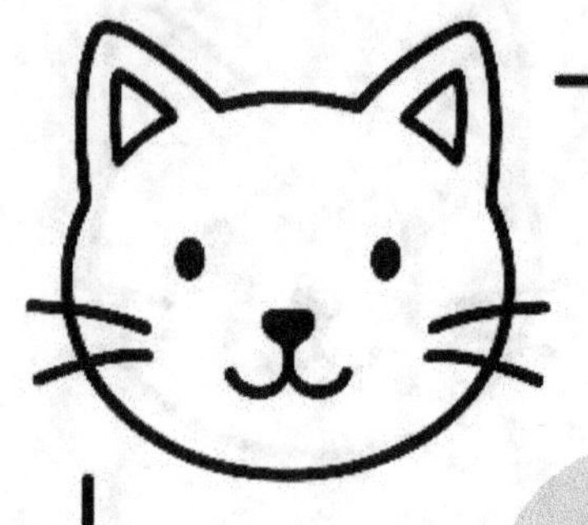
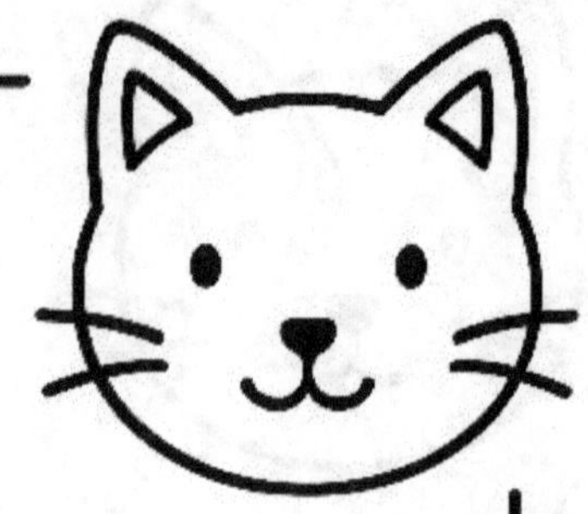

SOME CATS LIKE WATER—ESPECIALLY TURKISH VANS!

¡A algunos gatos les gusta el agua, especialmente a los Van Turcos!

Category 7: Fun & Global Cat Facts

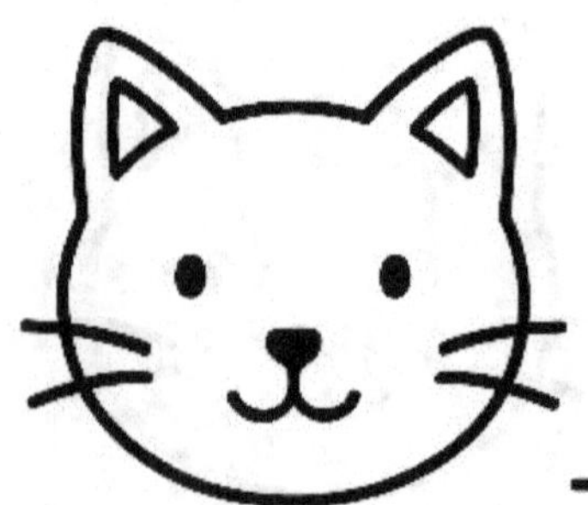
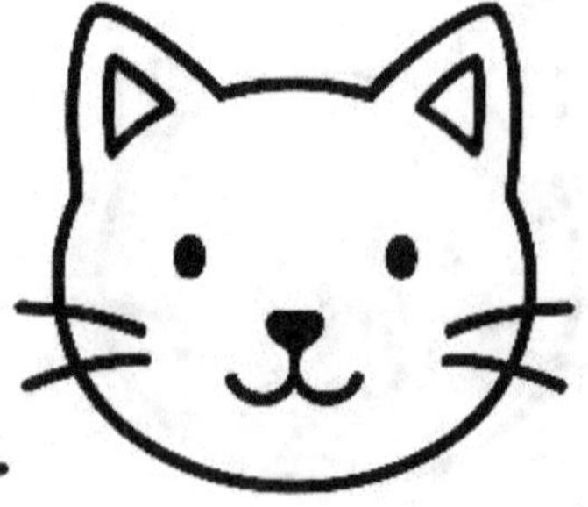

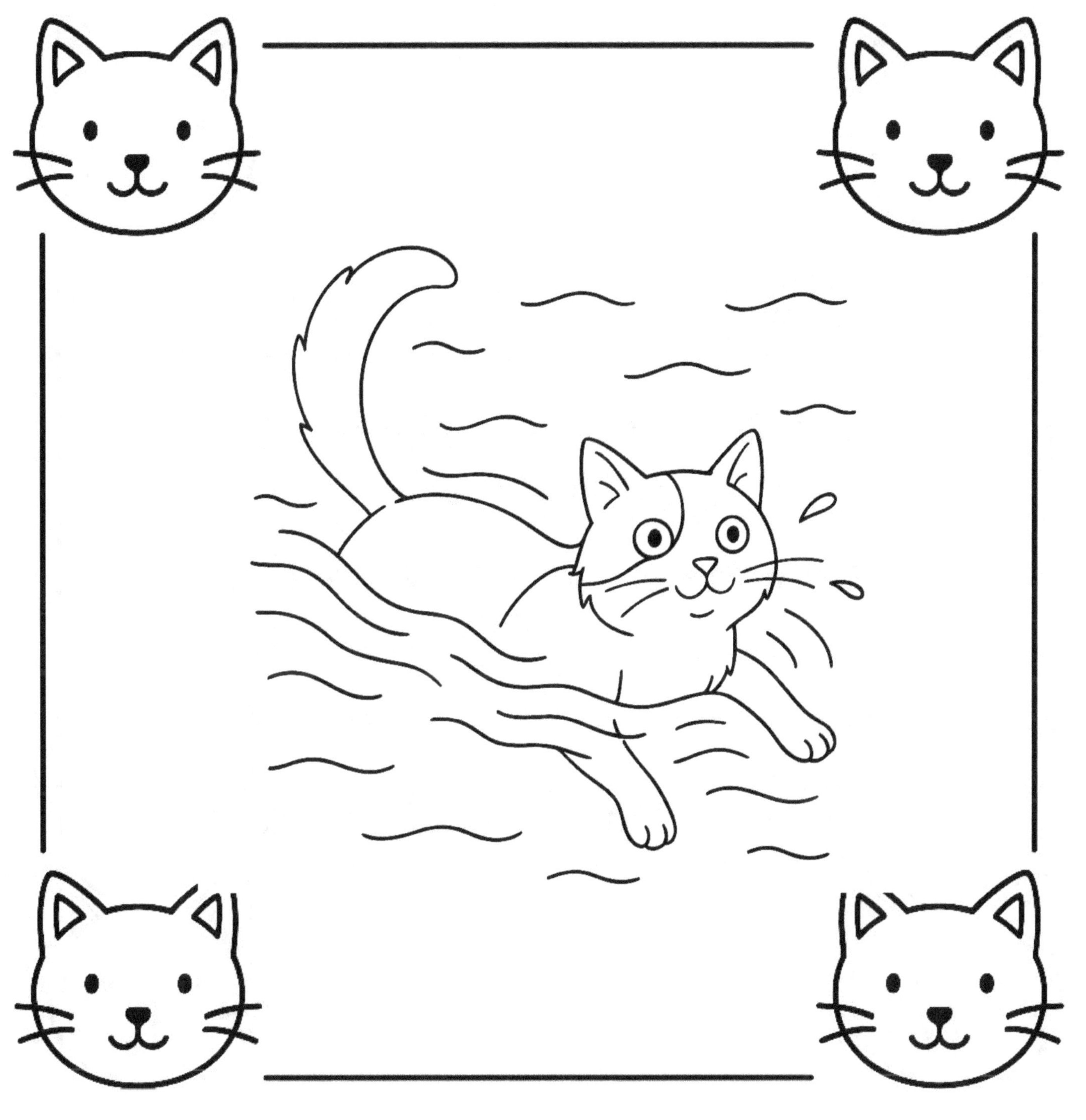

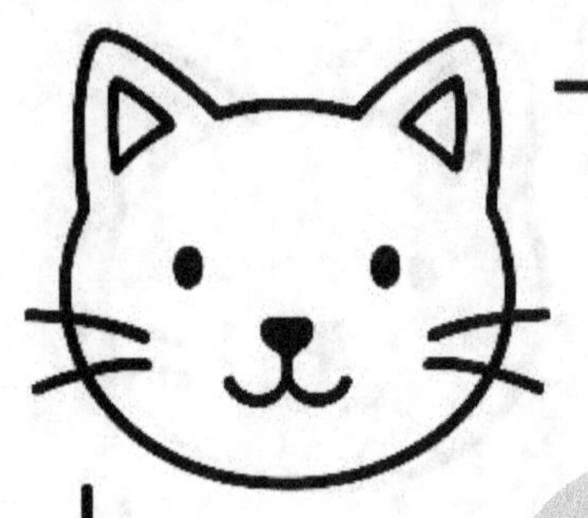 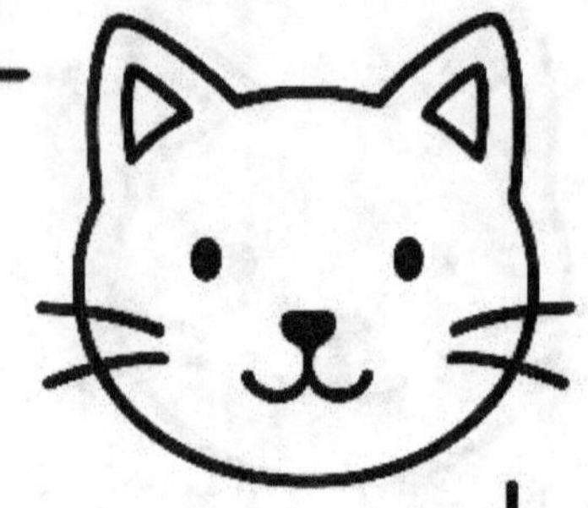

Fact #46

CATS CAN LIVE TO BE 15–20 YEARS OLD.

Los gatos pueden vivir entre 15 y 20 años.

Category 7: Fun & Global Cat Facts

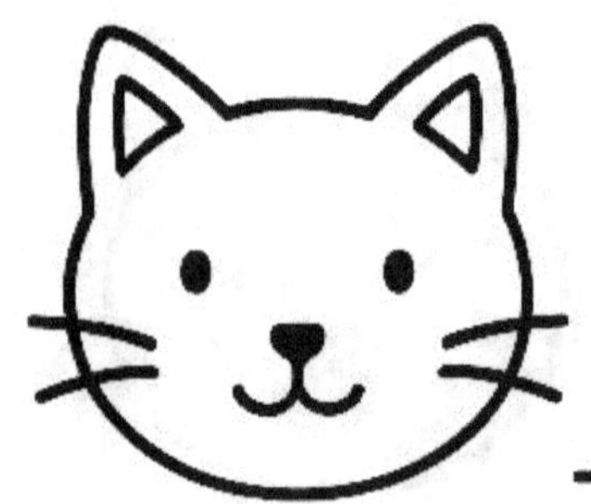 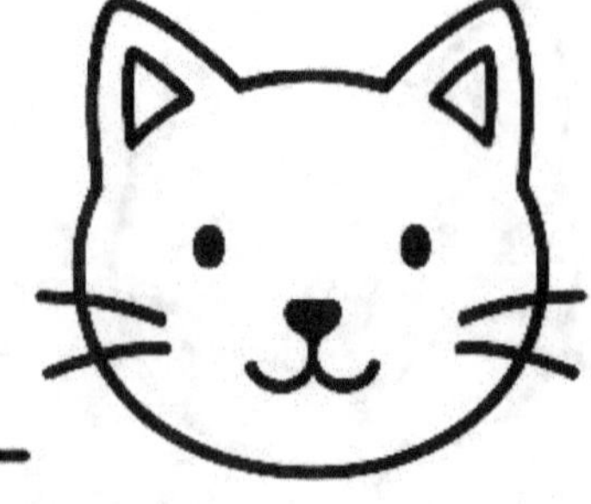

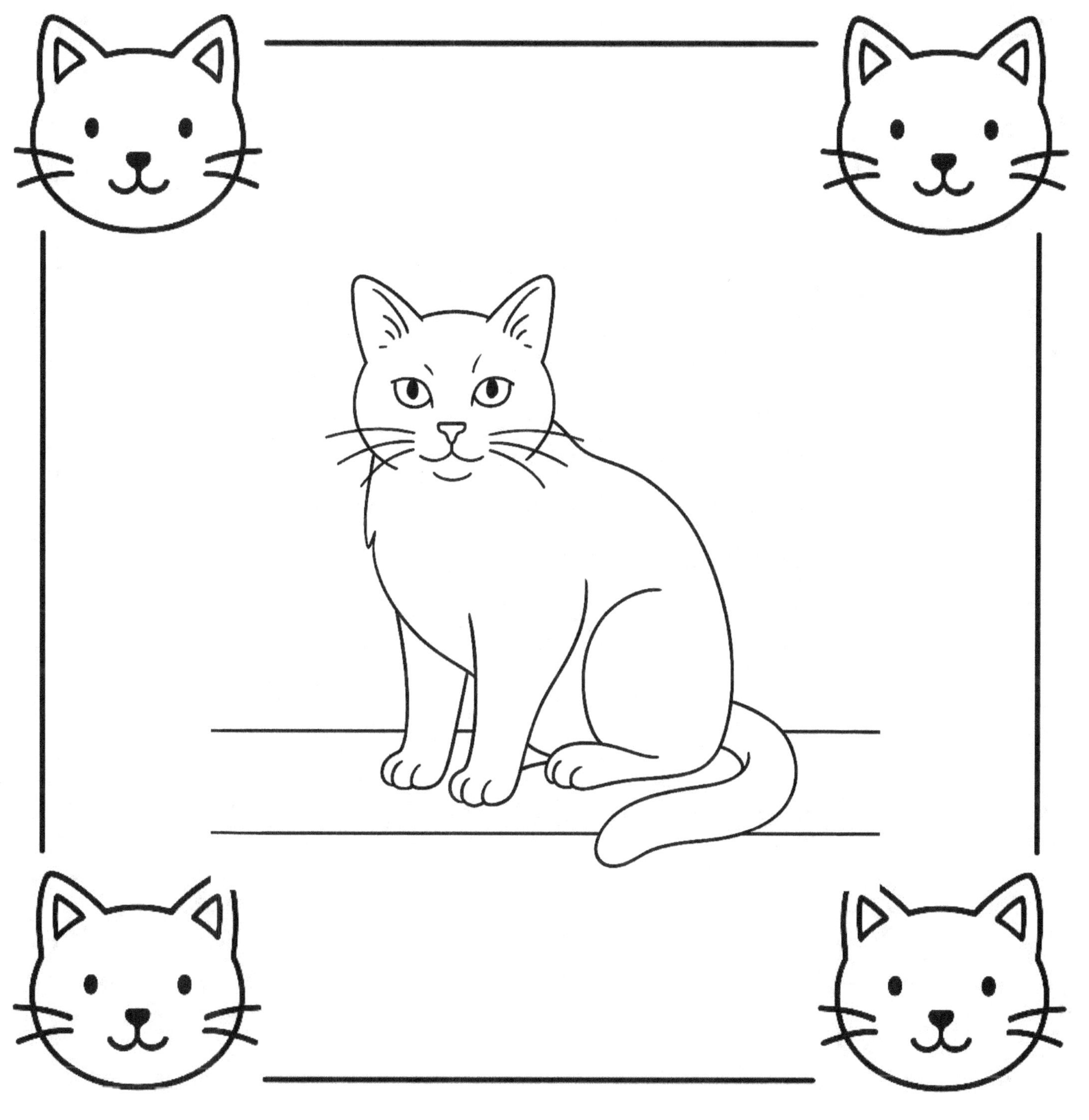

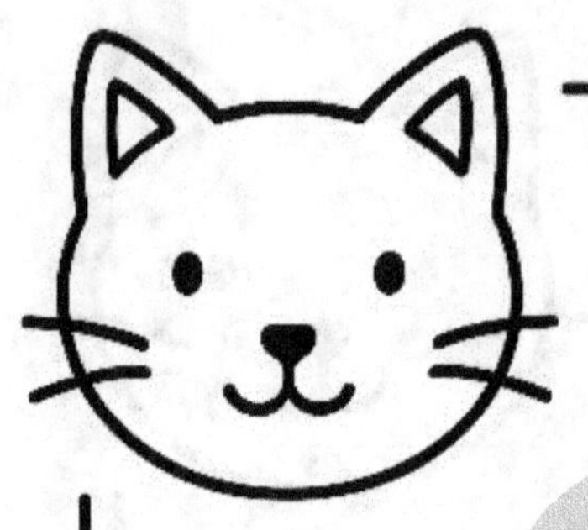
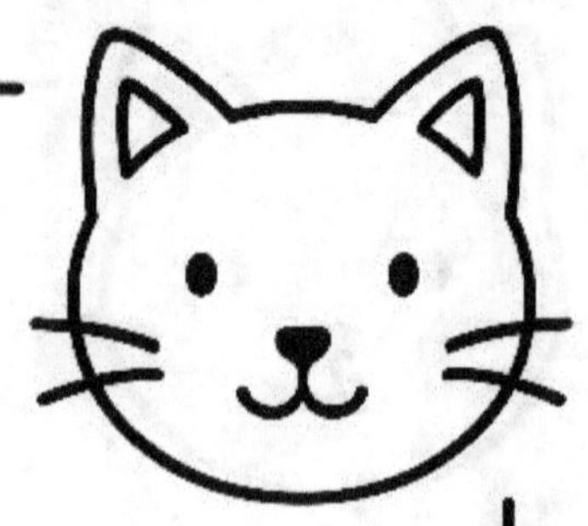

CATS LIKE TO NAP IN WARM, SUNNY SPOTS.

A los gatos les gusta dormir en lugares cálidos y soleados.

Category 7: Fun & Global Cat Facts

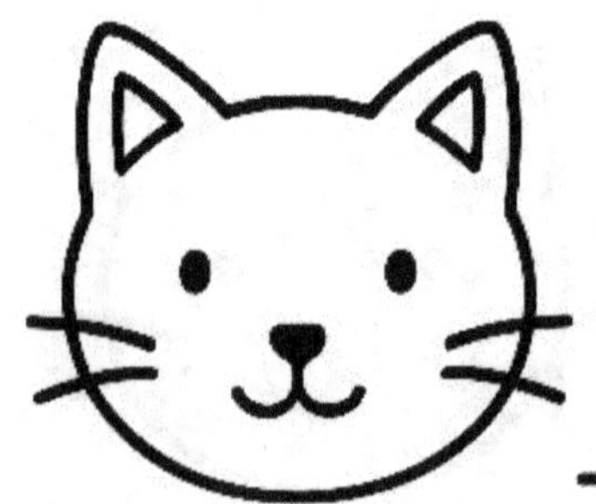
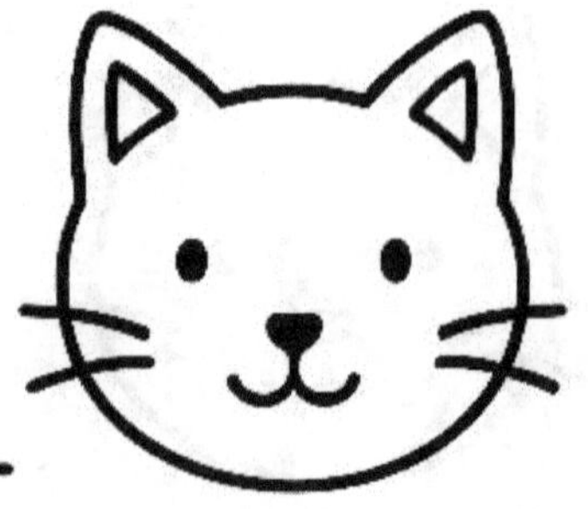

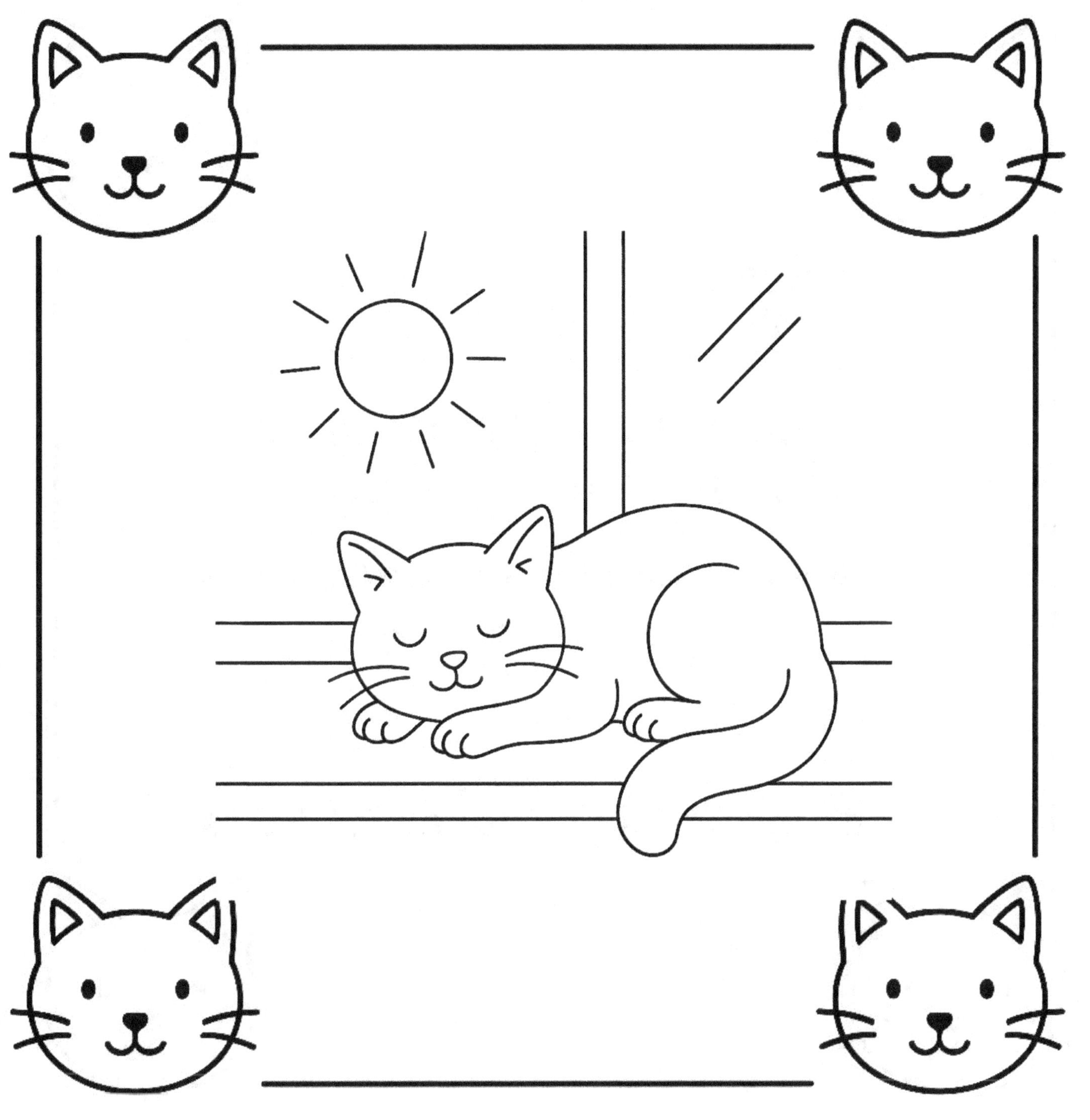

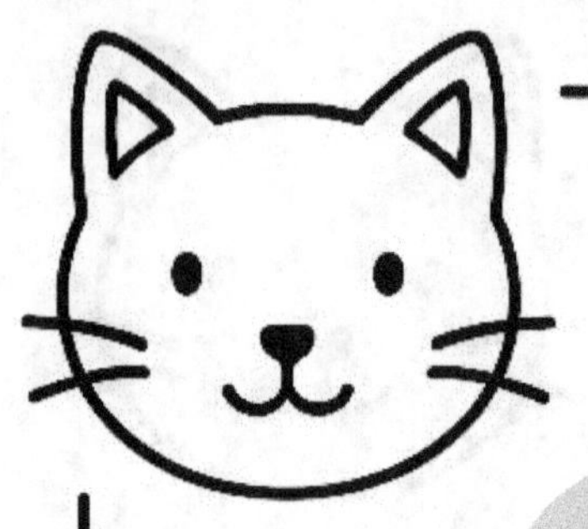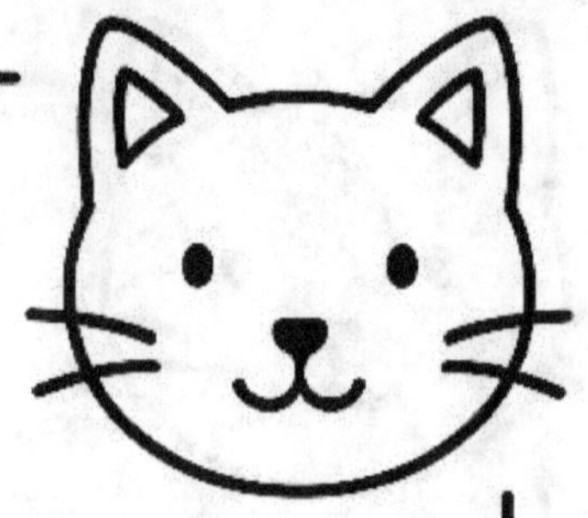

SCRATCHING HELPS CATS KEEP THEIR CLAWS HEALTHY.

Rascar les ayuda a mantener las garras sanas.

Category 7: Fun & Global Cat Facts

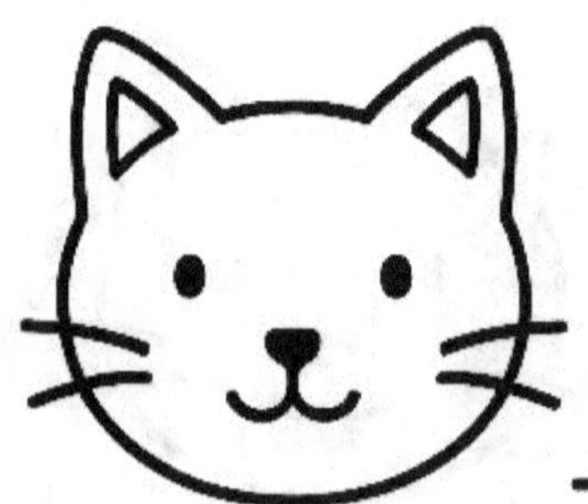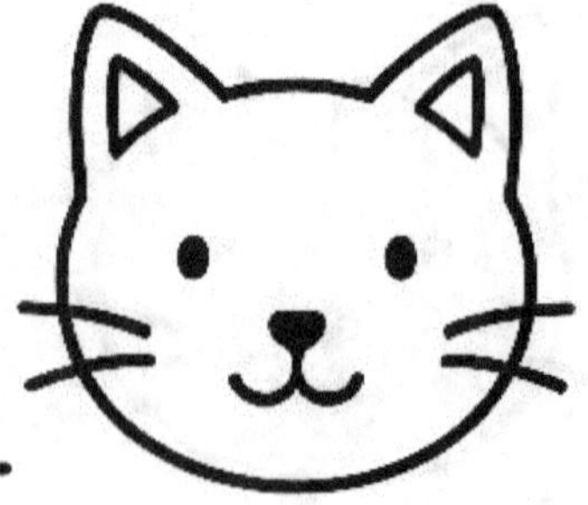

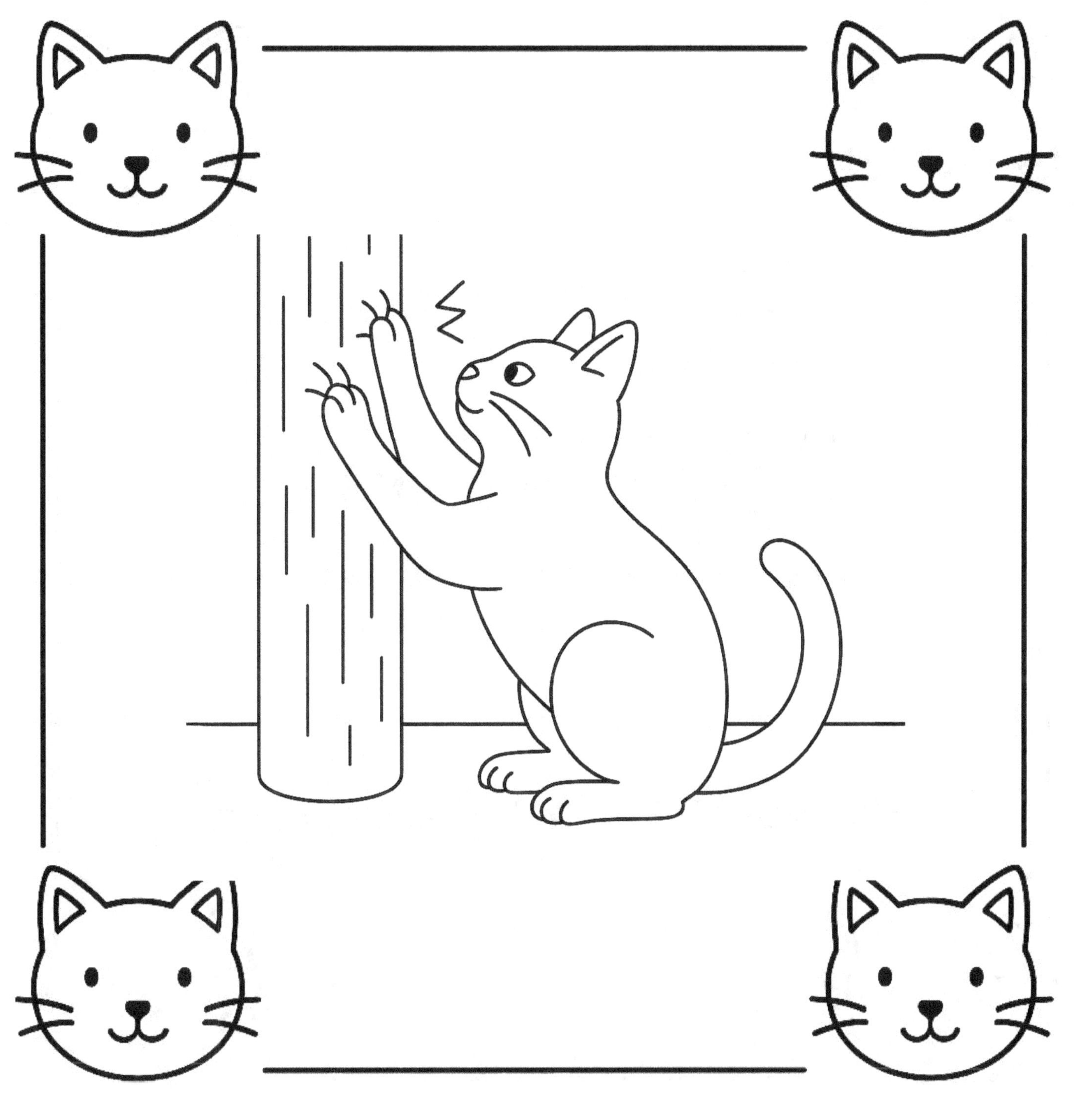

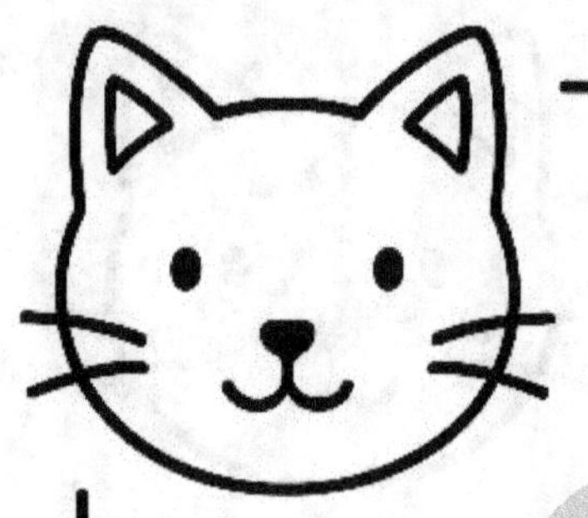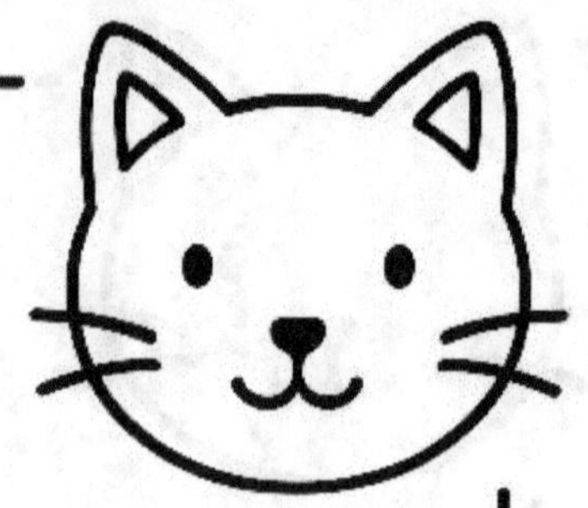

Fact #49

BRUSHING YOUR CAT HELPS REDUCE SHEDDING.

Cepillar a tu gato ayuda a reducir la caída de pelo.

Category 7: Fun & Global Cat Facts

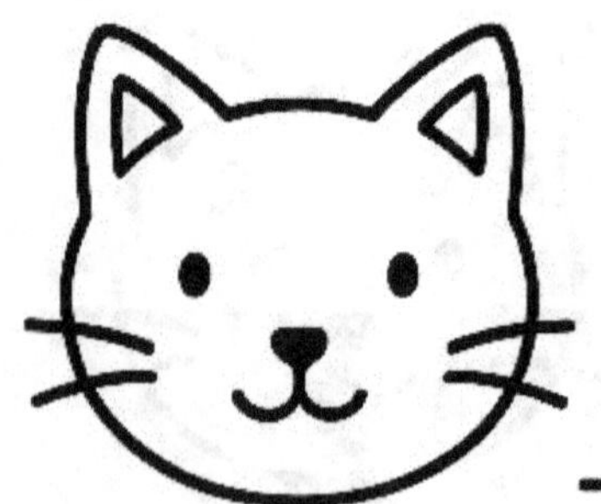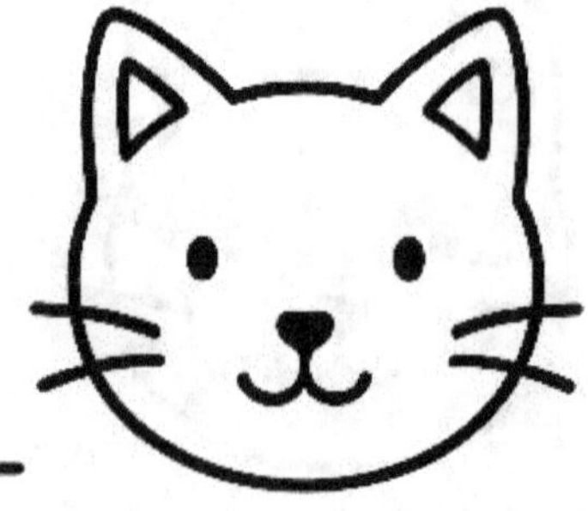

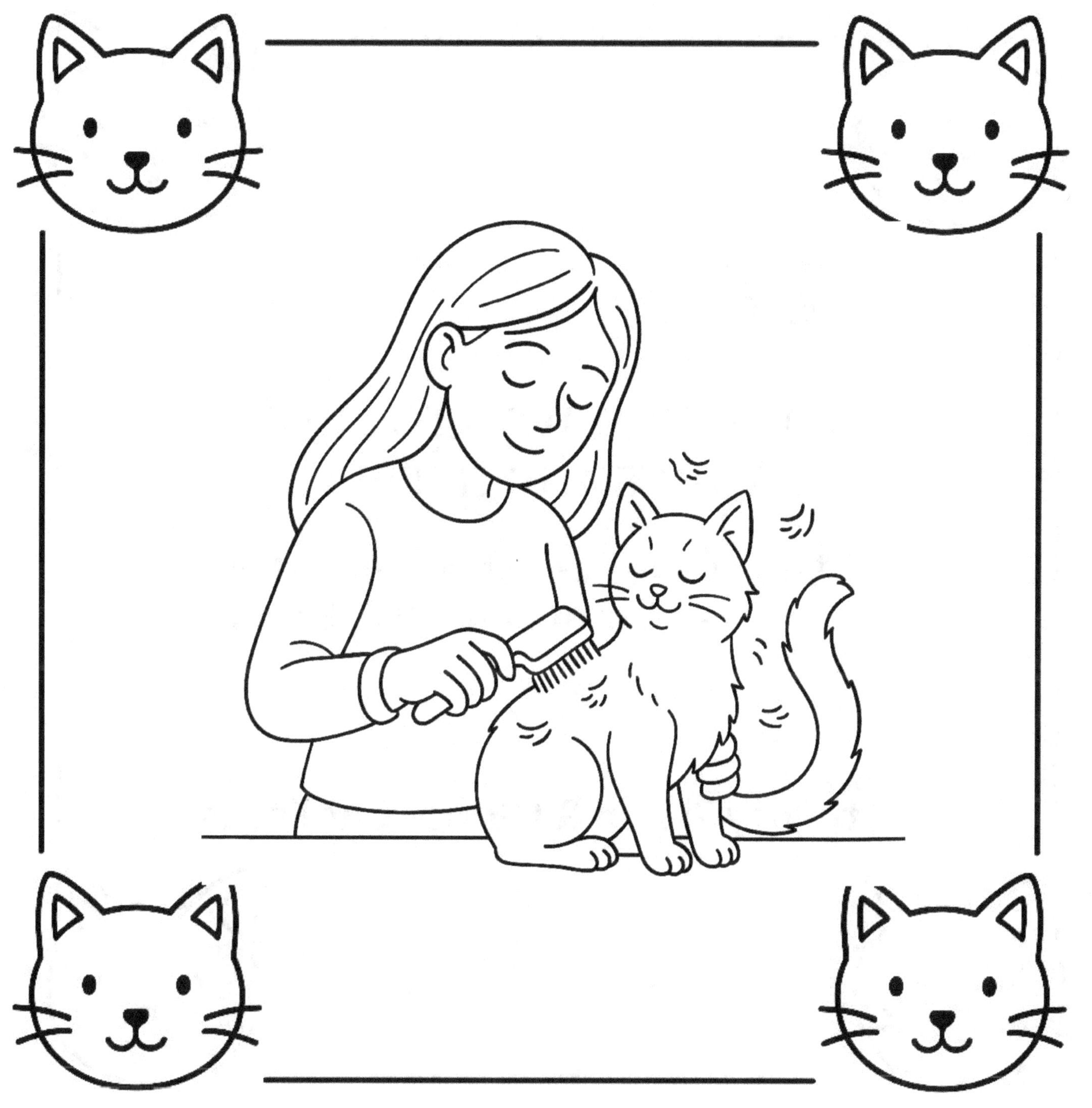

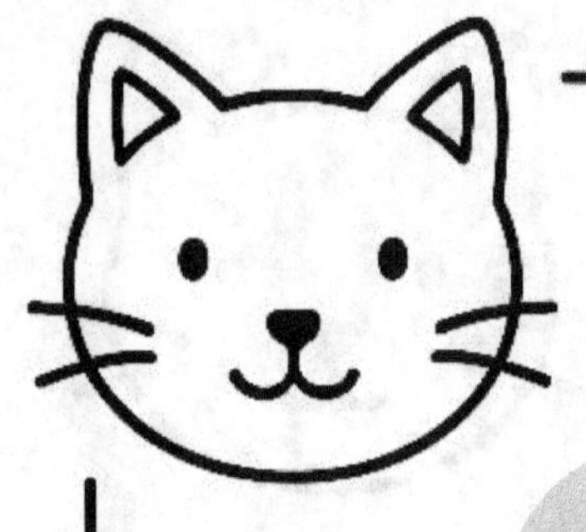
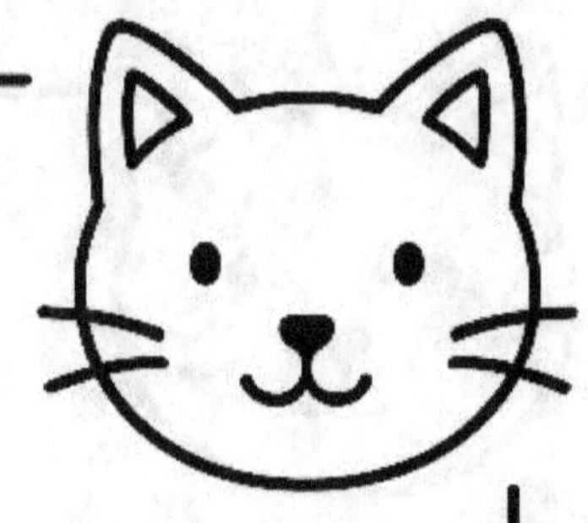

Fact #50

CATS NEED TOYS TO STAY ACTIVE AND HAPPY.

Los gatos necesitan juguetes para estar activos y felices.

Category 7: Fun & Global Cat Facts

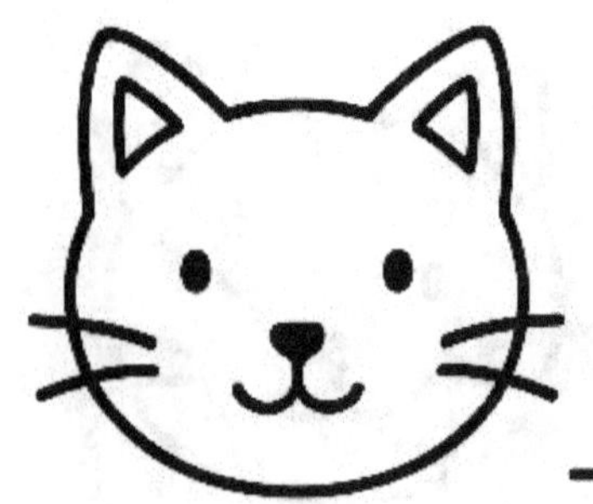
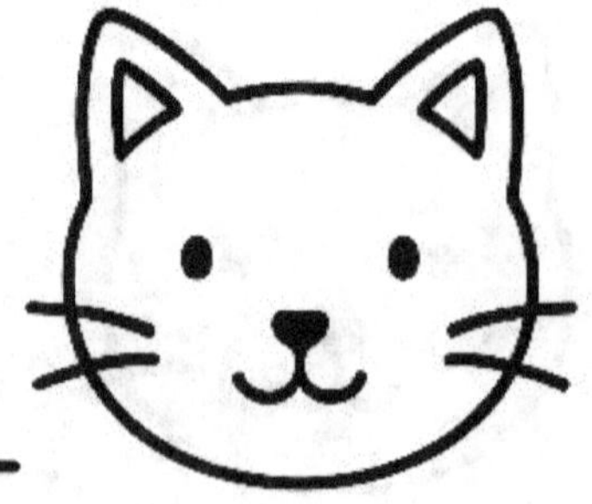

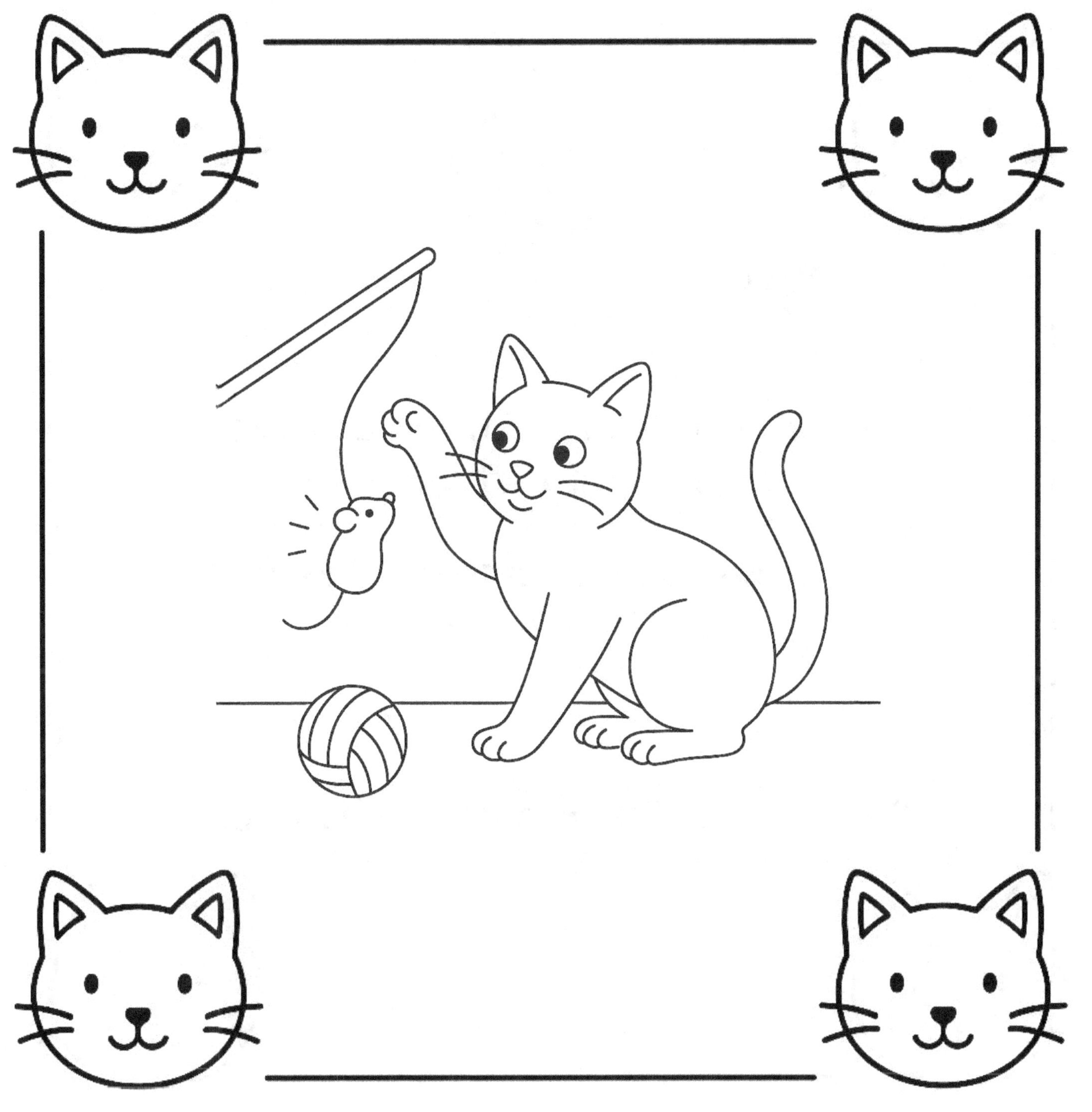

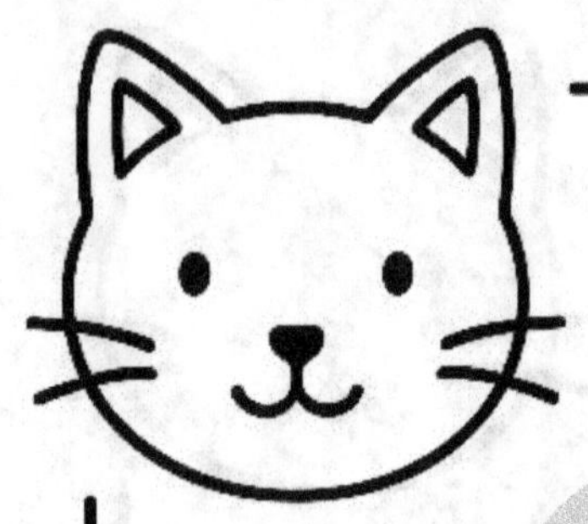

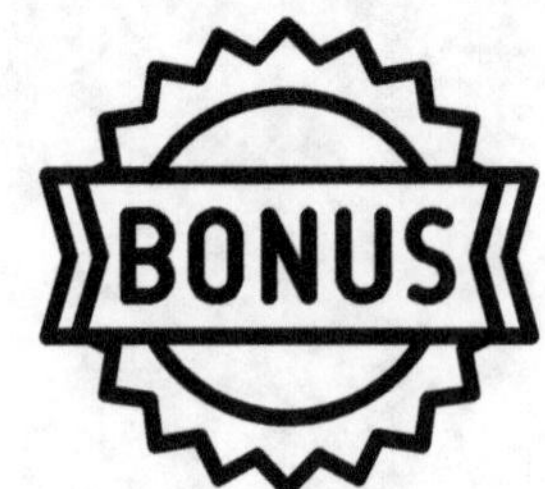

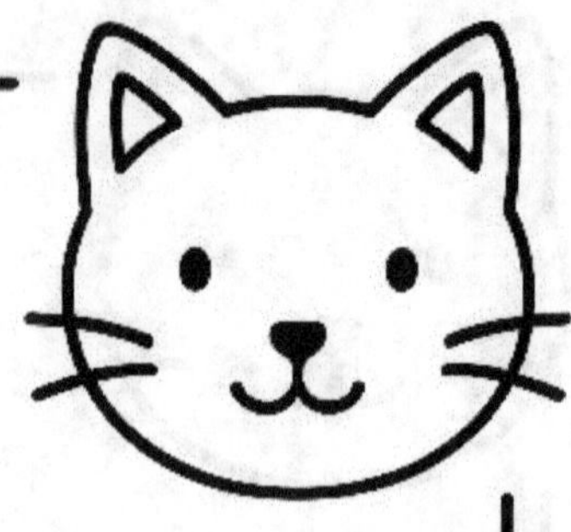

Fact #51

SOME CATS CAN OPEN DOORS OR DRAWERS!

¡Algunos gatos pueden abrir puertas o cajones!

Category 8: Surprising & Silly Facts

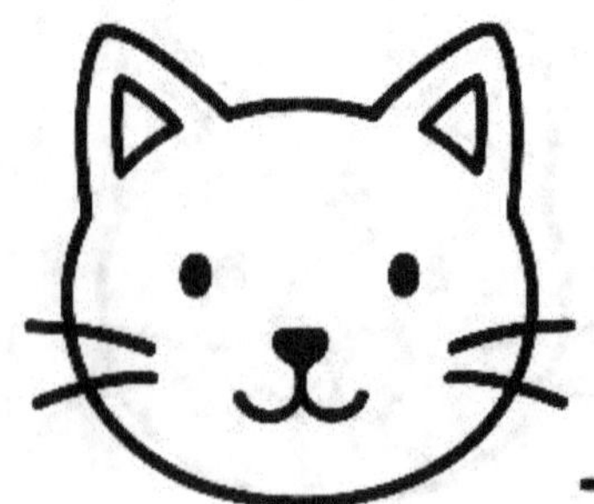

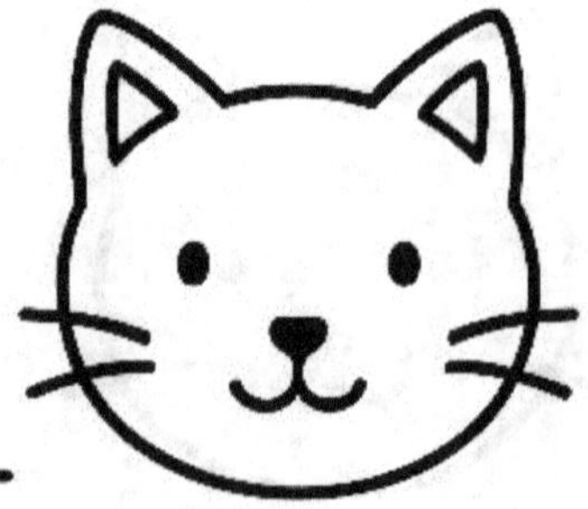

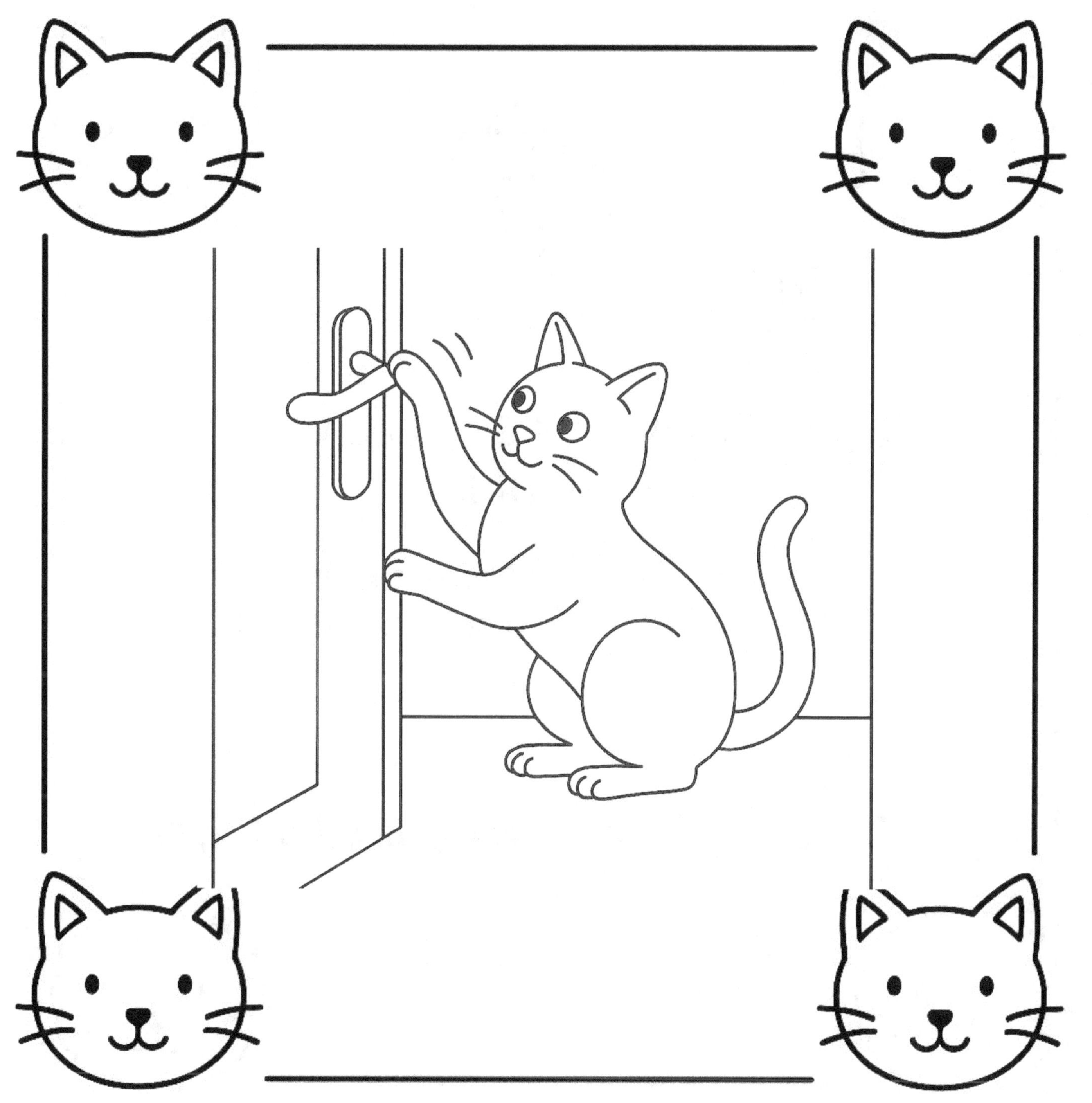

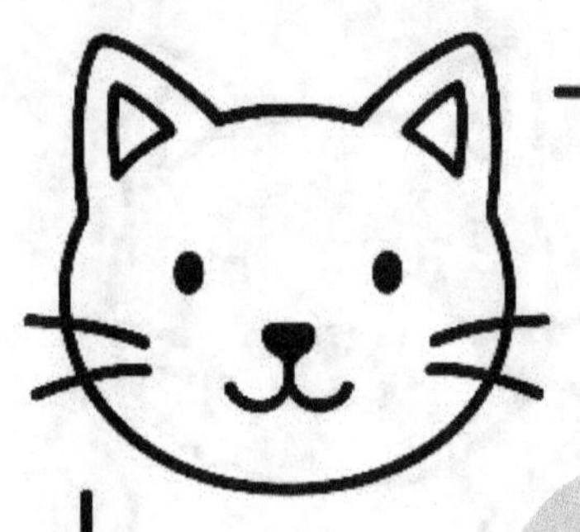
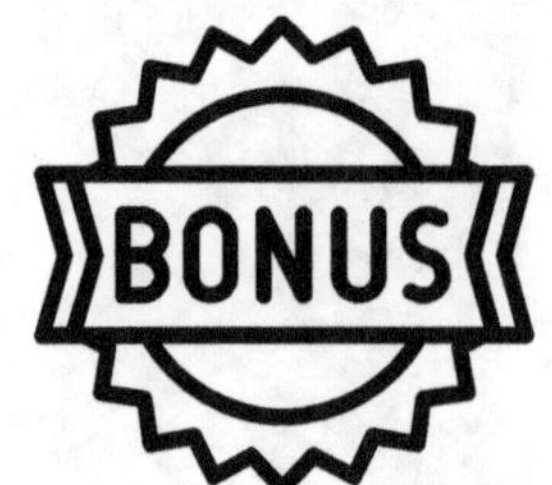

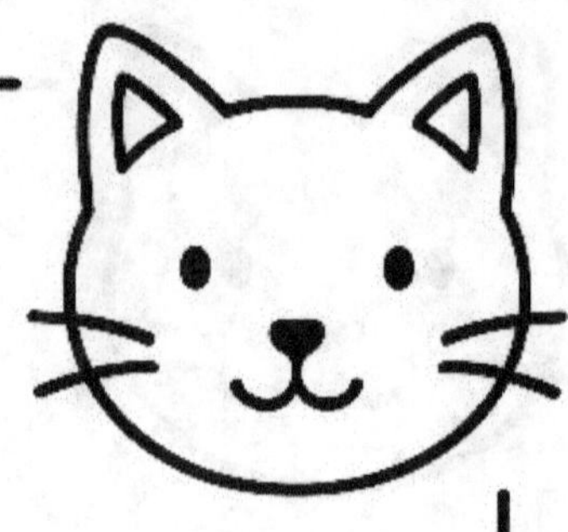

Fact #52

A GROUP OF KITTENS IS CALLED A KINDLE.

Un grupo de gatitos se llama "camada" o "kindle" en inglés.

Category 8: Surprising & Silly Facts

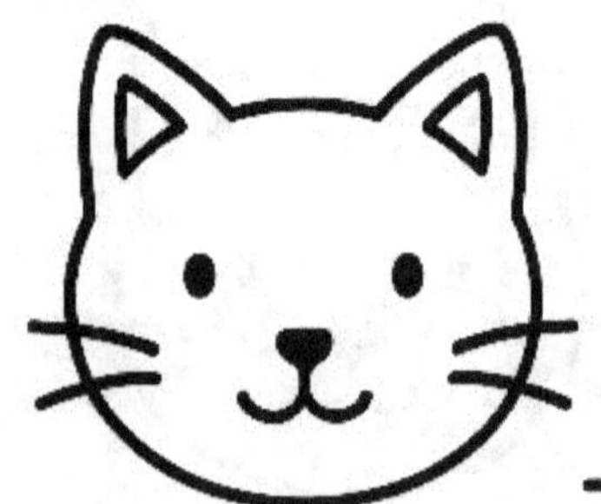
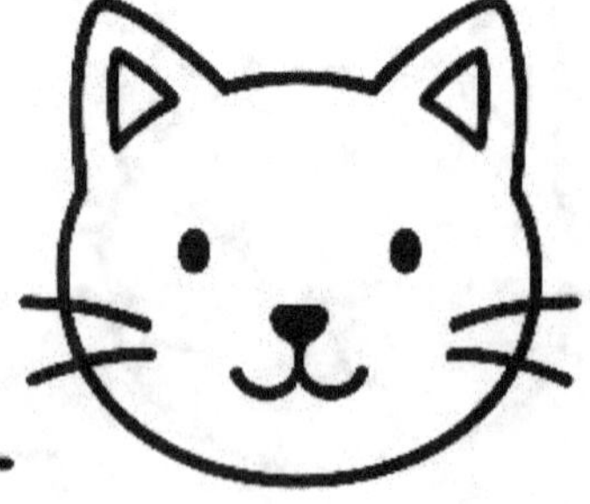

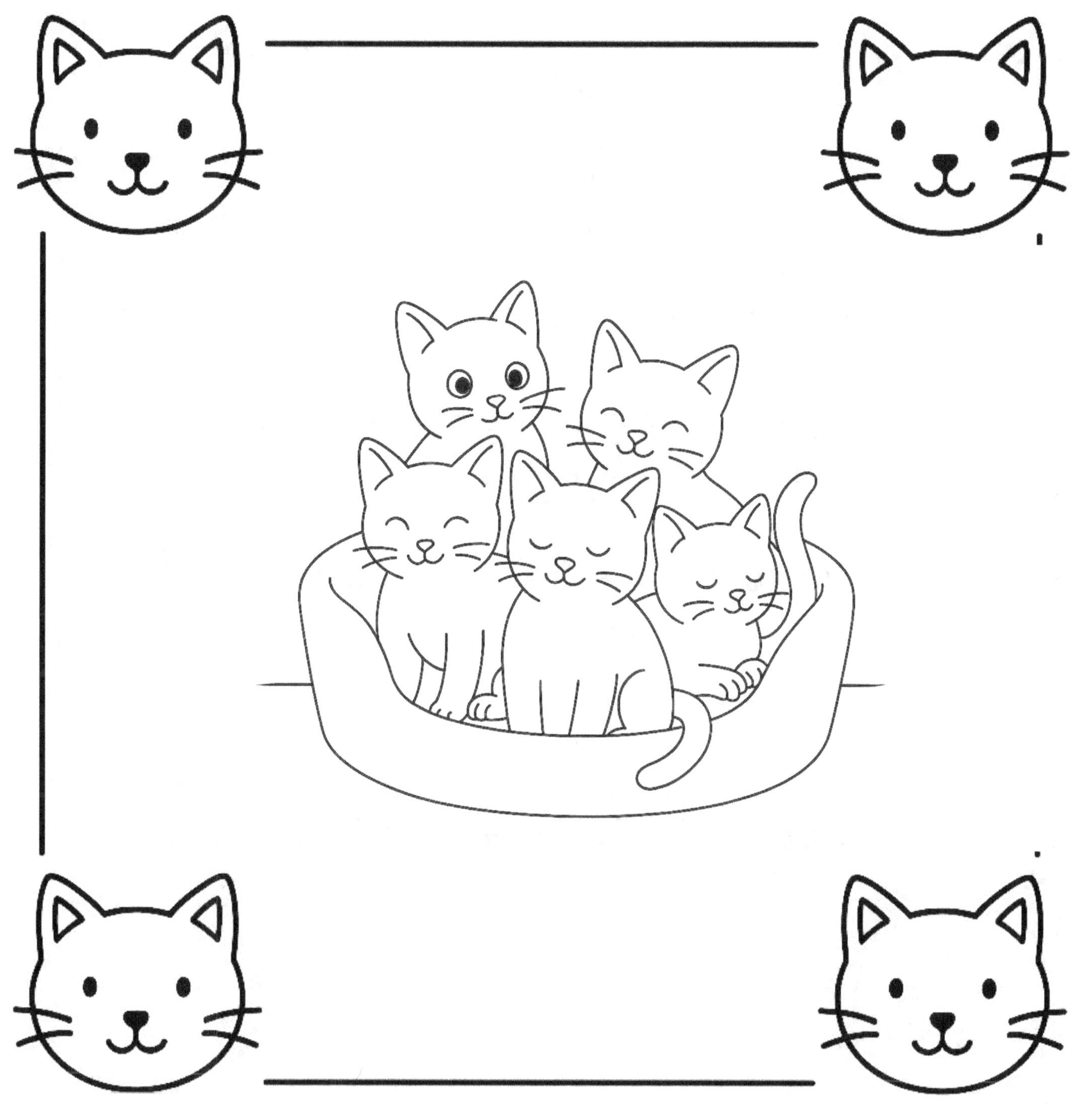

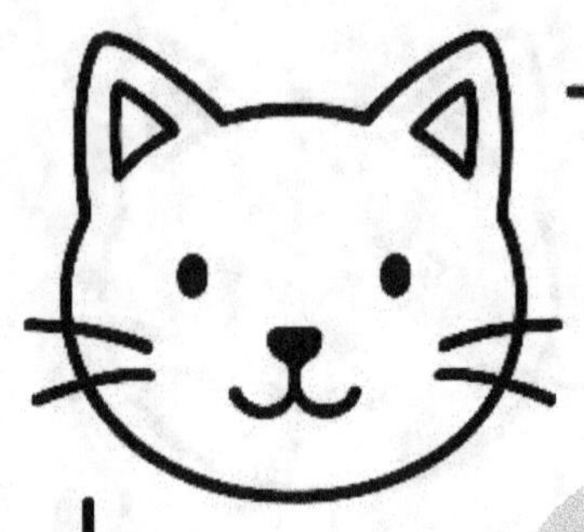 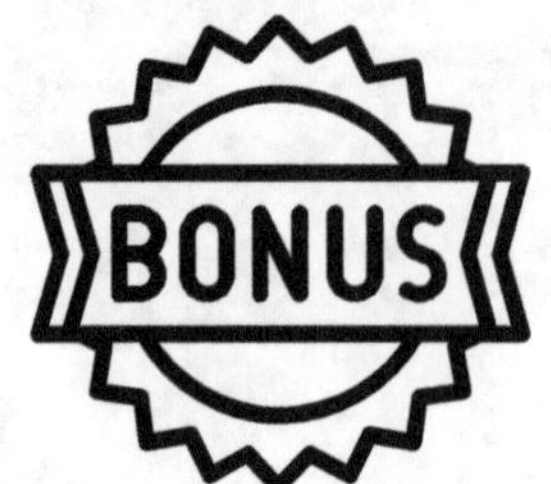

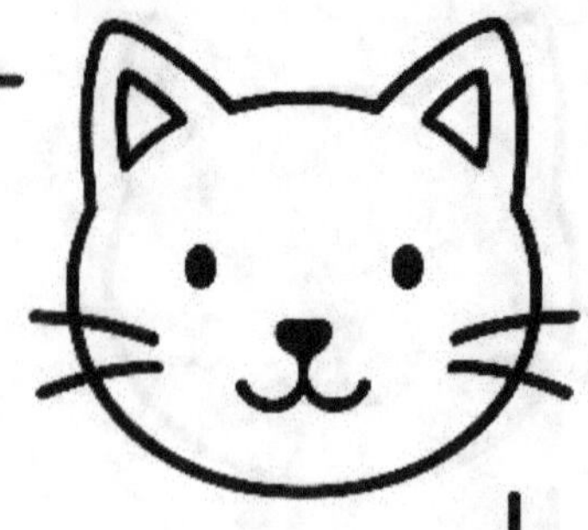

Fact #53

CATS CAN ROTATE THEIR EARS 180 DEGREES.

Los gatos pueden girar sus orejas 180 grados.

Category 8: Surprising & Silly Facts

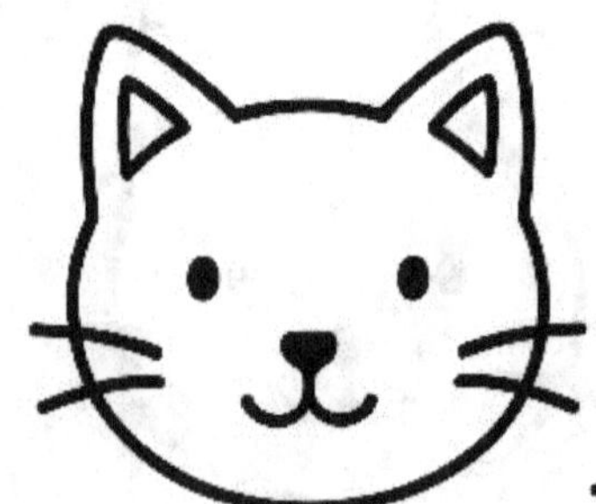 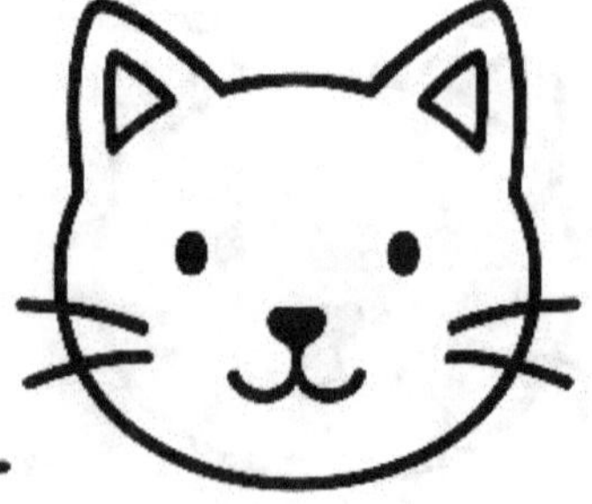

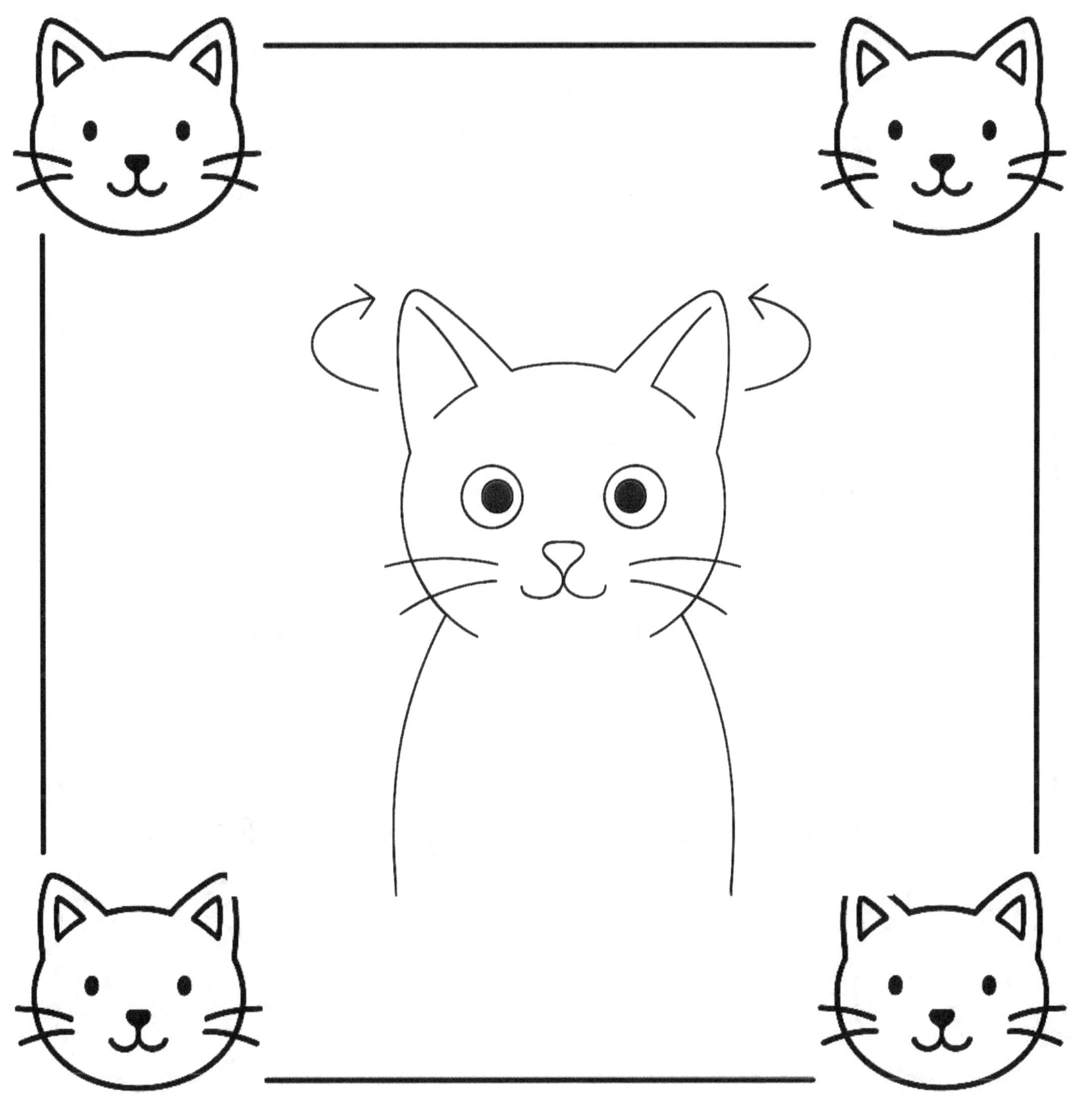

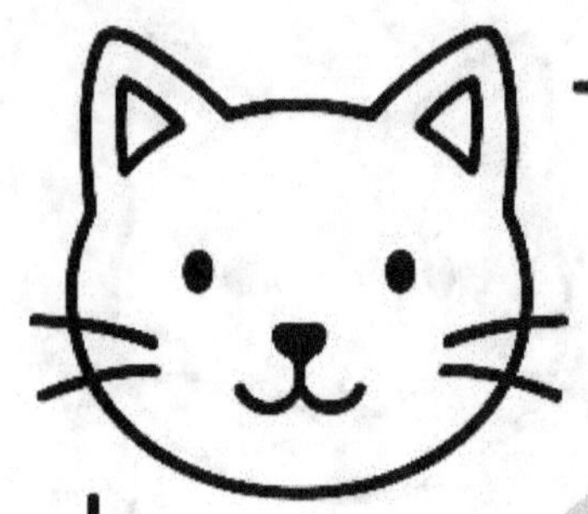
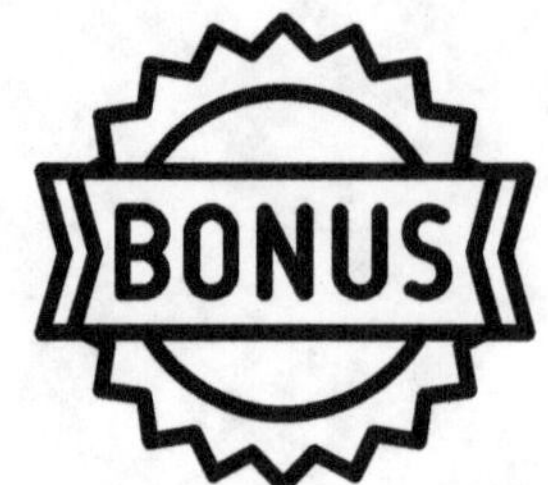

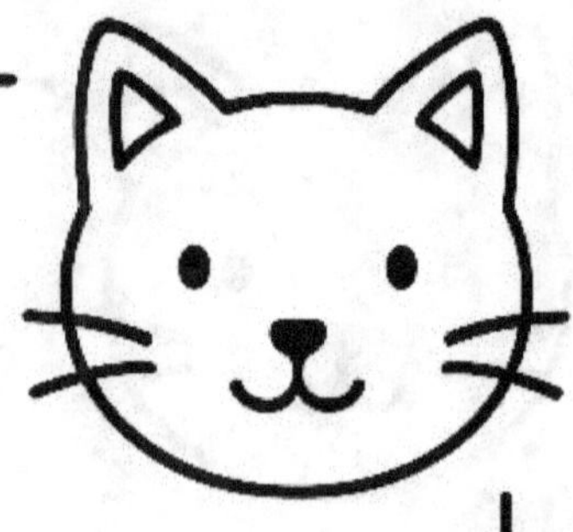

Fact #54

A CAT'S NOSE CAN CHANGE COLOR WITH THE WEATHER.

La nariz de un gato puede cambiar de color con el clima.

Category 8: Surprising & Silly Facts

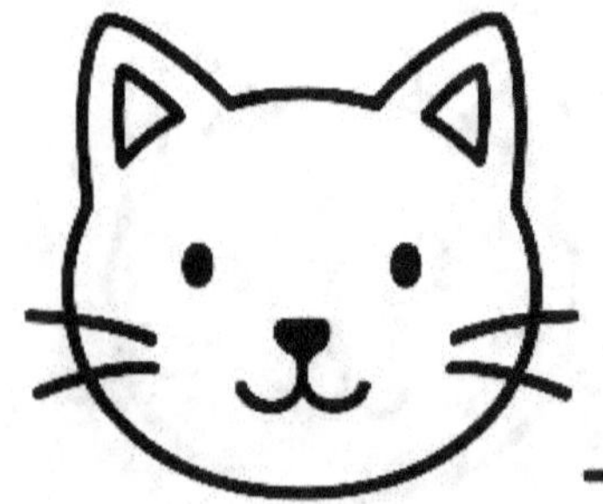
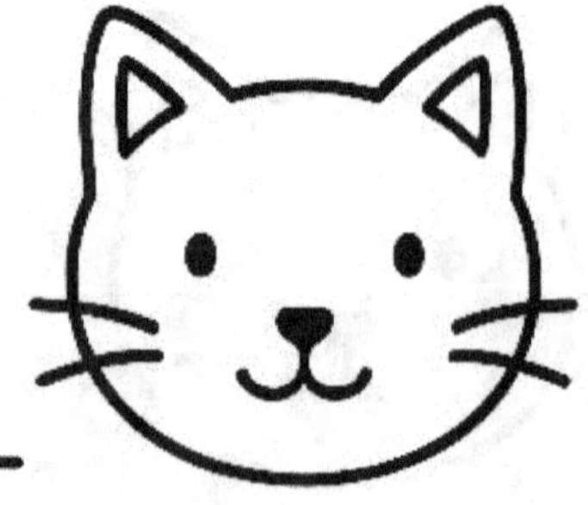

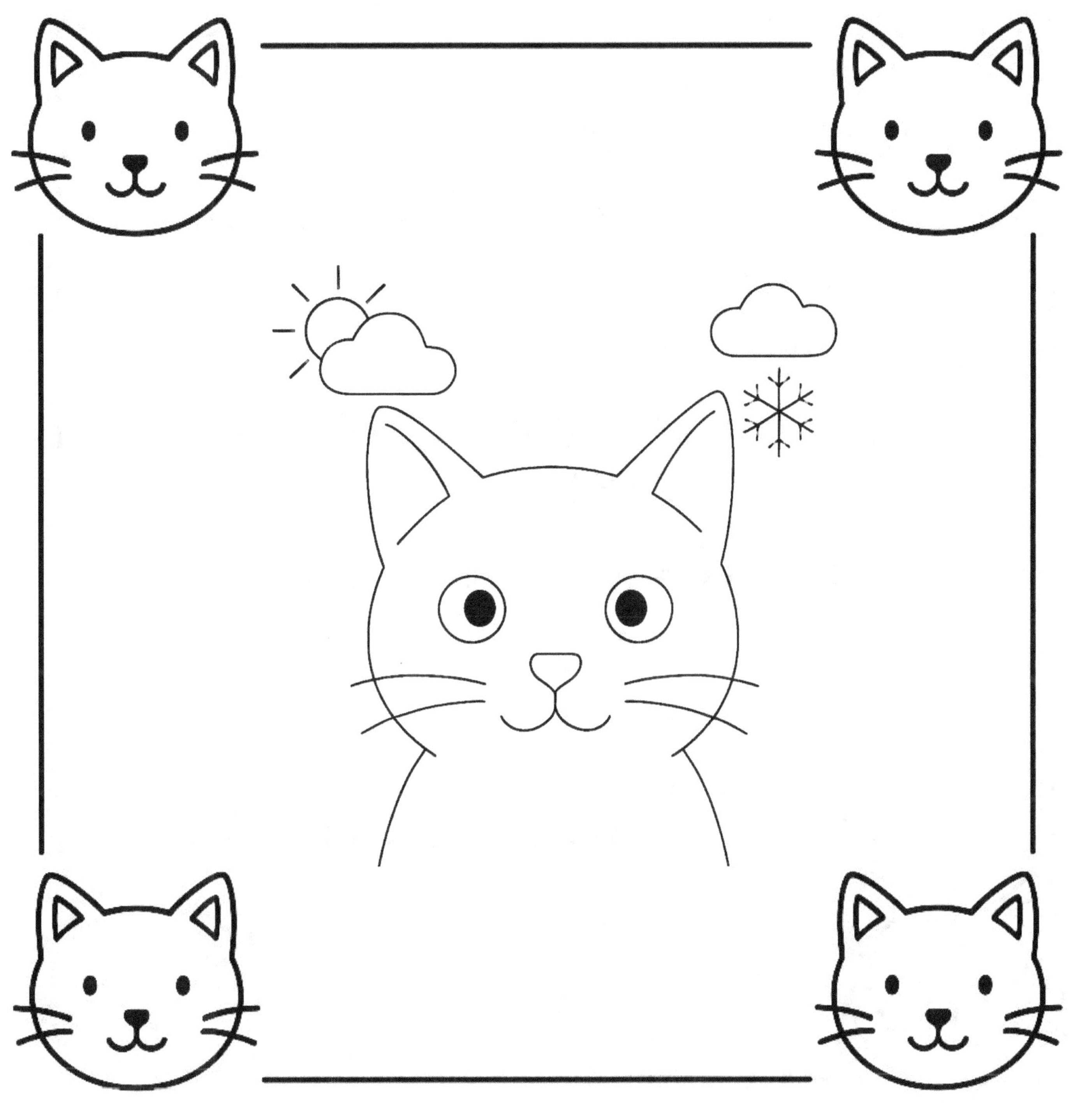

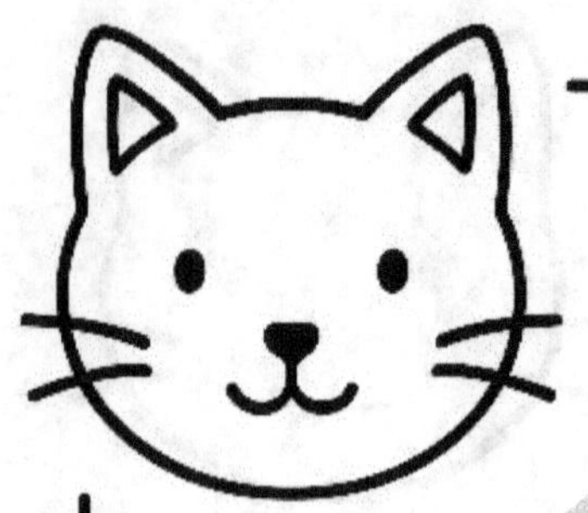
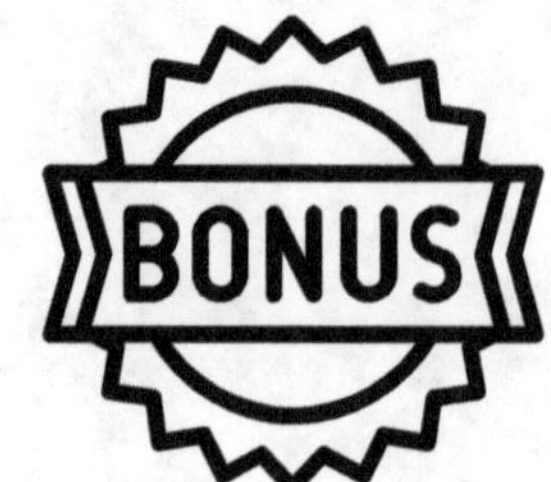
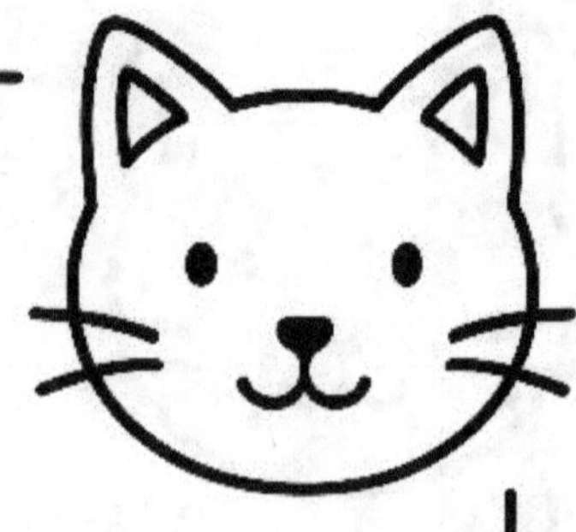

EVERY CAT IS DIFFERENT—JUST LIKE PEOPLE!

Cada gato es diferente-iigual que las personas!

Category 8: Surprising & Silly Facts

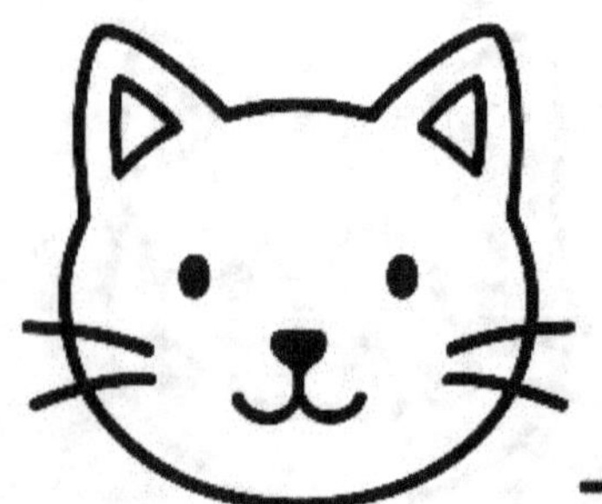
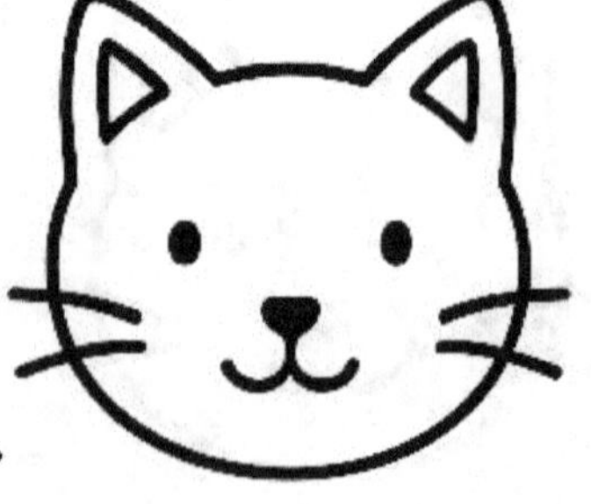

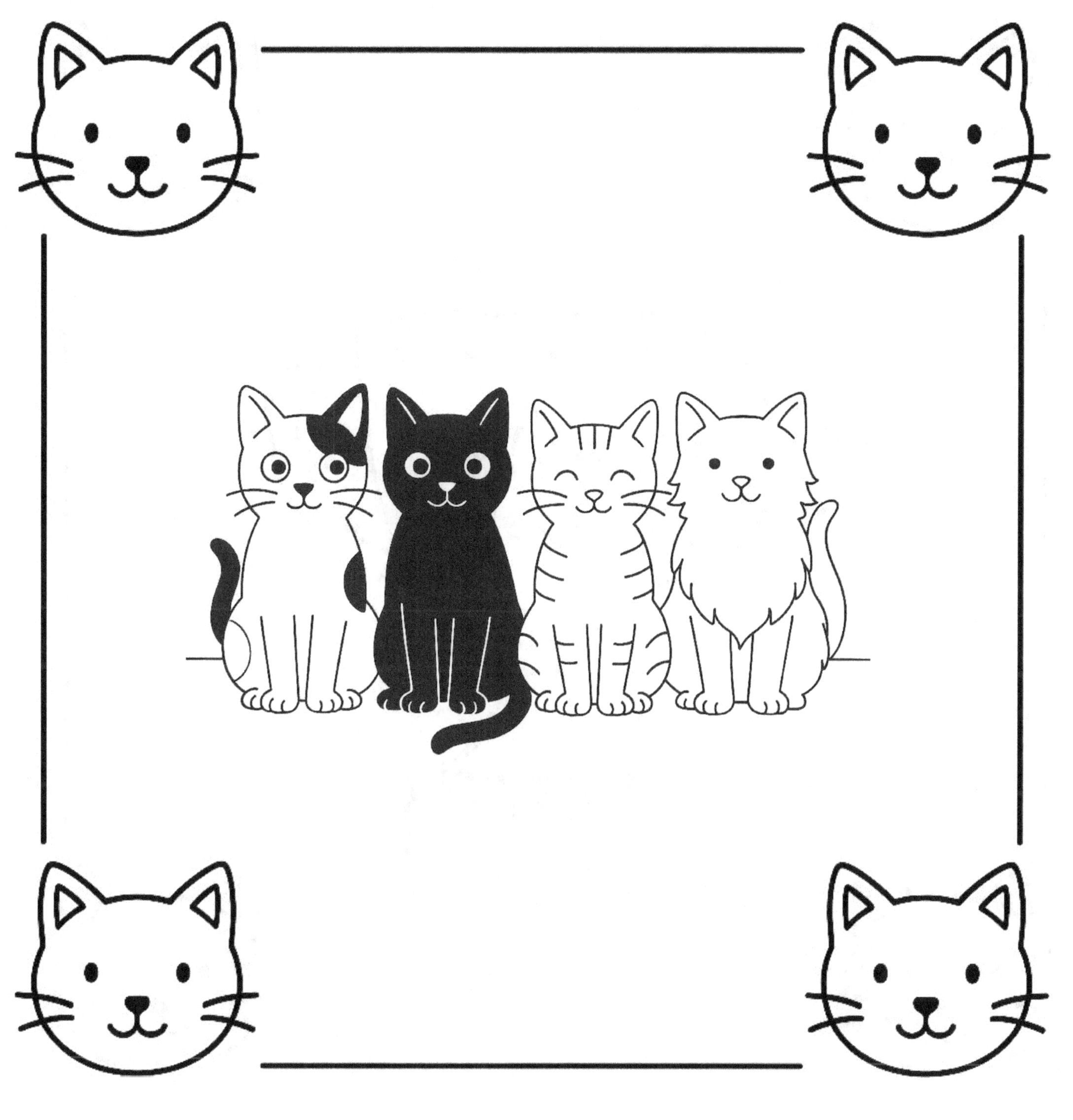

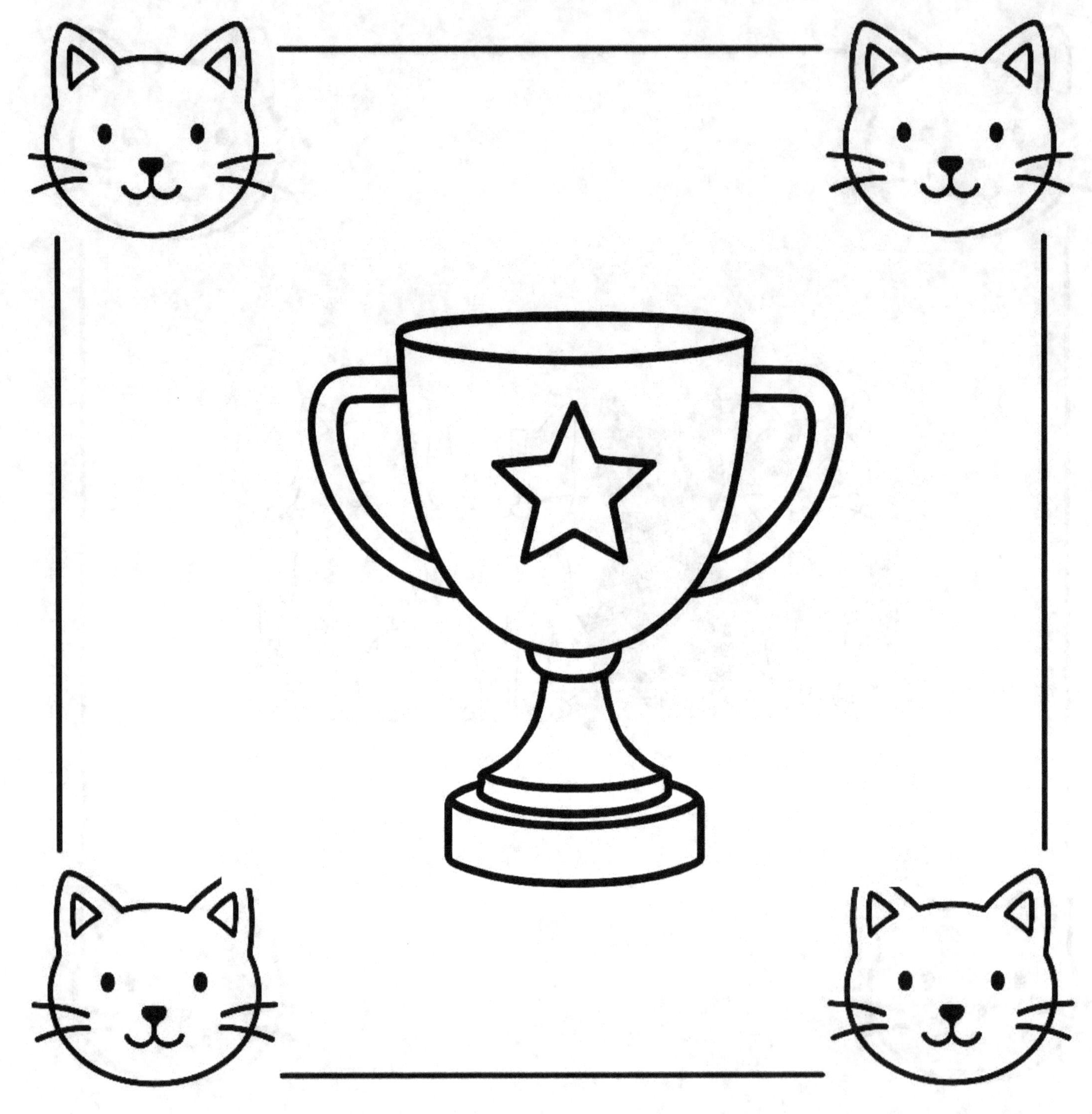

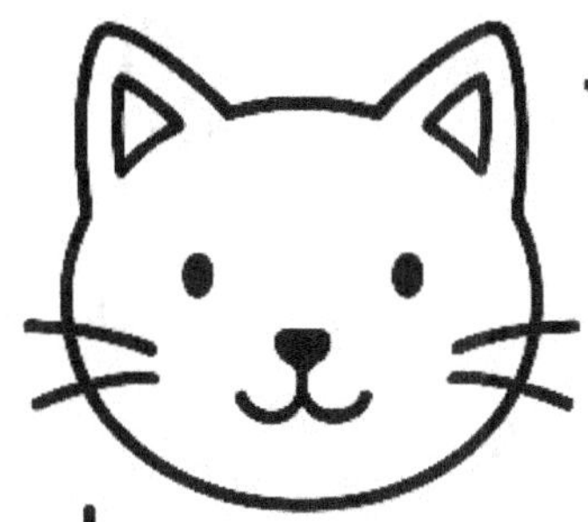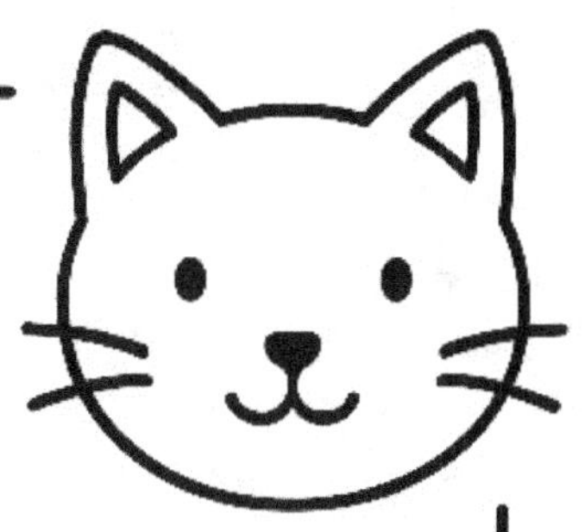

🏆 CONGRATULATIONS!
YOU DID IT, CAT-TASTIC COLOR CHAMP! 🐱🎉
THIS CERTIFICATE IS AWARDED TO:

____

(WRITE YOUR NAME HERE!)
FOR COLORING ALL THE PAGES, LEARNING COOL CAT FACTS,
AND SHOWING PAWS-ITIVELY AMAZING CREATIVITY!
YOU'RE OFFICIALLY A CAT EXPERT! 🐾
FROM YOUR FRIENDS AT
MYRAH & SHARKY ADVENTURES + LEARNING
📚🐾🎨

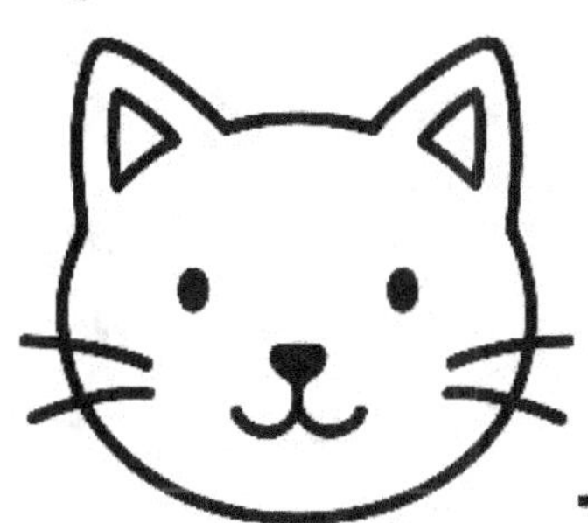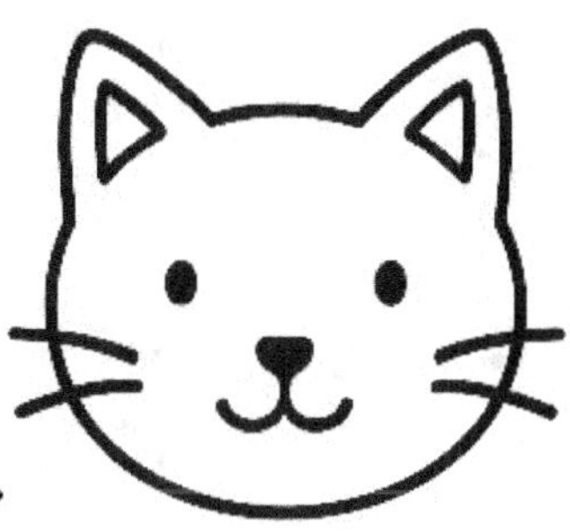

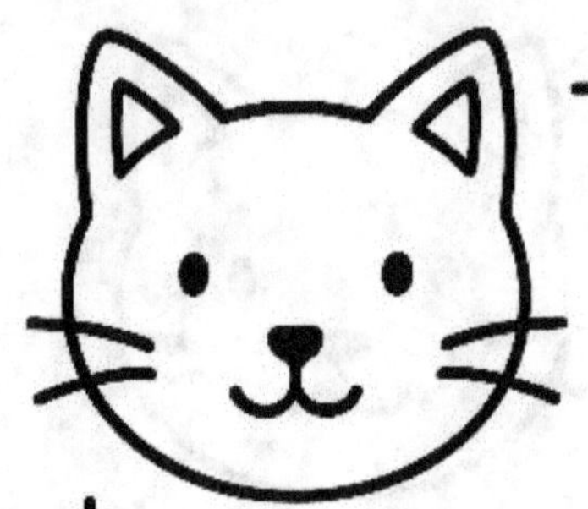
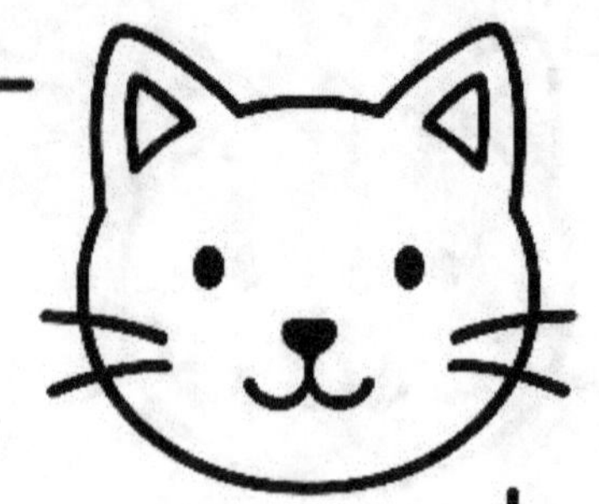

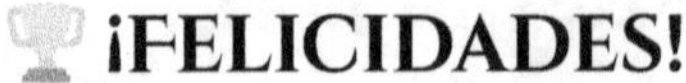

🏆 ¡FELICIDADES!

¡LO LOGRASTE, CAMPEÓN/A GATUNO DEL COLOR! 🐱🎉

ESTE CERTIFICADO SE OTORGA A:

____

(¡ESCRIBE TU NOMBRE AQUÍ!)

POR COLOREAR TODAS LAS PÁGINAS, APRENDER DATOS
GENIALES SOBRE GATOS
¡Y MOSTRAR UNA CREATIVIDAD VERDADERAMENTE
INCREÍBLE!
¡ERES OFICIALMENTE UN EXPERTO/A EN GATOS! 🐾🤍
CON CARIÑO DE TUS AMIGOS DE
MYRAH & SHARKY AVENTURAS + APRENDIZAJE

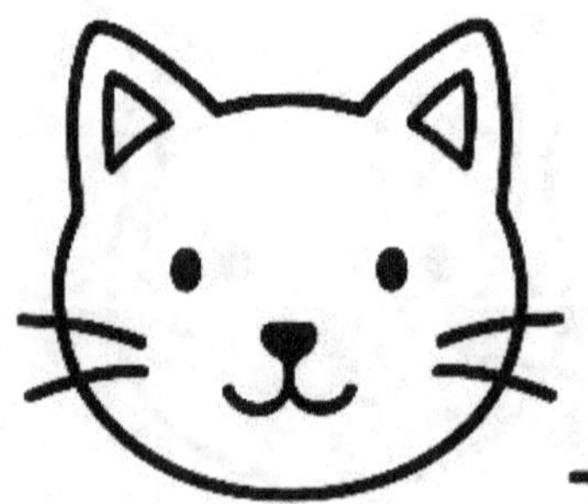
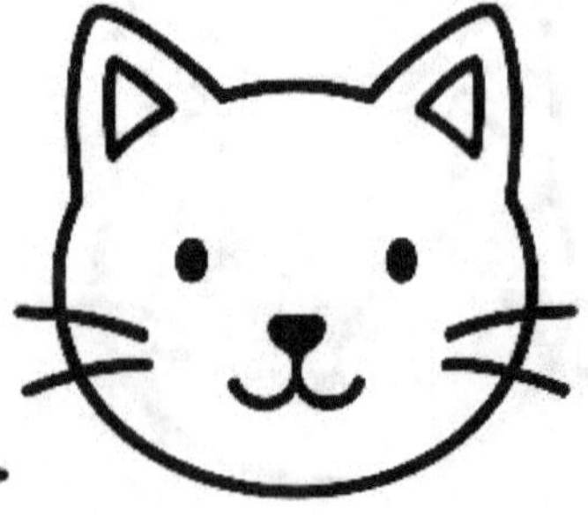

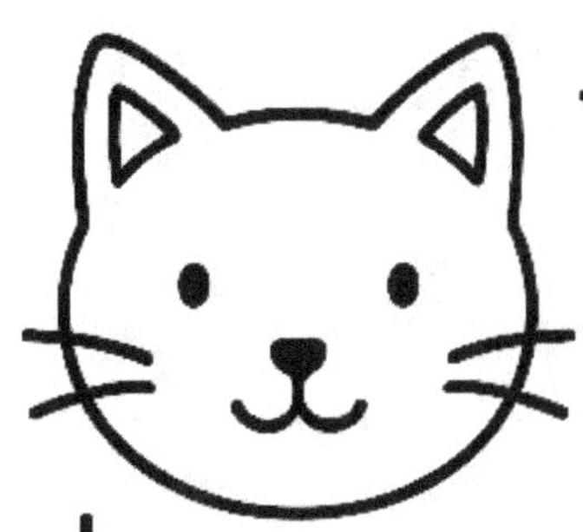
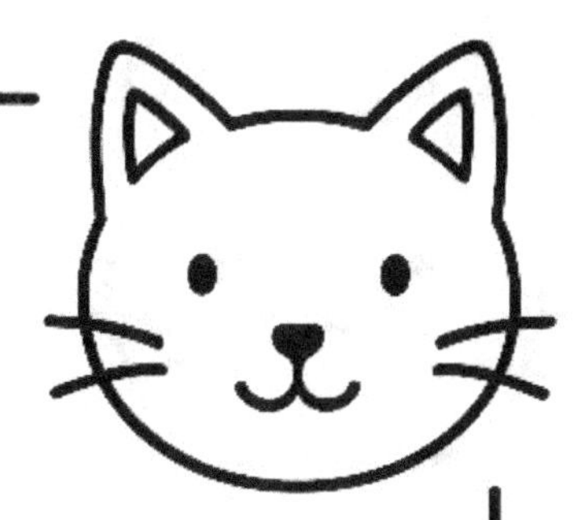

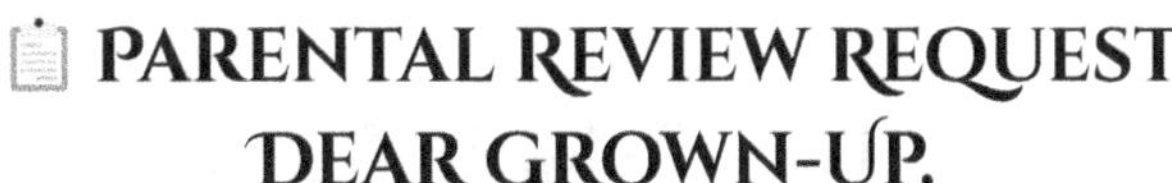 PARENTAL REVIEW REQUEST
DEAR GROWN-UP,
WE HOPE YOUR LITTLE ONE HAD A PAWS-ITIVELY FUN TIME
COLORING, LAUGHING, AND LEARNING WITH COLOR ME CATS –
KIDS EDITION: 50 FUN FACTS ABOUT CATS (BILINGUAL: ENGLISH
+ SPANISH).
IF YOUR CHILD ENJOYED THE BOOK, WOULD YOU CONSIDER
LEAVING A QUICK REVIEW?
YOUR KIND WORDS HELP US REACH MORE CURIOUS YOUNG
READERS
AND INSPIRE FUTURE ADVENTURES WITH MYRAH, SHARKY &
FRIENDS!
YOU CAN LEAVE YOUR REVIEW AT:
AMAZON LINK
THANK YOU FOR SUPPORTING BILINGUAL LEARNING,
CREATIVITY,
AND THE LOVE OF READING — ONE CAT FACT AT A TIME!
WITH GRATITUDE,
DR. BESS & THE TENDERNESSE TEAM

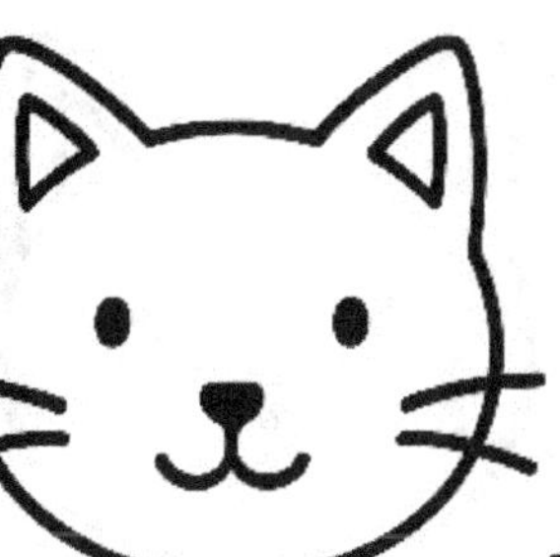
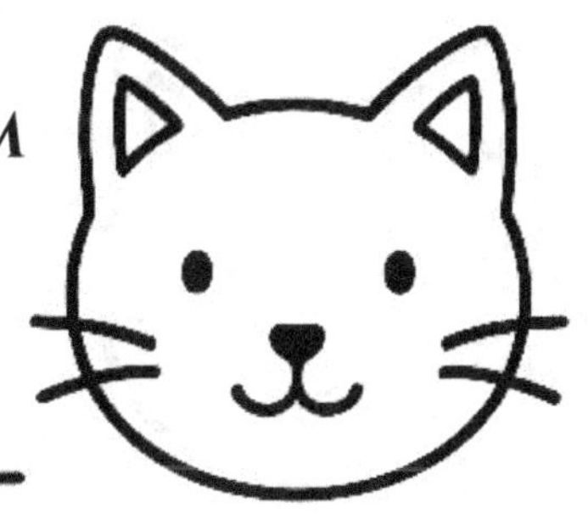

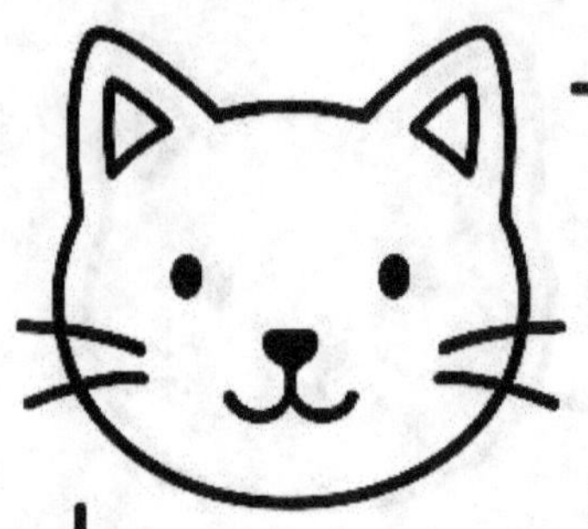
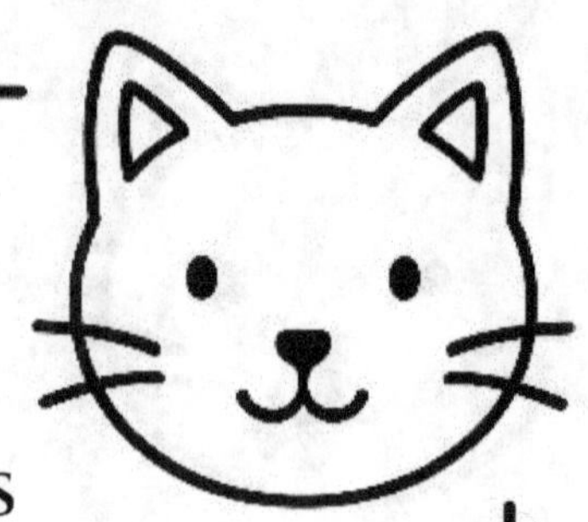

📋 SOLICITUD DE RESEÑA PARA PADRES
QUERIDO ADULTO:
ESPERAMOS QUE TU PEQUEÑO SE HAYA DIVERTIDO
COLOREANDO, RIENDO Y APRENDIENDO CON COLOR ME
CATS – EDICIÓN INFANTIL: 50 CURIOSIDADES SOBRE LOS
GATOS (BILINGÜE: INGLÉS + ESPAÑOL).
SI A TU HIJO LE GUSTÓ EL LIBRO, ¿TE IMPORTARÍA DEJAR UNA
RESEÑA RÁPIDA?
⭐ ¡TUS AMABLES PALABRAS NOS AYUDAN A LLEGAR A MÁS
LECTORES JÓVENES CURIOSOS Y A INSPIRAR FUTURAS
AVENTURAS CON MYRAH, SHARKY Y SUS AMIGOS!
PUEDES DEJAR TU RESEÑA EN:
📖 ENLACE DE AMAZON
GRACIAS POR APOYAR EL APRENDIZAJE BILINGÜE, LA
CREATIVIDAD Y EL AMOR POR LA LECTURA: ¡UNA CURIOSIDAD
SOBRE GATOS A LA VEZ! 🐾📚
CON GRATITUD,
DRA. BESS Y EL EQUIPO DE TENDERNESSE

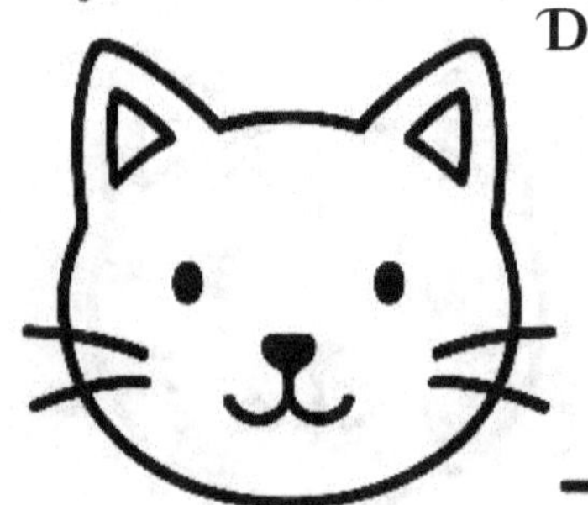
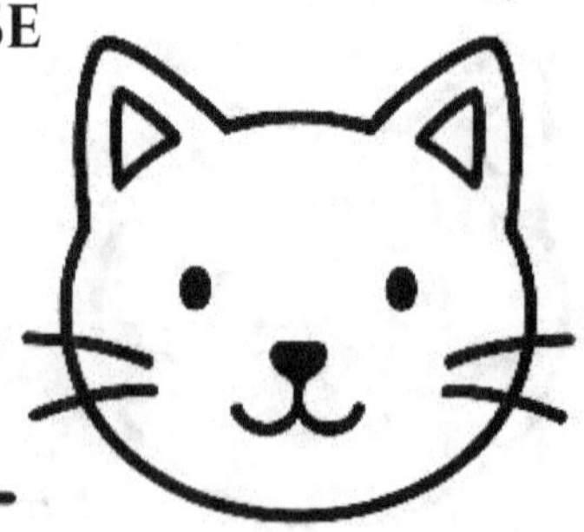

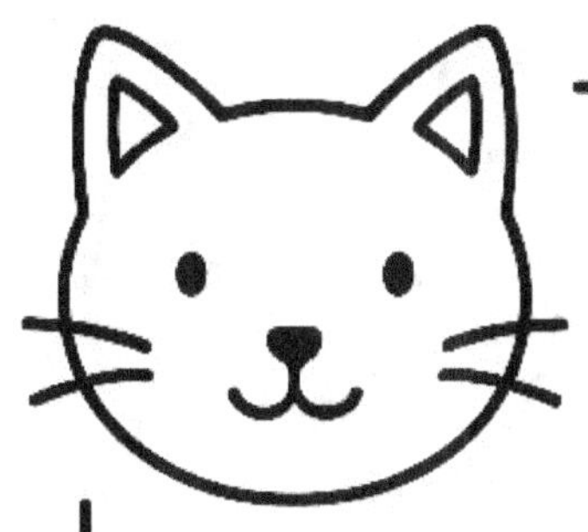
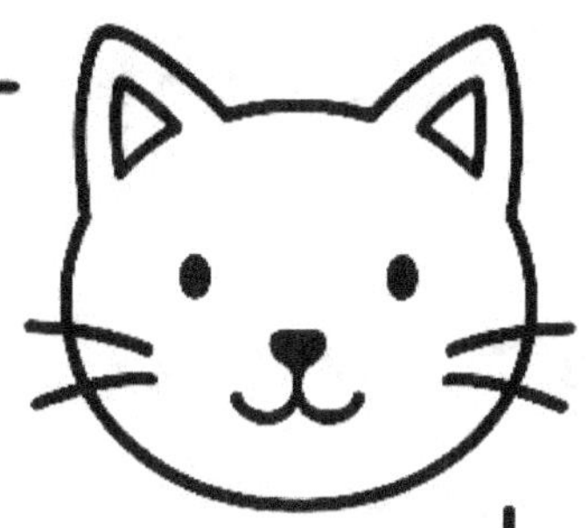

🐾 THANK YOU FOR CHOOSING COLOR ME CATS – KIDS EDITION!

WE'RE SO HAPPY YOU AND YOUR LITTLE LEARNER JOINED US ON THIS CAT-TASTIC ADVENTURE!
WHETHER IT WAS THE SILLY KITTY FACES, THE FUN FACTS IN ENGLISH AND SPANISH, OR THE JOY OF COLORING TOGETHER — WE HOPE THIS BOOK BROUGHT PLENTY OF GIGGLES, LEARNING, AND CREATIVITY INTO YOUR HOME.
FROM ALL OF US AT MYRAH & SHARKY ADVENTURES + LEARNING, THANK YOU FOR SUPPORTING PLAYFUL BILINGUAL LEARNING!

📚 KEEP EXPLORING, KEEP COLORING, AND REMEMBER...
YOU'RE OFFICIALLY A CAT EXPERT NOW! 🐱✨

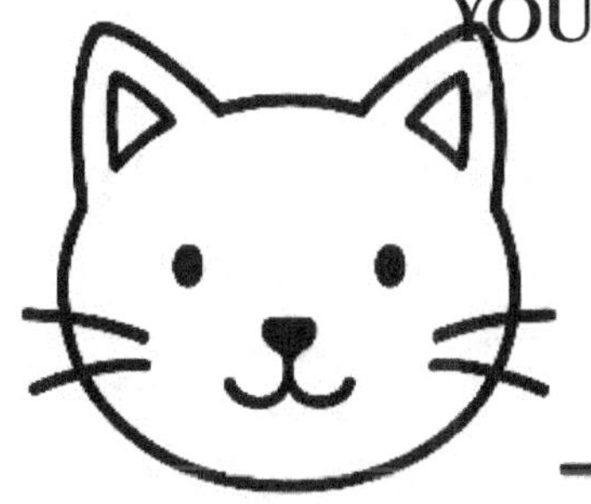
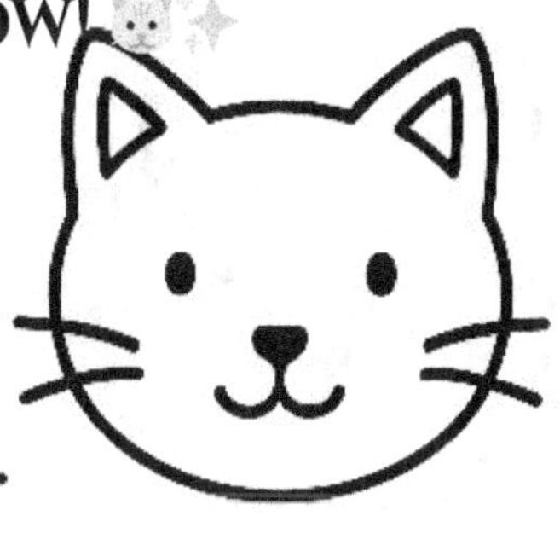

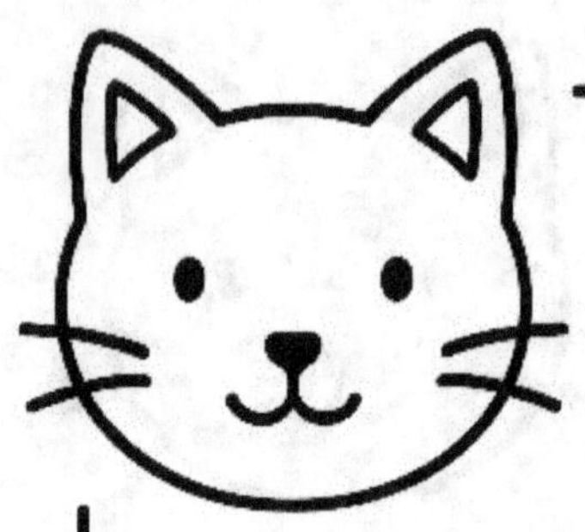
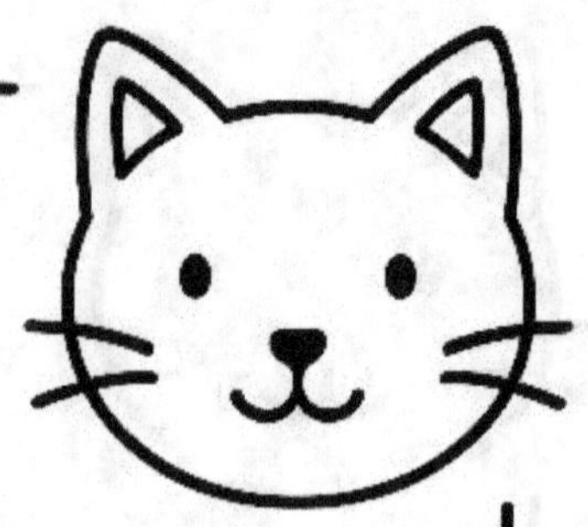

🐾 ¡GRACIAS POR ELEGIR COLOR ME CATS – EDICIÓN PARA NIÑOS!
¡ESTAMOS MUY FELICES DE QUE TÚ Y TU PEQUEÑO EXPLORADOR SE HAYAN UNIDO A ESTA AVENTURA GATUNA! YA SEA POR LAS CARITAS DIVERTIDAS DE LOS GATITOS, LOS DATOS CURIOSOS EN INGLÉS Y ESPAÑOL, O LA ALEGRÍA DE COLOREAR JUNTOS — ESPERAMOS QUE ESTE LIBRO HAYA TRAÍDO MUCHAS SONRISAS, APRENDIZAJE Y CREATIVIDAD A TU HOGAR.
DE PARTE DE TODO EL EQUIPO DE MYRAH & SHARKY AVENTURAS + APRENDIZAJE,
¡GRACIAS POR APOYAR EL APRENDIZAJE BILINGÜE Y DIVERTIDO!
📚 ¡SIGUE EXPLORANDO, SIGUE COLOREANDO Y RECUERDA...
¡YA ERES OFICIALMENTE UN EXPERTO/A EN GATOS! 🐱✨

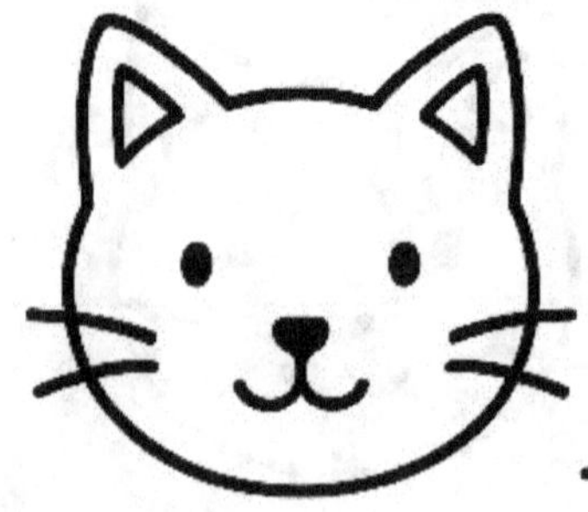
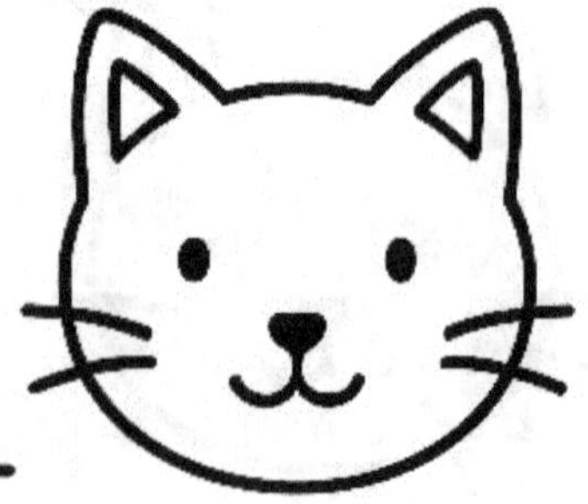